Leabharlanna Poiblí Chathair Bhaile Átha Cliath
Dublin City Public Libraries

Baile Átha Cliath
Dublin City

Leabharlann Shráid Chaoimhín
Kevin Street Library
Tel: 01 222 8488

Date Due	Date Due	Date Due

BIRDS
OF THE HOMEPLACE
THE LIVES OF IRELAND'S FAMILIAR BIRDS

To Neville McKee, for better help than Google.

BIRDS
OF THE HOMEPLACE
THE LIVES OF IRELAND'S FAMILIAR BIRDS

Anthony McGeehan
with Julian Wyllie

The Collins Press

First published in 2014 by
The Collins Press
West Link Park
Doughcloyne
Wilton
Cork

© Anthony McGeehan and Julian Wyllie 2014

A CIP record for this book is available from the British Library.

ISBN: 978-1-84889-229-3

Design and typesetting by Burns Design
Typeset in Goudy and Trade Gothic
Printed in Poland by Białostockie Zakłady Graficzne SA

Photograph on p. ii: male Linnet.

CONTENTS

AUTHOR'S NOTE

Professor Wolfgang Wiltschko is one of the pioneers of bird navigation research. Starling or Robin, all birds possess an astonishing global positioning system encoded in their genes. One of their 'secret senses' taps the pull of the Earth's magnetic field, which varies across the planet. When, during the 1960s, Professor Wiltschko proposed that birds had a magnetic compass, he was derided. He was told that 'you don't want a stupid little bird doing something you cannot do.' Years ago I became fascinated by the birds around my childhood home. To begin with, I wanted to know their names. Now I respect them as superior beings that leave Homo sapiens in the shade. Some have eyes that contain two focusing spots; others grow brain tissue to enlarge their memory capacity of where they hide food. Furthermore, all birds can manage without water to drink – because they metabolise it from their food. Yet they are patronised and belittled, mere birdies or feathered friends. Or, when 'taken seriously' as a litmus test of the environment, we justify our concern in an egocentric way, arguing that whatever happens to them could have implications for us. This book has been a reporter's journey to gather all the facts that underpin the way birds live their lives. I am a student, not an expert. The more I learn the more I feel like a graffiti artist in the presence of Van Gogh.

Anthony McGeehan

ACKNOWLEDGMENTS

Thank You! Everlasting patience: my wife, Mairead. Editors: Ken S. Douglas, Joe S. Furphy, Eleanor Keane, Alexander Lees, Frank Murphy, Neville McKee, Nick Watmough. Artistic assistance with plate design: Magdalena Zerebiec. Artists: Jennifer Baumeister (*Illustrations of band of polarised light* p. 84), John Quinn (*Earth's magnetic field* p. 82, *sonograms* pp. 102, 103 & 104). Designer: Alison Burns. Photographers: Victor Caschera (*Little Egrets* in flight p. 137); Eric Dempsey (*Dipper* juvenile p. 175); Jochen Diersche (*Stock Dove* in flight p. 153); John Doherty (*Lapwing* p. 78, *Swallow* juveniles, bottom left p. 179); Steve Ganlett (*Kestrel* male at rest p. 139, *Stock Dove* bottom left p. 153, *Barn Owls* p. 159); Norma Gleeson (*Swallow* juveniles p. 79 & back cover); Ingo Hartkopf (*Kestrels* in flight p. 139); Brandon Holden (*Merlin* male p. 140); Jane Kelleher (*Wheatear* p. 84): Craig Nash (*desert landscape* p. 80, *Swift* juvenile p. 179); Bruce Mactavish (*Peregrines* pp. 76, 77, 140 perched at right & 151 in flight); Ben Porter (*Chough* p. 2, *Cuckoo* p. 34, *Chiffchaff* p. 86, *Peregrine* juvenile p. 140, *House Martin* flying far left p. 180, *Blackcap* male lower left p. 185, *Linnet* red male p. 214); Rene Pop (*Buzzard* in flight top right p. 140 & at rest p. 140); Sindri Skulason (*Merlin* female in flight p. 140); Artur Stankiewicz (*Kingfishers* p. 174, *Cuckoo* pp. 36 & 157); Remo Savisaar (*Long-eared Owls* pp. 60 & 158, *Sparrowhawks* three in flight montage p. 64, *Estonia night sky* p. 82, *Estonia peat bogs* p. 122, *Great Spotted Woodpecker* p. 129, *Bullfinches* p. 219); Steve Young (*Rock Dove* in flight p. 151, *Great Spotted Woodpeckers* p. 160, *Jays* in middle row p. 163). Correspondents: Mike Bok, Dermot Breen, Lela Bolkvadze, Brian Cachalane, Jordi Calvet, Oscar Campbell, Anne Clarke, Graham Clarke, Seamus Concannon, Lady Dufferin, Martin Garner, Ricard Guttierez, Anne Hailes, Niall Hatch, Dennis Hawke, Flora Irwin, Jackie Jefferson, Kevin Mawhinney, Kathryn McGeehan, Tom McGeehan, Eugene McKeown, Richard Millington, Rachel Muheim, Julia Nunn, Ken Perry, Elizabeth Rice, Angela Ross, David Shawe, Stephanie Sim, Mark Smyth, Robert Vaughan, David Walker, D.I.M. Wallace, Pim Wolf, Jean Wood.

Peeping from a cavity in modern high-rise concrete, Feral Pigeons are ubiquitous among tall buildings in towns and cities. On islands in the west of Ireland small populations of Rock Dove – the wild ancestor – still survive, thanks to centuries of isolation.

1. BIRDS OF THE HOMEPLACE

WE, THE IRISH, are a standing army of lay birdwatchers. No matter where we live – on a farm, an island, in suburbia or in town – there is bird life. Home is our bosom and operates like a sense of smell, a key that unlocks deepest memories. With eyes shut, we are there. So too, not far away, are birds. Once you look, their faces become familiar and interest sparks. There is a whole new world to enjoy. This book attempts to instil perception of a shared existence that begins at the back door. We all love stories of ingenuity, escape from danger and intrepid travels to foreign lands. Your neighbourhood birds provide such derring-do in spades.

Unlike our grandparents, we live in a world of our own making. For the most part, older generations were rural dwellers and Irish farmhouses were part of a tapestry that gave expression to the ebb and flow of history and nature. Through the decades people cherished their roots and regarded them as a badge of identity that might embrace a parish, a townland or a single field. Seasons arrived every year, four new beginnings heralded by events that wiped the slate clean. Birds co-starred in this natural opera as tangible barometers; dots that joined twelve months together. People talked about them as though they were part of the family and enshrined their names with adjectives evoking kinship – House Sparrow, Barn Owl and Corncrake. The coming of spring's first Swallow, a sign that the grip of winter was broken, was an event told eagerly at the breakfast table. Life may have been hard but it was lived at a slower, less intense pace. 'All our yesterdays' are fading rapidly as rural Ireland merges with increasingly urban settlements. Ironically, the loss of an acre of monoculture grassland for new housing can result in an increase in overall numbers and diversity of birds. Trees, shrubs, lawns, water features, feeders and nest boxes combine to boost species that thrive in 'edge habitats'. Viewed from above, a collection of gardens may not be that different from a patch of woodland. Back yards become an outdoor theatre and when we spend time in them, we see and hear their other inhabitants.

The fact that birds are everywhere and can be found easily is an uplifting one. They do not hibernate or wilt like vegetation in autumn. As a class of living creatures they are phenomenally alive. Their body language is permanently set at 'Let's go!' When summer ends, Swallows leave Irish shores and head to sunny southern Africa. Conversely, most of Scandinavia's Blackbirds pass the winter under our noses. Rather than risk perishing in northern climes, two-thirds of all Norwegian Blackbirds travel to Ireland and Britain. However, this book is not a 'feed the birds' exhortation. Yes, Franciscan acts of providing food and lodging are of inestimable benefit. But what if you live on an island or way out west, dominated by ocean, sky and mountain? Your companions will be hardy enough already. For a Song Thrush it takes no more than a flight to Connacht to escape frozen Leinster; Galway's worms will sustain it until thaw sets in and it returns to leafy Wicklow. Then, a homecoming in spring: Estonia!

Facing page (clockwise from top left): Chough, House Sparrow and Lapwing. *Above (l–r)*: Wheatear and Stonechat pair (male, right). Depending where you live, 'working-class' House Sparrows may be the main entertainment; where farm fields escape intensification, Lapwings tumble overhead; along our Wild Atlantic Way, Choughs cruise over most homes with a sea view. Wheatears and Stonechats are, by nature, extroverts.

We live fixed lives that beat to a regular rhythm. Birds do not. The very core of their metabolism changes annually. Summer-visiting warblers, by converting insects to fatty deposits that double weight, fly directly from Ireland to the northern tropics in autumn. Some dispense with most of the digestive system to save space for the journey. Male sex organs regrow just for the mating season. Among the cast of male suitors, several change garb from Gothic to baroque in order to woo a mate. In simplest terms, sexual selection means that males display, while females choose. Do we share a unified approach to love and romance? Quiz anyone about the birds they see around home and stories fizz to the surface. It is like watching a nymph revive from the embrace of Pan. In this world that we think we know so well, great magic is playing right before our eyes – a wonderment beckoning us with both sound and vision.

Stumped by the challenge of recognition? Start by reading the whole being like a picture. It is better to absorb rather than grab a suspect in an identity parade. Tabbing a name is only half the battle. In tests, pigeons were found to be at least as good as humans at memorising and classifying images. While it is true that time is saved by checking diagnostic features, watching birds is more akin to appreciating art than studying science. Initial views should be regarded as an establishing sequence. Then, the trace elements of personality start to shine through. Blackbirds stalking worms employ a rugby scrum 'crouch, touch, engage' action. Chaffinches wander hither and thither combing the undergrowth for seeds and insects. Their hopping gait has a moronic air, lacking rhyme and reason. Hallmarks lie in such humdrum hopscotch. Observers who quit once identity is nailed down soon become no more illuminated than a low-wattage light bulb that tinkles when you shake it. The Reverend Gilbert White of Selborne in Hampshire wrote, in his introduction to *The Natural History and Antiquities of Selborne* (1788): 'If the writer should at all appear to have induced any of the readers to pay a more ready attention to the wonders of Creation … his purpose will be fully answered.' Above all, listen and the birds will tell you who they are.

Lamplight on roses and insects well hidden;
Old copper kettles and warm moss to nest in.
Brown earthy packages and still air to sing;
These are a few of my favourite things.

2. LANGUAGE LESSONS

BIRDSONGS ARE ANCIENT tunes that have been gilding the world's airwaves for millions of years. How far back do we have to go to find evidence that man was familiar with the same songs we hear today? Forty-thousand-year-old cave paintings and Egyptian hieroglyphs, some dating from around 2500 BC, are every bit as accurate in their illustrations as contemporary field guides. Specifically recognisable descriptions of sounds are more difficult to find. Aristotle, born in 384 BC, included rudimentary voice transcriptions for Jay and Crane in his *History of Animals*. In Ireland, hard facts started to crystallise sometime in the ninth century. An anonymous Celtic poet evoked a calling Corncrake by referring to its rasping tattoo as 'clacks' and left an apt encomium for Skylark: 'a timid persistent frail creature at the top of his voice, the lark chants a clear tale.' Carl Linneaus (1707–1778), a Swedish botanist and zoologist, founded a framework for naming nature called binomial nomenclature. All forms of life are categorised by family (equivalent to surname) and species (analogous to first name). Reflecting the scholarship of the time, most appellations were constructed using words from Latin or Greek. A friend of Linneaus considered him 'a poet who happened to become a naturalist'. Among his lexicon are phrases that he invented to describe several species on the basis of calls. Far from being an owlish academic with a powdered wig, he had both a keen ear and sharp wit. He used phonetics to coin *Pica pica* for Magpie, *Crex crex* for Corncrake and *Cinclus cinclus* – for realism, pronounced with a hard 'c' – for a fleeing, flying Dipper.

In evolutionary terms, birds have been around a lot longer than us. Are their voices set for all time? Within virtually every part of the human world there are accents and dialects. The same basic languages are being spoken but in former times isolation – separation by rivers and mountains or movement of people through nomadism and emigration – led to localised pronunciation. From this arose a myriad of regional accents, whether in English, French, Spanish or Mongolian. Birds, on the other hand, are highly mobile and few are truly resident. Many species switch hemispheres on a twice-yearly basis. For the vast majority a range of calls is used daily – but song is restricted in space and time and is usually the prerogative of males. Reserved for the breeding season, it serves to establish and defend a territory and attract a mate. Unless a species is

Dating back a thousand years, Irish monks, prompted by what they heard while painstakingly transcribing scripture, scribbled simple verses that celebrated birdsong – described as 'an amulet against loneliness' by an anonymous fourteenth-century scribe. 'A bird is calling from the willow / he is black and strong. / It is doing a dance, the Blackbird's song.'

The loudness of a Song Thrush is astonishing: not so much a crooner as a Martin Luther King orator. The sound exerts a strong pull and features in Robert Browning's poem 'Home-Thoughts from Abroad' (1845). Little wonder that English settlers to New Zealand introduced the species in 1867, where it is now common.

utterly isolated, might not its repertoire remain constant throughout its global range? By and large this holds true. Migratory divides can forge divergence and sedentary populations of 'mainland' birds on archipelagos sometimes develop a local twang. Timescales for this process are impossible to estimate. Wrens breeding on island outposts off Scotland's coast – Shetland, Fair Isle, the Outer Hebrides and St Kilda – differ subtly in plumage and overall size between each location and mainland Scotland. Yet, apart from a minor nuance in song delivered in Shetland, all sound the same as Wrens throughout their European range, including Ireland. When humans from Britain arrived in Australia and New Zealand they brought with them a selection of birds from home, including Blackbirds. In Australia, some Blackbirds are reputed to have developed a distinct accent. Similarly, Chaffinches in New Zealand are said to sing songs with fewer trills than their counterparts in the Old World. Can new voices emerge that quickly? Nowadays www.xeno-canto.org provides a vicarious testing ground. A user-driven, ever-expanding collection of calls and songs, it has a global reach. And its Southern Hemisphere recordings of both songbirds sound like traditional hymns, not different tunes. For the meantime …

Vocabulary is partly inherited and partly learned from parents and peers. Young Chaffinches isolated at hatching and then reared in silence deliver Chaffinch maiden speeches. Juvenile outpourings are soapy first drafts; accomplished song is achieved by listening to adults. Although young possess the raw material unique to their own kind, chicks raised by a foster parent of a different species will imitate and then adopt the song of the foster parent. Among individuals there is minor variation. In the same way that fingerprints are dissimilar, every vocal signature is unique. Birds are capable of distinguishing up to 200 vocal elements per second. To human ears, individual shards merge into homogenous notes at around 20 per second. Mimicry of other species and other sounds (including human voices) is testament to birds' intelligence. Neighbours know each other. Male territory holders listen out for interlopers; females do likewise, although often for quite different reasons – strangers in town always have a certain allure. Fast, dextrous wordsmiths pack a sonic punch whose complexity is, to our ears, the equivalent of a blur. Only by reviewing a graph of the output on a computer can we see the wealth of detail. Such analysis often reveals a further human failing – some of the notes are beyond our range of hearing.

Song can be defined as consistently repeated sounds that form a pattern. Its importance to a territorial male can be judged by the amount of time invested in singing. Unmated males sing most. They are setting out a stall that would pass muster as a curriculum vitae submitted to a dating agency. Except for short feeding breaks, winter singing by Song Thrushes in western Ireland can be continuous from dawn to dusk. Even when a partnership has been secured, the incumbent still feels obliged to defend his spouse and homestead. For this reason it can be difficult to be unequivocal about a songster's motives. Has he acquired a mate and thus broadcasting a 'hands off' to potential rivals? Or is he a lonely heart determined to succeed by expatiating endless arias? Observing singing Blackbirds offers some insights. Young males are subtly distinct in appearance (see p. 51). Over the course of a four-year study in the grounds of Oxford University Botanic Garden, Snow (1958) found that, during February

Male Willow Warblers sing endlessly as soon as they return from Africa. When females arrive, they find partners by song but then contemplate the worth of a male's territory before forging a tryst.

and most of March, youthful impresarios accounted for nearly all daytime song. Old hands sang sporadically at dawn and dusk, a time when cadets again threw their hat into the ring. Although the beginners' contribution was greater, few found mates. Established males quickly gained control of the airwaves and pair bonds were renewed with spouses from the previous year. Some new partnerships were forged eventually. Flushed with success, young husbands continued to sing, while a few old males hardly bothered. Spouting a cliché implying uniform song contests at dawn is, therefore, fallacious. In the case of Blackbirds (and probably others) the early spring song of young males is connected to asserting settler's rights. Because senior males are ensconced in territories at this time, they can rest on their laurels and devote less time to singing.

Is it fair to say that, for both birds and people, song is the food of love? Courtship overtures are undoubtedly best efforts, a sexual trait whose narrative conveys thoughts incomprehensible to us. On the contrary, science tends to take an impersonal view and reduces non-human actions to functions dictated by a struggle along the lines of a Darwinian survival of the fittest. In this scenario, there is no room for ascribing an aesthetic sense to either songsters or their listeners, especially females alleged to use singing prowess as a yardstick for selecting a beau. Interestingly, a relationship exists between drab looks and singing virtuosity. In place of a show-off costume, plain plumage comes with a fine voice. Male Reed Warblers broadcast a jumbled constellation of notes that is sustained, complex and melodic. Cadences and stresses define individuals and some emit twice the number of syllables than competitors. In closely related Sedge Warblers, females, in choosing a mate whose repertoire outdoes rivals', land a partner with a consistently higher food delivery rate for chicks (Buchanan & Catchpole 2000). Therefore, in the mind of females, singing ability appears to define the most worthy and a good voice impresses and has sex appeal. Yet a hearty voice also accords with a good bill of health, an attribute of considerable interest to any prospective mate keen to produce strong heirs. It transpires that the greater the burden of parasites, the poorer the singer (Muller et al. 2013). Male testosterone levels are reduced by parasite infestations and this leads to inferior song performance, such as less consistency in phrasing, resulting in *nul points* from female listeners.

Female Willow Warblers and Chiffchaffs, when they arrive in April, do not respect territories established by males over the preceding days. Instead, they exercise prerogative. Eager to please, males adjust territory boundaries but continue to sing relentlessly. In terms of maternal priority, choice of home trumps husband. Female Dunnocks do likewise. Having picked a core range, she awaits the arrival of a breeding partner and may enlist two suitors to father her brood, ensuring extra help to feed young. Dunnock song, a continuous quick-fire jumble, advertises the presence of males. Each troubadour is hoping to breed. Depending on his age, local sex ratios and female choice, he may achieve patriarchal status in a breeding hierarchy or his role might be subordinate – a toy boy – with clandestine copulation rites granted on the whim of a female. Song is his calling card and each male has a number of song types. Rather than recite full editions, truncated versions suffice. These incorporate snippets of neighbours' songs, thus elevating personal contact to a first-name basis. The scale of Dunnock 'intranet' outstripped researchers' ability to document its full complexity. One male used a minimum of four songs that contained excerpts from ten compositions derived from five neighbours. Impersonations enable each to recognise others by ear, one upshot being that a newcomer – and a potential rival – will stand out. Once breeding affinities stabilise, song becomes perfunctory and is downgraded to little more than a name-check. We blink like a hedgehog in April at the news that Dunnocks and many other species listen to each other's transmissions and comprehend sonic barcodes. Yet we instantly know a familiar human voice or laugh, even when we have not heard it for decades.

Calls perform a different function. If song is the equivalent of romantic poetry then calls are small talk. Compared to the wordy content of courtship, it is as though a subeditor has scissored out the padding. Brevity is important. When danger threatens, a fast hit of information is needed. On average, songbirds have about 15 varieties of short communications, equivalent to SMS templates. Of those studied, House Sparrow has 11 and Great Tit 20. Ravens, despite their gruff clucks and discordant muttering, scored highly with 23, a mark of undoubted intelligence. Research into Barn Owl nesting behaviour has uncovered a rule-based complex series of clicks, trills, barks and hoots which help coordinate family life, including altruistic food sharing by larger chicks with smaller siblings. For all species, standard functions include parental communications to young and shorthand that enables a pair or members of a flock to keep in touch even when they are out of sight. Lone airborne migrants use the notes as signatures in the hope of locating company.

Threat, alarm and distress calls are understood by more than just the species that utters them. Where mixed flocks are concerned, such as groups of tits, Treecreepers and Goldcrests in woodland outside the breeding season, the number of birds involved means that a predator is more likely to be noticed. Chaffinches emit a sharp *chink chink chink* when a static enemy is spotted, such as a perched Sparrowhawk. This general alert is common currency that summons other species and a cacophony ensues during which onlookers 'out' the danger. However, an airborne predator is a different matter. Escape is more important. A fast short *seet* is an urgent tom-tom instruction to flee or hide. Upon hearing it, others take immediate evasive action and many do so silently. If attacking, a predator is likely to be confused by birds fleeing simultaneously in different directions and may not be able to focus on a single target. Hence the quality of each call has a bearing on function. The emphatic, repeated *chink* draws attention to the caller's position; the brief *seet* is slurred and high-pitched, making it hard to pin down the messenger, although not the message. Separately or in tandem, Great and Blue Tits often perform security sweeps in the immediate aftermath of an alert. They intone an animated mantra. Short double whistles for Great Tit; Little-Bo-Peep trills for Blue Tit. If the intruder is a stalking cat they trail it as far as the edge of a self-styled exclusion zone. Only when their hubbub of calls subsides does normality start to return. Both are, by nature, bossy-boots. If, in the vicinity of 'its' feeder, either detects an unwanted human visitor, the vigilante may well dash off a chiding churr (see VOICES OF BLUE, GREAT AND COAL TITS). In terms of threat level, the trespasser has been rated as 'moderate' and has received an aural Yellow Card, thereby bringing the intruder to the attention of all and sundry.

By nature, Blackbirds are alarmists. In fact, what sounds like bedlam is cleverly orchestrated. When faced with a potentially lethal predator, short series of worried, sotto voce *chuck chuck chuck* calls emerge like a slow-transmitting fax. There are pauses between each delivery. Vigilantes closest to the danger call continuously, however, using higher-pitched, strident metronomic notes that get on human listeners' nerves. These calls are more agitated, as befits a spectator making a first-hand report. Thus a twofold commotion accompanies movement by the bête noire. Short flights by an invisible Sparrowhawk can be followed and the whereabouts of a slinking cat can be pinpointed exactly. When the nemesis makes a threatening move, flight alarm calls split the air like a row of exclamation marks. The shriek is a Mayday to flee.

There is a rough correlation between the size of a bird and the pitch of its voice. As a general rule, large species have low-pitched voices and small songbirds have high-pitched voices. Birds living in dense vegetation, such as reed beds or thick woodland undergrowth – a typical haunt of Wrens – have loud and persistent voices. Vegetation reduces broadcast range by blocking and absorbing sound waves. Corncrakes are especially loud. They live in dense undergrowth and hope to attract a partner passing overhead on nocturnal migration. Little wonder they crake loudest and longest during the middle of the night. Their voice registers around 100 decibels and carries up to 2km. Put in context, an ambulance siren registers 150 decibels. How come the caller does not damage his hearing? During bursts of calling a

To articulate a burry trill, male Swallows open the mouth. The trill's pitch is fixed for life. Males with deeper trills weigh more and have higher testosterone levels – and have more robust immune systems.

mechanical action adjusts the tension on the eardrum, muffling the bird's perception of its own voice. A further reflex that accompanies bill opening is the drawing of a translucent membrane – the nictitating membrane – over the eye. All birds possess this translucent eyelid. When extended, it makes the eye look misted. Normally the membrane is used to protect the eye, such as when a Dipper peers underwater. Quite why a calling Corncrake simultaneously covers its eye is a mystery.

Song posts offer uninterrupted acoustic conditions and disperse sound widely. Where no perch exists, songsters take to the air. Skylarks and pipits nest on the ground in open terrain and hover aloft to declaim sustained bursts. Lapwings perform aerial displays set to a soundtrack using voice and wing noise. Wind and, to a lesser extent, rain curtail song and even run-of-the-mill communications pipe down. In one study, when wind strength touched 24km/h Blackbird vocalisations ceased. In calm, sixty-eight calls were heard. Incontestably, stillness is best. It is also true that sound carries particularly well in early morning air. In spring, the rising sun warms the sky. Frigid air closer to ground level is slow to accumulate warmth. For several hours it sits as a chilly blanket, sandwiched between cold earth and summery sky. A peculiarity of sound waves is that they are repelled by a temperature interface. Rather than deflect upwards, waves travel laterally. For this reason, dawn is Happy Hour for songsters. Furthermore, until daylight warms the air, insects remain largely hidden and inactive – another reason why insectivorous birds use chilly first light to sing.

In birds, sound is produced in a structure called a syrinx. It is the equivalent to a human larynx. Located at the lower end of a bird's windpipe, the syrinx's resonance ability depends on its length, diameter and the hardness of its tissues. Membranes are arranged like pleats and can vibrate independently. As air is blown forwards from the lungs and into the syrinx, muscles within the organ contract or expand to generate sound. Options are infinite – from a monosyllabic whistle to a complex, pulse-generated phrase. In Canaries and other studied species, nerves on only one side of the syrinx are connected to the brain. Just like humans, language acquisition by birds seems to be centred exclusively in one cerebral hemisphere. Whooper Swans are one of several species that possess enormously lengthened windpipes that generate loud trumpeting. Collared Doves and Woodpigeons inflate their neck sides with swallowed air to increase the resonance and effectiveness of their calls. In addition, Woodpigeons and Long-eared Owls wing-clap and Great Spotted Woodpeckers drum as a non-vocal means of generating sound.

As listeners, we can enjoy birdsong from a purely aesthetic standpoint. Springtime is all the more uplifting when sight and sound combine to convey a sense of renewal in the world around us. If we pay attention, every species will reveal its identity. We are exceptionally good at facial recognition. Birds possess a similar faculty but the most immediate and deeply ingrained way that they know each other is through voice. Recognition is particular not only to species but also individuals. A chick reared in a noisy colony distinguishes its parent from the din of many competing voices. From our perspective using sound as a means to identify birds has an advantage over sight. Often birds can be heard when they cannot be seen. Our field of hearing encompasses 360 degrees, far more than our field of view. Beginners used to looking for visual characteristics as a reference point tend to struggle to find a framework that classifies voices. We need to connect the song to the songster. To learn a song, it helps if there is a 'stand out' feature to metaphorically point at. Often there is. A key phrase may be repeated, a featureless spiel may finish in a distinctive flourish or there may be an unmistakeable rise or fall in pitch. A first step is to visualise what we hear. This is easier than it seems. By constructing a blueprint in our mind, a few 'field marks' emerge that can even be reproduced as crude squiggles on a page.

Flight calls given by Greenfinches are commonplace in most gardens. Although few people are able to differentiate them from similar sounds made by other finches and sparrows, yet they amount to a unique series of around four identical flat notes. Given in quick succession, they form a loose trill with a distinctive judder, represented on paper by four look-alike spikes. Job done? Not quite. A crucial next step is needed. By visualising the spikes – four blocks of flats, a four-masted vessel or The Beatles crossing Abbey Road – a personal 'handle' cements the sound into a mental image. Just as Linnaeus did, try using phonetics to describe a vocalisation. But be sure to invent an analogy for what it sounds like. To many ears the terminal flourish in Chaffinch song suggests the words 'ginger beer' and the song of a Yellowhammer has a rhythm that fits the metre of the phrase 'a little bit of bread and no – *cheese*.' The cooing songs of Collared Dove and Woodpigeon can confuse. But only Woodpigeons sound like they are calling through a gag. If a tremolo quality strikes you as noteworthy, such as the quavery ending to Blue Tit's alarm call, conjure up an image. Perhaps a violinist holding the note with chin pressed tight against the instrument in earnest concentration? By painting a mental picture, the sound and the caller's identity will soon become clear. Several bird names were coined in this way. Wagtail and Dipper are derived from actions; Cuckoo and Chiffchaff are phonetic representations. No matter how frivolous, if an analogy works for you then you have a sure-fire shortcut to identification. There is no need to be overawed by the terminological spaghetti of rows of consonants and vowels that are used in most field guides to describe bird vocalisations. Although sometimes the only option available, they are someone else's attempt to transcribe the raw data. Sounds made by the birds in this book can be heard online at www. xeno-canto.org. To hear them, click 'About' on the tool bar; next, click as follows: 'Meet the Members', 'A'; 'Anthony McGeehan' [click name]; scroll through recordings; click 'Cat.nr.' to select a sound (e.g. XC179944 for Corncrake).

Greenfinch calls are monosyllabic repetitions that merge into a short trill. Congratulations if you understand that! Instead, try visualising the sound graph. Does it suggest a block of flats?

3. FROM DINOSAURS TO DOVES

LONG BEFORE DARWIN, naturalists observed that birds and reptiles shared many traits: birds' legs are scaly and reptilian; crocodiles hatch from eggs and chirp like chicks. Young can, if threatened, clamber into the lower branches of trees, indicating that they might once have been less terrestrial. And their fossil record reaches further back in time. Somewhere among reptile lineage, was there an ancestor of birds? If so, there ought to be a link between the two: a prototype half-bird, half reptile. *Archaeopteryx* – the word means 'ancient wing' – seemed to be that missing link. At first flush it resembled a small reptile. However, other features said bird. Its bony forelimbs resembled wings and had feathers. The breastbone was keel-shaped, a sign that chest muscles operated the wings for active flight rather than holding them spreadeagled like a flying squirrel that unfurls folds of skin to turn its torso into a paraglider. Pterodactyls, which developed limited powers of flight, did so by supporting flaps of skin across light wing bones. It was the evolution of feathers that gave birds mastery of the air. *Archaeopteryx* was alive in Jurassic times, 145 million years ago – the days of the dinosaurs.

Are birds descended from dinosaurs? Several scientists have expressed this opinion. The mists of time have not, in truth, yielded enough evidence to be certain. But several facts are

Woodpigeon outer tail feather. An aerofoil that creates lift, a feather also protects, insulates and glamorises.

clear. Several small dinosaurs were covered – some only partially – with primitive feathers. From this starting point, whatever title you wish to give tree-dwelling feather-clad forebears, evolution went viral. Modern birds leave *Archaeopteryx* in the shade. It breathed in and out through mammal-like lungs, meaning that it could probably only manage several airborne minutes before running out of puff. We use the same system. Our diaphragm drives air in and out of the lungs. Birds' respiratory systems are ingenious. Breath is drawn non-stop through the lungs, allowing oxygen to be extracted constantly, during both the inhalation and exhalation of air. The air sacs act a bit like bellows. Breathing happens by expansion of the body cavity that causes the network of air sacs to expand, thereby sucking air through the lungs. When the bird breathes out, the air returns through the lungs. The returning air is still high in oxygen so that the gas exchange in the lungs is far more efficient than in mammals: because it happens with both inhaled and exhaled breath. Mammal lungs are a cul-de-sac containing unused space and near-stagnant air. The difference in extracted oxygen between avian and mammalian lungs is remarkable, all the more so because the lung volume in birds is proportionately less. To reduce weight further, bird bones are hollow.

Birds have come a long way in 145 million years. The demands of flight have altered the skeleton. Many bones that are separate in other vertebrates are fused to promote lightness and strength. Bill development replaced teeth, a further saving in weight. Because the forelimbs became wings, the bill and feet do the work of paws. Neck muscles need to be strong and flexible, enabling the bill to reach all parts of the body. Small, seemingly short-necked species such as Coal Tit can twist and extend the neck to reach deep inside confined spaces. Nest-box inspections, body outside but head and neck inside, are made in this way. In birds, the number of neck vertebrae varies from 11 to 25. We possess 7. Feathers form more than just outer plumage. Effectively, birds live within a duvet. Downy layers provide 'eiderdown' insulation and a hidden gap in belly plumage allows adults to swaddle eggs and incubate them against hot skin. Feathers come in several styles and each has a quill embedded in the skin. Blood supply nourishes the feather during growth. When growth is complete, the quill is sealed off and the feather becomes a dead structure, although it is still operated by muscles in the skin and performs vital functions from flight to repelling water. A central shaft extends from the quill and rows of barbs form a two-webbed vane. Depending on the feather's role, the webs may be broad and of similar width either side of a straight shaft (central tail feathers) or of unequal width on a curving shaft (leading feathers at the wing's tip). The webs' barbs interlock and create a smooth surface. Feathers of the wing and tail are stiff and strong. Because they are the largest they take longer to grow than any others and are designed to last at least a year.

All birds change plumage by regular moults (See MOULT p. 67). Adults often change into drab non-breeding plumage after nesting (although their feathers, being relatively new, are anything but drab) and assume swanky dress again early in the following year. It is as though they shop at Brown Thomas for spring fashions and revert to Penneys in autumn. Youngsters have a succession of moults and some species may not reach breeding age for several years. During adolescence, costume changes steadily alter their outward appearance. Others, such as Wrens and Dunnocks, fledge in almost identical garb to their parents. Colour is derived either from pigment cells within the feather's structure or from light reflected off the surface of the web. Dark feathers, because they are full of pigment, wear better than others. Hence, black wing tips may fade but the feather remains intact and less tatty than paler plumage elsewhere. Feathers also change by a controlled, phased process of abrasion. In finches, buntings and sparrows, the ends of feathers start to rub off in late winter and early spring to reveal underlying colours. In this way courtship livery is acquired without resorting to moult. Plumage is kept in condition by meticulous preening: zipping the barbs of the feathers together with strokes of the bill. Lubricant is applied in the form of oil that is smeared over the bill from a gland located at the base of the tail. As part of daily grooming, some species also use toes. Herons have powdery down among chest plumage and rub the head and neck through it, presumably to clean off oily residue from their prey of fish and amphibians. A further refinement is a serrated edge on the claw of one toe, which combs slimy detritus from feathers.

As wear abrades feather tips, colours may alter. By summer (right) male House Sparrows have a more extensive black bib than in autumn (left), when their costume is new. Some species use the process in a controlled way to acquire bright breeding plumage.

4. TERRITORY AND NESTS

Male Blackbird in spring. The regal stare is backed up by a swanky cock of the tail upon landing or an exaggerated upstretched neck.

Territorial behaviour fluctuates with reproductive activities, increasing in intensity during courtship and reaching its peak during nest building, then tailing to its lowest ebb just after breeding when adults start to moult, an annual necessity that constitutes the real break between one year and the next. At some point during late winter, harmonious relations break down among songbird buddies that spent the winter peaceably, either in a flock or by sharing habitat on *modus vivendi* terms. Where once several Blackbirds co-existed, a male bossyboots emerges and routs rivals. He struts, inflates body plumage and strikes a heraldic pose, even snootily tilting his bill. Should he see his reflection in a mirror, he will wage war upon himself. Old males become intolerant of young pretenders. It is an advantage for seniors to retain territories where they bred before. They know them intimately.

Young Turks only succeed by taking over vacant plots or inserting themselves along interfaces between occupied territories. Surviving pairs from the previous season renew acquaintance; some will have been together throughout the year. A proportion of adult females move away but return to breed in the same area – preferably with the same partner. Colour-ringing and four years of scrupulous observations (Snow 1958) revealed unexpected platonic relationships. During winter, apparent pairs proved not to be true pairs. Female Blackbirds deserted boyfriends and returned to natal areas where they linked up with husbands that spent the winter home alone, beating territorial bounds. By the end of February the stage is set for breeding and, irrespective of age, couples now have amorous intent. However, established adults do not drive out intruders indiscriminately. A certain amount of communal use of foraging habitat is accepted. Neighbours are recognised. But not all are welcome. Mature males are often tolerant of peers, less so of young hopefuls. Presumably, debutant males are deemed to pose a potential threat to the owner's patch and partner.

In all birds, male sex organs enlarge after winter dormancy. Depending on species, they may swell to become 300 times larger than at other times of the year and, among certain wildfowl, they can account for one-tenth of body weight. In male House Sparrow, the scale of change is from winter pinhead to springtime baked bean. Female change sees the oviduct increase in

Defence of winter territory is unusual. Keeping interlopers at bay saps energy. Beach-master Pied Wagtails will take on a sidekick, provided the helper is a good bouncer with a small appetite.

diameter from a gossamer thread to a thickly muscled conduit. Lengthening daylight triggers all these momentous changes. Increased light levels stimulate the production of hormones in the brain, setting in motion a sequence of reproductive organ growth and, for males, song. All males of breeding age undergo the same transformation but only some breed. During autumn and winter, most species circulate over a wide range and few defend a discrete feeding zone. Robins and Wrens are exceptions and both use voice as a year-round declaration of property rights. However, while most Wrens are resident, many Robins are not and sing to proclaim ownership of a feeding redoubt. Robins are unusual in that song is used as an offensive weapon. Rather than engage in posturing or fisticuffs to preserve ownership, the inevitable 'first come, first served' result is achieved by the most economical means – song. Rules can, however, be broken. In hard weather hatchets are buried and, gingerly, several share a feeding area such as a garden replete with an *embarras de richesses*.

Pied Wagtails, ostensibly free and easy with a high-stepping gait and sunny disposition, struggle to find enough food to survive the winter. Despite what appears to be a phenomenal feeding rate of seizing tiny prey, the bird barely meets its energy demand. Short days require constant foraging. Depending on food availability a territory may be established and defended single-handedly, usually by an adult male, or with the assistance of a subordinate, often a young bird. The territory holder faces a dilemma. His beat might yield an adequate food supply but is subject to intrusions. Trespassers test his rights and need to be excluded. Exchanges and evictions are noisy time-consuming interruptions. Vocal declarations are used as a signal of ownership of a territory. Upon arrival, a prospective owner is edgy and broadcasts *chissick*, a standard salute, also commonly used as a flight call. To rebuff an intruder, the owner-occupier replies *chu-wee*, analogous to 'Get off my land!' With this, the passer-by departs. Because enforcement is onerous, the resident male tolerates a sidekick. Upon arrival, a wannabe batman appeases the owner with special gestures. If accepted, the newcomer is free to stay so long as there is enough food for two. A bargain is struck. The guest undertakes roughly half of all defensive duties thereby increasing feeding opportunities for the owner, a gain estimated at one-third more. But if times are hard the tenant is ousted. Quite how the resident male calculates the carrying capacity of his domain with the presence of a lodger is unclear. Probably, hunger governs his forbearance. Tenants may share territories with several males and can leave voluntarily. In a way, they too are opportunists. Should a boom in prey occur elsewhere, such as an insect hatch during a mild spell, the territory owner temporarily vacates his patch and joins a Klondike flock, gambling that when he returns he will be able to wrestle his holding back from potential squatters. Overnight roosts are postulated to serve as information exchanges whereby the location of feeding hotspots is communicated among peers. Quite what signalling system the birds use is yet to be understood (Broome *et al.* 1976). In the spring a sudden increase in food supply relieves pressure. Territory owners stop evicting intruders and accept the presence of others, the result of which will be a breeding partner.

For all species, occupancy of a territory means that its owner has the wherewithal to woo a female and, with her, enjoy something of a monopoly of resources sufficient to raise a family. In truth, rather than safeguarding a select foraging area, defence of a territory is more to do with defence of the female. Feeding sites are tapped both within and outside the area defended by a male. Size of the actively defended part of the territory differs between habitats and is also dependent on the density of neighbouring rivals. The adornment of breeding plumage in males serves a twofold purpose: dapper looks to impress females combined with war paint to face down competitors. Moreover, the psychological benefit of possessing a territory bolsters hubris. Territorial males rarely lose disputes with interlopers when played out on home turf. Ironically, if the gamekeeper turns poacher, he will probably be vanquished. It seems that the 'moral right' of owner-occupiers infuses them with zeal. For the duration of the breeding season the male becomes a stay-at-home property-owning conservative with attitude. Rivals are attacked belligerently and he becomes paranoid about his partner's fidelity. Male Swallows frequently issue false alarm calls to locate absent partners. In many species, both sexes are promiscuous and second broods often have a mixed parentage.

While, for some, house and home evoke a do-or-die defence, the writ of others runs no further than the immediate vicinity of the nest. Pigeons and doves do not defend a homeland. They disperse widely to feed, often in loose company with peers. Wheatears nest in holes at or close to ground level. The same accommodation is used annually but the occupiers change. A safe breeding site scores highly when surrounding habitat is homogenous. Rooks, although

Rook nests are fixed abodes, despite swaying precariously in high wind. The first sunny days of the new year usher in quarrelsome spring cleaning. Repairs and upkeep result in pursuit flights and bickering.

colonial, still have a proprietorial streak. Rook society is hierarchical and tyros that attempt to build on the margins of existing rookeries are attacked and their sticks commandeered. Unapproved start-up colonies suffer the same treatment. Territory size is modified by, among other factors, local food supply. Provided there are trees and bushes, Chaffinches breed throughout Ireland. Density varies enormously. Food is hardest to find in mature coniferous plantations, where Chaffinch territories are eight times larger than in deciduous, well-timbered gardens. Territorial adults exclude non-breeders and push members of this floating population to the margins. Some try their luck by attempting to breed in substandard habitat. Although a few pioneers succeed, most bide their time and test the resolve of mature adults. It is tough at the top.

The survival of a species depends on producing enough young to compensate for adult mortality. Rearing a new generation is of paramount concern but the means of doing so have to be balanced against assessing the chances of success, notwithstanding endangering the lives of those that knuckle down to breed. Strategies vary enormously. One tactic is to raise few young at a time and lavish them with concentrated care for a long period while they hone survival techniques. Birds of prey rear a small family in a single brood. Hunting theory is

instilled over the course of many hours of 'copy mum' instruction. To offset anticipated heavy losses inflicted during a tortuous migration, Swallows pump out several broods. Parents and first-fledged juveniles care for siblings reared in subsequent broods and all come together as a band of brothers to face migration. Apprenticeships in snatching flying insects are conducted by older hands that catch and then release stray feathers as target practice for juveniles. Young Swallows have cinnamon faces, the equivalent of an L-plate.

Determination of breeding age is, by and large, a function of size. Sexual maturity is reached at an earlier age in small birds, a logical expression of shorter life expectancy. For this reason most breeding pairs of small birds do not consist of the same individuals from one year to the next. Even if both members of a pair return to the same locality, the urgency and ardour of males to attract mates means that courtship is a frenzied ritual rather than behaviour imbued with love and devotion. Nonetheless, emotional attachments are a reality and some larger species mate for life. Jackdaw society is extremely well ordered. New couples are betrothed in the spring following their birth, despite not reaching breeding maturity until a year later. In pigeons and doves, pair faithfulness is remembered. Memory is based on visual recognition. In experiments, breeding partners were separated at the end of one season and kept apart

(L–r): underside view of Blue Tit nest; topside view; same nest in use. The female builds the home. A circular grassy foundation anchors a cushion made from moss and fibres. White feathers and wool garland the circumference, a habit peculiar to Blue Tit. Over a thousand trips are made to complete the nest which can be built in as little as three days.

until the onset of the next. Despite the opportunity to choose new partners, 75 per cent of pairs reunited. A number of species that are usually monogamous occasionally shift into polygamous pair bonds if there is potential to rear an additional generation. Male Dippers may mate with a second female but not assist with rearing her brood. Female Sand Martins frequently switch colonies, leaving males in charge of one-parent families. In most species the female undertakes incubation, for which she acquires a brood patch on the breast or belly for warming eggs. The patch develops shortly before a clutch is laid. Hormonal changes cause some feathers to fall out, making a bare-skin 'hot-water bottle'. Where incubation is shared, males also develop a brood patch. However, in general, females undertake the lion's share of the big sit. A songbird clutch requires at least a fortnight of constant heat to hatch. During this time the sitting bird has limited time to feed. Depending on species, males contribute by bringing food to their nest-bound mate.

Perhaps the greatest dilemma faced by a bird is the selection of breeding site. Although males, in varying degrees, attempt to influence choice, females are the final arbiters. Indeed, male Wrens are known to construct several 'cock's nests' to advertise real estate and hope for a tenant. Key features are concealment, stability and strength to withstand wear and tear imposed by growing chicks. The development of cryptic patterns designed to harmonise nest and surroundings amount to camouflage evolution. Chaffinches and Goldfinches craft exquisite homes. The exterior is embroidered with moss and lichens, woven to create the illusion of a protuberance on a branch. A deep cup is lined with thistledown and the inglenook is snug and waterproof. Perversely, inadvertently trapped rainfall can drown chicks. Attempts at concealment were doubtless the primary impulse that drove Blue Tits, Jackdaws and others to place their nests in holes.

Nests come in many types but all share a theme: no human is capable of such skilled handiwork. Frequently used building materials include mud as a solidifying lining, grass stems

Female Goldfinch is the sole architect and builder of a tiny nest draped with lichen as camouflage and located out of squirrel reach near the end of a spreading bough. Apart from Bullfinch and Chaffinch, finches prefer to breed in loose groups of two or three pairs. Information on food sources can be pooled and more eyes watch for approaching enemies.

to form a cup and spider-silk or cobwebs for interweaving materials together. In general, male songbirds that vigorously defend well-defined territories play no part in nest construction. Self-serving arias and a swashbuckling lifestyle enforcing homeland security keep them busy. In these species, evolution has gifted architectural ability to females. Among the roll call of female master builders are Blue, Great and Coal Tits, Willow Warbler, Chiffchaff, Robin, Blackbird and Song Thrush. Great and Blue Tits install deep bedding material and, during building operations, deposit their eggs among the dishevelled mass. Only on the eve of incubation are the eggs 'excavated' before being snuggled against the brood patch.

Mistle Thrushes, perhaps because they lose some vigilance when preoccupied with nest building, have been observed in some detail. Building commences in the early morning and finishes around midday. The foundation block consists of a clump of vegetation. The female stands on this and, using her feet, shuffles and tramps fresh material into the crotch of adjoining branches. As more is added, the body, wings and chin come into play. Once a mould starts to form, she presses like a potter spinning a pot, deepening the shape while rotating her body step by step to ensure a symmetrical outcome. Rotations progress in small increments. Gyrations are rapid and the bill is only used to pull stray strands into the weave. When a tight-fitting grassy cup has been sculpted, wet mud is plastered to cement its shape. A final layer of fine vegetation is then added. The dimensions and contours of the cup are derived, not from measurements, but from the builder's rotational movements. In some cases, males attempt to make themselves useful by proffering building materials although the majority are mere onlookers.

Male Woodpigeons leave their partner 'parked' at the selected nest site and fly off to procure sticks. He searches and returns with a single spar that he places close to or under the female before departing for more. Her role is to press the growing stick-work into a trestle. She squats, rotates and pushes. After many hours the structure consolidates and acquires a shallow concave centre. Operations last at least a week. Looked at from ground level, the finished product appears flimsy and almost see-through. Even when new, it resembles a mouldering platform of broken twigs, hardly likely to attract attention. Yet it resists gales and holds young securely. Grey Herons use a similar building technique.

Observing a scene of industrious parents delivering mouthfuls of food to clamouring chicks is the apogee of a nuclear family. But sometimes such a conclusion is wrong. Long-tailed Tits resemble each other, so the sex and age of those attending a brood cannot be told. However, by careful examination of individuals and subsequent colour-ringing, it emerged that kibbutz-style cooperative breeding is normal. Life is complicated for this tiny insectivorous bird. Weighing around 6 grams and needing to keep body temperature at a constant 40 °C, it is vulnerable to cold weather. Unlike hole-roosting Wrens and other tits, Long-tailed Tits minimise the effect of overnight cold by roosting together in groups. In extreme cold they huddle in a ball. Sociability and communal defence of a large winter territory is based on family ties. Neighbouring clans are kept at bay. In spring, some females switch clans to find a mate who is not a blood relative, the only time of the year when pairs rather than flocks can be encountered. Nest construction is also a product of joint enterprise, the pair working in unison. The elaborate nest is made of moss, cobwebs and hair. Its external covering consists of an adornment of camouflaging lichens; inside, it is warmly lined with up to 2,500 feathers. Large families are accommodated by the nest's pillow-cushion ability to expand. Moreover, the lodging's temperature is maintained, an important consideration because adult body size is small and not all chicks can be brooded. Access is through a peephole side entrance, from which the tail of a sitting adult sometimes protrudes. Builders operate in relays, one chattering with impatience while the other works rapidly and assiduously. Up to a month may pass before the breeding quarters are completed. Finally, eggs are laid on top of the featherbed lining and incubation begins. Unfortunately, most attempts fail due to predation. A meagre 15 per cent of nests yield fledged young. With so few offspring produced the post-breeding tribe is in danger of being reduced to a skeleton band. The implications are worrying. The wintertime troop of brothers and sisters may not be large enough to keep each other warm. Going to roost solo during a big freeze may be tantamount to suicide. To bolster numbers, failed breeders help at other nests so long as they contain chicks. In other words, when successful fledging has a chance, all hands rally and fledging rates are doubled by helpers. Hence territorial ambitions in springtime are eclipsed by the need to produce the maximum number of bodies to hunch up against a chilly winter wind.

5. DULL AS A DUNNOCK?

BASED ON OUTWARD APPEARANCE, Dunnocks are tweedy. Sober plumage, a shy disposition and modest, unobtrusive shuffling among vegetation evoke the persona of a librarian. Such virtues were extolled by Reverend F.O. Morris (1856): 'Quiet and retiring, the Dunnock exhibits a pattern which many [people] of a higher grade might imitate, with advantage to themselves and benefit to others through an improved example.' However, to succeed in rearing a new generation, the bird tears up Garden of Eden principles and resorts to avant-garde sexual mores. Although some relationships are monogamous, most are polygamous. Dunnocks feed from the ground by turning over leaf litter. Quarry is tiny, at times bordering on microscopic. Were it not for the Dunnock's industrious body language, many food items would be invisible. Dunnocks are capable of breeding from nine months of age and most live for just one or two years. Reproduction is, therefore, an immediate and pressing priority. Rearing a family places a strain on a parent because the habitat, while providing adequate food, imposes a high workload when items are small. Although both sexes aspire to raise young, a caveat applies: any mating system can be used in the battle to monopolise a breeding partner or partners. In fact, the more the merrier, provided reproductive success is achieved.

Defence of territory by females appears to be the catalyst for subsequent outcomes. Domains are independent of male distribution and females compete among themselves to carve out a

To our eyes, all Dunnocks look the same. Yet the drab lookalikes have complicated sex lives. A common arrangement is for a female to utilise two breeding partners, both of whom think they are the father of her brood.

breeding niche. Each resides in her own space and, during the breeding season, seldom leaves. Like a spider in a parlour, she waits for a fly to arrive. Males usually outnumber females as a consequence of what happened during the previous winter. Nearly half the adults perish, with males surviving better. Females suffer greater mortality because, after they vacate breeding territory, they occupy a lower position in the pecking order at wintertime feeding sites. As a result, cold weather exerts a greater toll. The exigencies of the breeding season also claim more female lives than male. In Oxfordshire, during a study spanning each of nine breeding seasons from 1981 to 1990, predation was documented (Davies 1992): 'Adult females were more likely to die than males, probably for two reasons. First, females did all the incubation and brooding of young and some were killed on the nest (probably by cats). Second, incubating females were easily recognised because they fed at a noticeably higher rate when they came off the nest and were probably less vigilant and so more susceptible to surprise attacks by predators.' Davies ringed 453 nestlings during 1981–1984. Of these, 32 were taken from the nest and killed, mainly by cats.

Therefore, in many areas, the annual round of courtship commences with an imbalance between the sexes. When adjoining male territories overlap, one defers and the territories merge. A male axis is formed and allies keep rivals at bay. Although brothers in arms, they are not equal. One is dominant, especially with regard to wooing a mate and rearing a family. Adjacent female territories may offer mating opportunities for the subordinate male – or for the dominant male. Permutations abound. Occasionally males may be in short supply and two females share one partner. Single-handedly, she builds a nest. The male, as pragmatic as ever, assists in the rearing of just one family. What seems heartless to us is, in fact, probably a well-founded calculation. Rather than risk losing two broods, one is favoured. Not surprisingly, one-parent families are the least successful.

In polygamous arrangements featuring one female and two males, the female, far from being the underdog, draws the subordinate male into a ménage-à-trois by granting him mating rights. By so doing, she is assured of his help in feeding chicks. Because he has fertilised the female he is convinced that at least some of the brood are his own. Without this certainty his contribution to the family's welfare wanes or ceases entirely. His role is an open secret. The dominant male mistrusts him and pursues him on sight. Were the female to do likewise, he would, presumably, move away. Her affections ensure that, instead of going, he prefers to hide. Often she hides with him. Trios of Dunnocks are a common sight during spring. Stand-offs, signified by a dominant male bullishly flicking one wing, continue until young fledge. In truth, the top dog has a tough time. Despite being the alpha male, he is constantly on edge and attempts to guard the female. This is impractical. When she is out of sight, he becomes paranoid and suspects that she is in the company of the subordinate. Usually she is. Quickly, he looks for her. His searches have real urgency because males are adapted for high copulation rates, fuelled by unusually large testes. Couplings are rapid and frequent. The duration may be a mere tenth of a second but rates reach 100 times a day. The female has, at her disposal, a powerful idiosyncrasy. She can eject a rival's sperm, encapsulated in a pinhead-sized droplet. Far from performing this act discreetly, the gesture is performed for the benefit of her chosen beloved. Thus, for the greater good of feeding her chicks, his affections are manipulated. Little did Reverend F.O. Morris know!

The blatancy of such 'in your face' girl power is a relatively recent discovery (Davies 1983), although the first hints of a strange pre-copulation display were noted by Edmund Selous in *Evolution of Habit in Birds* (1933). 'I made a curious and very intimate observation on the nuptial habits … A pair of these little birds came out from the shrubbery … after hopping about a while, in a state of great sexual excitement, the hen elevated her rump and stood still, when the male, hopping up, made … wanton-looking pecks in this region, that is to say into the actual orifice.' Close but no cigar. Selous missed the denouement encouraged by the ardent male – the sight of a jettisoned sperm capsule.

6. COUNTING THE EGGS

How can a Collared Dove that lays just two eggs be more reproductively efficient than a turtle that lays hundreds of eggs, buried in a pit for added security? Turtles, when they hatch, are unguarded. If they successfully run the gauntlet of beach predators and reach the sea, they have only made it from the frying pan into the fire. While enough reach adulthood to maintain the species, losses are astronomical. Through a slaughter of innocents, a handful survives but may continue the line for centuries. Birds lay few eggs in sheltered nests and chicks are fed and mollycoddled through infancy. Many parents synchronise incubation efforts to ensure that hatching is almost simultaneous. Lapwings, like most shorebirds, lay four tapered eggs and point them inwards like slices of a pie. The arrangement fits the bird's brood patch. Moreover, compact positioning means that no heat escapes during incubation.

In doves and pigeons, both sexes produce high-protein crop milk to wean squabs. Milk quantity and brood patch size impose a two chick ceiling. Nonetheless, the ability to produce milk emancipates the parents from a need to obtain suitable wild 'baby food'. Offspring grow rapidly and fledge in three weeks. As they grow, the percentage of crop milk is steadily reduced and replaced by grains and seeds. Division of labour is also shared and the household is run in shifts. The male feeds young from mid-morning to afternoon; the female takes charge at other times. Within hours of the first brood becoming independent, parents are free to commence a

To avoid detection by predators, Ringed Plovers lay eggs that mimic stony ground. Before hatching, chicks communicate with parents and other siblings by cheeping from inside the eggshells.

second. Ergo, small clutch size and independent means of food production facilitates fecundity. On top of this, young reach breeding maturity within a year – small wonder the Collared Dove's spread westwards was so rapid.

Other species face more perplexing problems. Swifts arrive from Africa in May and attempt to rear a single generation of up to three chicks fed exclusively on flying insects. But what if summer is wet and cold and food supplies fall short? Adults respond to deterioration in weather by removing one or more eggs from the nest. Such drastic intervention makes sense but how does the savant know when to trim potential losses? Titmice lay large clutches – before abundant food is available. A seven-year study of Great Tits showed that not only do clutches increase in size in those years when caterpillar prey is plentiful, but that offspring hatch just as caterpillars emerge in numbers. Each year both events synchronise, yet peak numbers of prey vary by as much as a month. Research established a link between early spring temperatures and caterpillar life cycle (Perrins 1979). Are Great Tits cognisant of the connection?

Geographical variation in clutch size also occurs. Length of daylight curtails foraging activity and exerts influence over clutch size. Basically, a shorter day limits the amount of food adults can collect to feed chicks. Goldfinches transplanted by British settlers to Australia have become widely established. Latitude determines daylight length and Antipodean populations of Goldfinches have a shorter working day than their British counterparts and Australian clutch size has shrunk to an average of three eggs. In Britain and Ireland, average clutch size is five. Across Europe, a similar situation applies to Robins. Populations on the Canary Islands lay an average of three eggs, Spanish birds produce four and in Holland the normal quota is five, whereas Finnish Robins lay six eggs. Robins in the Canary Islands and parts of Iberia are chiefly resident. On the other hand, northern populations of Robins are migratory.

Anticipated losses inflicted on migration and during the course of a year spent in disparate parts of a continent-wide range take a toll of numbers. Therefore, northern Robins attempt to compensate by producing as many recruits as possible.

Wheatears possess an almost completely global range across the higher latitudes of the Northern Hemisphere. Apart from a gap in the central Canadian Arctic, tundra is universally occupied. At home on short turf with rock outcrops, the small songbird also occurs in temperate regions where habitat requirements are met. All populations return

Juvenile Wheatear. Huge importance is placed on sprouting wings. Maiden flights are executed in under a fortnight.

to ancestral winter quarters in the semi-deserts of sub-Saharan Africa. Arctic breeders make an epic journey and perform single-hop flights over the North Atlantic. Individuals nesting in Canada, Greenland and Iceland fatten up in preparation for airborne marathons of 48 hours or more. Mortality is high. The age of spring migrants indicates that most of those destined for higher latitudes are one-year-olds. Breeding is not only possible at this age, it is also desirable and clutch size is doubled. Whereas Irish breeders lay between three and five eggs, as many as ten are laid in Greenland and Canada. High productivity is possible because insects are abundant in the brief Arctic summer, making it feasible to rear a large brood. If food was not bountiful, not enough descendants would be produced to maintain the population and local extinction would result. To compensate for being born into a kamikaze population at the far reaches of the globe, northern fliers are equipped with longer wings than their Irish cousins.

For parents, breeding exacts a high price. To face the rigours of egg production, female Blue Tits increase body weight by one-quarter. Males lose weight due to courtship feeding. Egg production requires at least one-tenth of the female's daily energy consumption. Feeding young is energetically expensive and parents may lose almost one-fifth of their body weight during this period. Nonetheless, the commitment to breed eclipses everything. So it is a sad day when a clutch is destroyed. Contrary to some popular belief, the laying of a replacement clutch is not simply a case of replicating what was lost. First clutches reflect optimum timing and attempts by males to ensure that just one top-quality set of genes produce offspring. Young reared in second broods show higher rates of mixed parentage and fledging rates are often lower. The first brood is a pair's best shot at seed corn. Losses of clutches to Magpies and other nest predators entrain a slow process involving repeating all preliminaries from courtship to nest building, egg production and incubation. Forced to undergo hardship and self-sacrifice a second time, the strain on the health of parents is considerable. In a study of House Sparrow mortality in Britain, more adult deaths occurred during the breeding season than in the rest of the year combined (Welty and Baptista 1988).

In Starlings, maternal duties account for a sex-differential mortality. Young females, breeding for the first time at one year old, suffer a death rate of 70 per cent. In males of equivalent age, less than 40 per cent die. Novice males are deemed to be greenhorns and are left in the lurch by older matriarchs, but by hook or by crook, younger mothers are keen to start breeding. A single azure Starling egg lying on a dew-covered lawn is not an uncommon sight. How did it get there? Whether intact or broken, it was dropped. Presumably, a nearby nest had been raided. The real explanation is an eye-opener. The culprit was a female Starling parasitising the nest of another. Just like a Cuckoo, the raid was meticulously planned. The femme fatale knew that the occupant was not at home. Quickly, she removes one egg, replacing it with one of her own. Her circumstances go some way in justifying this behaviour. Although capable of breeding, she is immature, probably a year old. Male Starlings are polygynous so, although mated, she has no intention of rearing a family single-handedly. If discovered by the returning female a battle royal ensues. When two combatants are seen locked in a vicious struggle, this is often the reason for the dispute. Indeed, occasionally the outcome is the death of the interloper. Research into the phenomenon has revealed that it is a regular facet of

Adult male Starling (left) and first-winter female (right). Photographed in January, the male is at his finest for courtship in spring. Born the previous summer, the brown-eyed, dull-billed female is around seven months old. One fleck of mouse-brown juvenile plumage, above her eye, remains to be moulted.

behaviour for females in this peer group. Twelve 'floaters' were fitted with radio transmitters and followed for up to two weeks. None had a nest. Instead, they trespassed among other females' breeding sites, checking for broods and looking for a chance to offload an egg. If an egg is added to an uncompleted clutch, the real mother rumbles the deception and removes the foreigner. However, if incubation has commenced then the ruse succeeds. Statistically, it appears that attempts at 'cuckoldry' could be made on as many as one in three nests each year (Davies 2000).

7. THERE IS ALWAYS ONE

CUCKOO IS THE ODD MAN OUT. Rather than accept the responsibility of rearing its own progeny, it palms off chick-rearing responsibilities to others. By cheating, it does not have to spend time defending a nest or finding food for hungry offspring. Speculation about motives does not, however, abate the infanticide executed by junior. Or, for that matter, the 'outrage on maternal affection' (Gilbert White 1788). At around ten hours old, the hatchling instinctively wriggles within the confines of the nest. Its bare skin is touch-sensitive. Upon encountering an egg, chick or random small object, it squirrels below the cargo and heaves it overboard by means of a concave depression in the centre of a disproportionately broad back. The behaviour persists until nothing remains. This is no mean feat because the pink pimpernel weighs a mere 3 grams and is toiling with a load equalling one-third of its body weight. Lest its foster parent is in the throes of completing a clutch, ejections continue even during matronly brooding. Indeed the surrogate mother will stand aside to enable the chick to accomplish its grisly task, transfixed and idle as the demon jettisons the unborn family.

The saboteur gained admission to the brood because its natural mother perfected mimicry of the host's egg. Females produce just one type of forgery that ties them to a first-preference host. Each year adult Cuckoos return to the same district to work their deception. For females, site fidelity spanning seven years has been proven by an examination of characteristic egg patterns. Nests are located through a combination of watching from a hidden perch or, over open habitat, slow overhead circling. If a dot in the sky, the bird copies the posture of a soaring hawk or harrier. The ruse conned experienced birdwatchers and prompted a flurry of correspondence to ornithological journals in the 1960s (Ash 1965). At rest or in low-level flight, the bird's likeness to a bird of prey is designed to cause panic among songbirds that react by mobbing the fake predator (see p. 156). In doing so, they provide a steer to the whereabouts of nest sites. Unwittingly, they have anointed their home place with a Judas kiss. With play-acting over and intelligence gathered, sleuthing begins. During perched reconnoitring the female remains motionless for periods of an hour or more and adopts a prostrate pose in an

Four Irish Cuckoo eggs paired with eggs of host species. In each pair, Cuckoo egg is on left. Host eggs, clockwise from top left: Reed Bunting, Sedge Warbler, Meadow Pipit (two on bottom row).

attempt to resemble an inanimate object. When a nest is discovered, surveillance is conducted from a discreet distance. If the spy has a suitable command post, she can monitor activities from 100m or more.

Several nests are raided and one or more eggs or small young are removed and eaten. On the one hand, this supplements the Cuckoo's diet and the added calcium boosts egg formation. On the other hand, selected nests are being manipulated. Because hosts attempt to make good for the loss of eggs or young, they commence a replacement clutch. Such attempts, having been instigated by the Cuckoo, suit its ends. In effect, the robbing spree means that the laying of replacement clutches ripe for parasitising have been synchronised. The scale of skulduggery can be considerable. In countryside near Hamburg, Germany, up to 30 per cent of Marsh Warbler nests were robbed in readiness for the addition of a Cuckoo egg in the replacement clutch (Gartner 1981). Another European study documented raids on 159 Reed Warbler nests, 48 per cent of which were robbed of 158 eggs. Of those Reed Warblers that laid a second clutch, one Cuckoo inserted a succession of eggs (Gehringer 1979). Unfortunately, preparatory nest grooming often results not in the production of a new clutch but in desertion by the host. This is of little concern to the usurping mastermind, which steals a march on the remaining active nests by laying an egg already partially incubated in her own oviduct, thereby giving the embryo a head start and enabling it to hatch just before, or around the same time as, the host's own offspring.

A juvenile Cuckoo: to disguise itself from enemies, it fledges in a costume akin to a Sparrowhawk, even mimicking the hawk's whitish blotches on the nape.

The fatal raid is usually carried out on a warm afternoon when the nest is unattended. Furtive and fast, the femme fatale planes low to the ground and, by means of a distensible cloaca, lays her egg directly into a nest cup too small to support her body. Less than a minute is spent in the vicinity of a nest and egg deposition is accomplished in an average of nine seconds, sometimes as few as four. She is at pains to leave no clues and treads lightly, balancing on the outside of the nest. In Germany, Cuckoos have laid eggs directly into nest-boxes by clinging to the entrance. Some canny hosts spot the slightly larger alien egg. They strike it in an attempt to perforate the shell and prevent hatching. Even in this endeavour, most are thwarted because the shell is thick. Further deception falls to the infant. Its begging calls match those of a live brood. The intensity is amplified and, as an added stimulus, the inside of its gawping mouth is emblazoned with tongue spots that mimic those of the host's chicks. So pleading are the cherub's cries that prodigious food amounts are ferried, not just by foster parents, but sometimes by onlookers. As a testament to the begging calls' potency, a young Cuckoo taken from a Meadow Pipit nest and brought into captivity attracted the attention of Wrens that made their way through a broken window into the house from where the youngster's cries originated. Another juvenile, captured by James R. Garrett in June 1821 (Thompson 1849–52) prompted a momentous observation: 'For several weeks after the Cuckoo was placed in confinement, it uttered, when in want of food, a note so closely resembling that of the Meadow Pipit, that it would have been almost impossible to distinguish between them. By degrees, however, its voice became more harsh, and latterly its only call has been a discordant one, uttered in the evening, and but once daily. This is very like the bark of a dog, repeated four or five times in quick succession. Whether all young Cuckoos have, in the first instance, the same note or acquire for a time, that of the foster parents, I have been unable to ascertain.'

As a result, the blind and naked foreigner mushrooms from 2 grams to 100 grams in just three weeks. Fully grown, it begins to resemble its real parent. Like hypnotised dummies threatening to wake up, the revelation risks bringing the foster parents to their senses. To maintain its façade the chick redoubles its begging calls. If anything, the coquettish whimpering becomes even more solicitous and continues to mesmerise the foster parents until the fledgling starts to roam and seek out larger prey better suited to its burgeoning bulk. Finally flying off strongly, it begins foraging for caterpillars, a food choice governed by a genetic instinct. All types are accepted including numerous colonial, hairy and warningly coloured species avoided by other birds, such as those of the Cinnabar Moth, whose black-and-yellow caterpillars appear in July and feed on the poisonous leaves of ragwort. Not only is the Cuckoo immune to toxic caterpillars, its gizzard is also adapted to deal with noxious hairs from hirsute species, which are periodically ejected in pellets.

In Ireland, Meadow Pipit is Cuckoo's first-preference choice of foster-parent and lays an olive egg overlain with profuse fine speckles. Except for slightly larger size, a Cuckoo egg is an excellent match. Pied Wagtail, Robin and Wren are among other recipients and are most likely to be conned if the duplicate is not markedly different or if, in the dark recesses of a domed nest (such as a Wren's), the strange addition might not be noticed. Female Cuckoos can only produce a stereotype egg specific to the first-choice host – a 'horses for courses' strategy amounting to an Achilles heel when it comes to finding alternative surrogate parents. Given the less convincing match to the eggs of second-preference hosts, the female Cuckoo may simply be indulging in a hopeful, rather than cunning, deception. More inexplicable is the use of Dunnock as a host. In Britain, 2 per cent of all Dunnock nests examined as part of the British Trust for Ornithology (BTO) nest record scheme contained a Cuckoo egg, making Dunnock one of the four favourite British hosts. In Ireland, except for Meadow Pipit, information on the range of host species is sparse. Indeed, based on numerous examples in the collection housed at the Ulster Museum in Belfast, no Irish Cuckoo egg appears to deviate from a standard Meadow Pipit pattern (see examples in photograph on p. 33). While Dunnock may be chosen with some regularity, a search of published literature yielded just one reference, from Monkstown, near Cork, in the early nineteenth century (Thompson 1849–52). Dunnock eggs are plain sky-blue and despite the 'sore thumb' conspicuousness of a large patterned Cuckoo egg among an azure clutch, the deception succeeds. One study established that, roughly, a mere 5 per cent of Cuckoo eggs are rejected by Dunnocks (Aviles & Garamszegi 2007). In Britain the loss during historic times of extensive greenwood has enabled Dunnocks to thrive in resultant scrubby habitats, a trend that might have brought the species to the attention of Cuckoos. Dunnocks may, therefore, be recent victims, still naïve

Adult Cuckoo: the wandering voice of summer. Cuckoos fly low with fast shallow wingbeats; the wings are not raised above the back. Perched, they droop the wings and raise the tail, splaying feathers to reveal white tips.

when it comes to rejecting an egg that does not mimic their own. Quite how long this time lag in developing host defences will last is unknown.

Similar acceptance of glaringly obvious misfits has been shown experimentally for Meadow Pipits in Iceland. There, Cuckoo is absent and local Meadow Pipits did not bother to discriminate when odd dummy eggs were added to their clutch (Davies 2000). Confronted with the same dummies, British Meadow Pipits were not fooled. Initially, are hosts less likely to reject if they are unaware of a threat? Over time, the situation changes and protagonists learn, resulting in Cuckoos perfecting ever more sophisticated copies of hosts' eggs in a kind of avian arms race. Rather than basing arguments on a human subjective assessment of mimicry, recent research quantified pattern matching as seen through bird eyes (Stoddard & Stevens 2010). It transpires that several criteria apply and that complex patterns in host eggs demand the best counterfeits. Away from Ireland, Cuckoos that attempt to match Pied Wagtails face a stern test because the eggs have a unique 'granular' template of markings based on size, density and distribution. Not surprisingly, rejection rates of fakes are high and range from 71 per cent to 91 per cent (Aviles & Garamszegi 2007). Nonetheless, as some success accrues, Cuckoos evolve better mimics and by a process of elimination, only the best duplicate-producing females continue to outwit their specific hosts.

Cuckoo behaviour bends many rules. Outsmarting a host is one thing but another consequence of the birds' actions is the need for the juvenile to recognise its own kind, rather than imprint on the species that reared it. Normally, when birds raised by a stranger become adults, they attempt to mate with members of that species. This phenomenon is known as sexual imprinting. Female waterfowl occasionally 'dump' surplus eggs in broods of other, unrelated, wildfowl. Imprinted ducklings become confused for life. Some attract mates and hybrid young are produced. Juvenile Cuckoos avoid this pitfall because they imprint correctly. But how or when does imprinting occur? It is possible to construct a hypothesis, based on a study made with a related species, Great Spotted Cuckoo (Soler & Soler 1999). Great Spotted Cuckoo breeds in Iberia and is a brood parasite of Magpie nests. Subterfuge tactics are broadly similar in both species of cuckoo but there is a critical difference: adult Great Spotted Cuckoos make erratic contact with fledglings while they are being raised by Magpies or shortly after they have gained independence. In fact, contact may be between adults unrelated to the fledgling. Communication is, in the first instance, vocal. In this way the youngster learns to recognise its species. The timing of the chick's sensitive phase for imprinting appears to be delayed until triggered by an appropriate call. In other words, the youngster may only be receptive to calls of its own kin, irrespective of when it first hears them. In North America, Brown-headed Cowbirds are, like Cuckoos, brood parasites. When cowbird chicks were played calls of their own species at six days of age, they responded to them, despite never having seen their real parent. Indeed, the simplicity of Cuckoo's basic two-tone call might make it easy for the embryo's brain to store it – a genetic trait, rather than something that has to be learned.

Adults depart in summer for winter quarters in Africa and leave the new generation in their wake without any apparent hint to their true parentage. Logic suggests that when contact is eventually made, feasibly in Africa, vocal cues precipitate a Eureka moment. Perhaps adult Cuckoos, upon randomly encountering migrant youngsters either en route or on wintering grounds, emit 'password' calls? In all birds, chicks are hard-wired to react to certain vocal commands that demand a specific response. Skylark chicks, because they hatch from ground nests and are vulnerable to predation, leave the nest well before they fledge, some in as little as six days after hatching. When the time comes for them to leave, the female utters a single unique note. The call is described as short and shrill and is believed to be reserved as a one-off instruction. Upon hearing it, chicks were observed leaving the nest immediately (Donald 2004). Intriguingly, for the juvenile Cuckoo, there is a slim basis for believing that imprinting might sometimes occur during summer. A passage in *The Birds of the Western Palearctic* (Cramp 1977–94) dealing with Cuckoo flock behaviour and autumn emigration reads: 'At Dungeness (England), mid-June, feeding flocks of 8–12 adults, perhaps mainly males, commonly occur; from July, females and juveniles appear better represented, and from around 20 July, flocks entirely juveniles; birds typically silent and unobtrusive (N. Riddiford).' From the use of the word 'flocks' it could be inferred that the juveniles already recognised their peers. In other words, even though each youngster had had continuous contact with foster parents, it had not imprinted on them but had met its own species. Sadly, given a sharp decline in numbers of migrants at Dungeness, with a mere three adults and one juvenile recorded during July and August 2013 (www.dungenessbirdobs.org.uk), there is little prospect of repeat observations.

8. JUNIOR DINNERS TO Á LA CARTE

SONGBIRDS ARE BORN NAKED. Blind and too weak to stand, all they can manage is a laboured twist of the head. To our eyes they are the essence of vulnerability. Yet the ingénues have already achieved much under their own steam. While inside the egg, chicks communicate by clicking to each other. This serves as a pre-hatching signal between the brood and helps to synchronise emergence. Frequency of clicks varies between species. Baby Song Thrushes make an average of 35 clicks per minute. In preparation for liberation two tools are developed. A temporary collar of muscle swells around the nape. In conjunction with a small gritty tusk – called an egg-tooth – on the bill's upper tip, the muscle is used to force the head and egg-tooth upward and perforate a membrane inside the egg chamber. Around three days before hatching, the baby splits the gelatinous envelope and accesses poor quality air trapped between membrane and shell. When the egg's surface is pierced, energising fresh air fills the chick's lungs. Communication is established with a parent and, if alerted by adult clucking, piping calls that might alert a predator cease immediately: wariness is a basic instinct. When free of its calcium prison the infant gapes and hopes to be fed. Even the vibration of an adult landing on the perimeter of a nest stimulates gaping. Begging calls are produced and the chick imprints on the first moving thing it sees, under normal circumstances a parent. Until it grows wings and can fly, the youngster is confined to the nest. Fledging times vary and are linked to overall size. For example, small warblers fledge in a little over a fortnight. The cries of hungry young may sound like a homogenous racket to human ears, but adults can distinguish the hungriest and rotational feeding ensures that none is overlooked.

Ground-nesting birds follow a different system. Their young have a better chance of survival if they evacuate and scatter as soon as possible. To flee and hide, tiny-tot young need legs, not wings. In Skylarks and pipits, leg development is extremely rapid. Although born blind, their eyes open during the second full day. As well as sound, they now have vision. Pin feathers begin to erupt on the third day and by the fourth day the soft flesh of the legs starts to harden. At the end of the newborn's first week the legs are virtually fully grown, well ahead of feather growth. In unison, the brood responds to a specific 'abandon ship' penetrating whistle from their mother (Donald 2004) and move away from their birthplace. They spread out – as much as 50m from the nest and 20m from each other – and parents continue to feed them until they can fly and feed themselves. Full independence is reached around three weeks after hatching, despite flight powers being wobbly.

Lapwing young go one stage further and become precocious within a matter of hours, not days. They hatch covered with down and instinctively struggle to their feet and blink, bleary-eyed, at their surroundings. Although camouflaged, they could still be in danger if they remain together. Teetering steps are made behind one parent who leads them away from the patch of ground where they hatched. Sometimes the brood is split by the breeding pair and then reunited when nerves settle. The brood are self-feeding, learning danger signs and

Lapwing chick. The well-developed head and stout legs reflect priorities. The downy baby feeds itself but is tightly chaperoned by a parent until its feathers emerge. Once it can fly (in three weeks) it fends for itself.

copying parental feeding techniques. Unlike songbird nestlings, they are not born with an empty stomach. They retain up to one-third of the egg's yolk. This augments nutrition for up to seven days. For the same reason, domesticated poultry hatchlings do not need to be fed for three days. Young birds of prey take a middle course. They are born down-covered but are unable to leave the nest. Because the nest is a relatively open structure lacking a deep cup or wind-breaking walls, down provides a duvet that cotton-wools them against the elements. As a result, both parents are free to hunt. For the female, this often means watching for prey from a nearby perch whilst keeping an eye on the kids. As a general rule, females of all species spend more time brooding delicate young than feeding them. Males are breadwinners, even though they may be required to pass provender to the female who dispenses dinner. Predators need to tear up prey and tease out morsels for tiny mouths. Male Kestrels are incapable of shredding food into small bites. If mother dies, young also succumb, as they are unable to swallow entire prey delivered by the male.

Skylark, juvenile. No more than a fortnight old, this Skylark can fly but only a short distance. For safety and to ensure that some survive in the event of a crisis, chicks of ground-nesting birds leave the nest and scatter. Downy shorebird chicks, such as Lapwings, stagger clear of where they were born in a matter of hours. Naked baby Skylarks quickly grow feathers and sneak away in just over a week. Each hides in vegetation and is fed separately by a parent.

In order to grow, chicks require bodybuilding protein rather than high-calorie carbohydrates. Adults are cognisant of infants' requirements and amend food selection to suit. Breeding season analysis of House Sparrow diet revealed 70 per cent insects for nestlings but only 3 per cent in adults. Fledged young gradually cranked up seed intake until it was similar to adults (around 70 per cent). Young birds seem to be instinctively aware of the need for protein. Given a choice, ducklings choose insects over vegetable matter despite the fact that aquatic plants become a staple when the ducks are fully grown. Captive young Blackbirds that were fed exclusively worms grew more rapidly than those whose diet was manipulated to contain 50 per cent ivy berries. Several species of warbler switch diet prior to migration. By concentrating on easily digested, energy-rich food, calorie intake is boosted. Like a marathon runner preparing for race day, they mainline fruit that contains a high proportion of carbohydrate and unsaturated fatty acids easily converted to body fat. The main drawback of most fruits is a low percentage of protein. Olives and elderberries are exceptions and are eagerly consumed. An advantage is that berries can be guzzled with minimal effort. Insects are mobile and calories are expended in their pursuit. However, caterpillars, because they are relatively large and slow moving, are singled out and, in reed beds, a glut of aphids can almost be grazed.

During autumn migration around the Mediterranean, fruit-eating Whitethroats and Blackcaps increased in body mass about twice as rapidly as insectivorous Willow Warblers and Chiffchaffs. The watery pulp of berries is processed rapidly and seeds are excreted in as little as twelve minutes. Pavement below Waxwing flocks in berry-laden trees rapidly turns purple. A captive Song Thrush fed elderberries completed digestion and passed seed in thirty minutes, testament to the powerful digestive juices of all birds. Regurgitation vents seeds. Blackbirds spit out undigested ivy seeds, explaining germination hotspots in ground level undergrowth. Some plants depend on birds to broadcast seed. Not only do seeds emerge unharmed after passage through the alimentary canal but also their exterior has been moistened and research showed that germination rates were higher for seeds that took this route. Tiny seeds may, inadvertently, become attached to part of a bird, especially the legs and feet. In 1859 Charles Darwin planted the seeds taken from mud attached to the leg of a Grey Partridge. Eighty-two seedlings of at least five species germinated from the parcel of soil.

Swifts are tied to an aerial existence and a diet consisting of aerial plankton – insect 'krill'. If supply fails adults move elsewhere, leaving chicks to face austerity. In response nestlings fast and, echoing reptilian living, revert to cold-bloodedness. Core temperature and heart rate drops and offspring fall into a state of torpor, a suspended development that can be maintained for up to ten days. Adults can invoke the same tactic. However, their fasting limit is shorter: no more than five days. When feeding resumes, food is delivered as a 'bug burger'; the catch is solidified into a ball. Parents with a marble of food in the mouth are easy to recognise, such is the modification to a normally svelte, sylph-like silhouette. Swifts do not possess a crop. In those species that do, food remains there for a variable time and becomes softened by salivary glands before passing into the stomach. Finches possess storage pouches either in the mouth cavity or on the sides of the oesophagus. In the breeding season, the pouches are used as miniature shopping baskets, accumulating supplies of seed or insects to be regurgitated inside babies' mouths. Outside the breeding season, finches and other seedeaters use the crop as a means of gathering food quickly in order to roost early. In effect, they retire to chew the cud, thereby shortening their exposure to enemies. All birds complete digestion by using both a stomach and a gizzard. Both operate using strong muscular actions and many species swallow small pieces of grit to aid the gizzard's abrasive grinding. Grit-gathering crows are a common sight on motorway verges. Because the grit particles wear away they are regularly replaced.

Where diet differs markedly between seasons, the stomach and gizzard alter structure. A toughening of the stomach walls and a greater volume of ingested grit parallel a seed-based winter menu. To break down grains, the bird develops the constitution of a cement mixer. In summer, when the diet of most finches and larks contains a higher proportion of insects, stomachs shrink. Digestive organs also become softer and the gizzard lacks grit. In birds of prey and owls, the gizzard acts as a trap that prevents indigestible material from the last meal – teeth, fur and feathers – from proceeding into the alimentary canal. Grebes face a similar difficulty with fish bones and get around the problem by swallowing feathers to line the

Linnet is a small finch with a short, stocky bill. It feeds mainly from plants such as docks, whose seeds are either directly attached to the stem or, like dandelions, are enclosed within pods or capsules.

stomach wall. Hunters, however, meld the remains together and cough them up as a pellet. Study of the fragments tells much about diet. Dentition identifies species of toothed prey and various fragments from insects are equally diagnostic, albeit requiring microscopic scrutiny.

Seeds are a vital resource for many Irish birds. They contain concentrated nourishment and have a staggered availability throughout the year, each season delivering a different bounty. Consumption is tackled in various ways. Pigeons and doves guzzle raw product and pound it up in the gizzard. Crows and tits grip capsules with their feet and chisel through the tough exterior. Great Spotted Woodpeckers sometimes wedge acorns in bark crevices and rain blows to gain entry. Finches use a different technique. They have short, stocky bills operated by powerful jaws. The edges of the bill are sharp, much like the blade of a potato peeler. Parallel ridges and hollows lie inside the lower mandible. These act as a vice against which the seed can be rolled and held secure. Once clamped, it is split against the edge of one mandible. Simultaneously, a hard muscular tongue pushes from below and rotates the seed using jaw movements. Once under way, peeling or 'shucking' is accomplished with rapid, almost imperceptible gyrations of the lower mandible. Like frayed shavings dangling from a pencil sharpener, discarded husk starts to emerge from the side of the bill. When the kernel is swallowed, dribbling ceases and the lower mandible reverts to a stationary, clean state, but only until the next bout of foraging commences.

Opportunists exploit situations where other wildlife acts as a beater to reveal food. Robins have had to switch allegiance from extinct topsoil-disturbing Wild Boar to human gardeners. Coyness and fear of humans has been subsumed by the greater need of being close to the scene of disturbance before prey dashes for cover. Pipits and wagtails invoke much the same strategy by hanging out with grazing animals that attract insects to dung as well as disturbing them from vegetation. Storing food is another option. For resident birds, seasonal fluctuations in food supply can turn a feast into a famine. Few, however, attempt to make a cache that will tide them through lean periods. Making a larder is difficult. Foodstuffs may not keep and the energy spent laying down supplies may be wasted if the booty is discovered. To ward against theft, perhaps items could be secreted in many locations? Which raises a further problem – remembering whereabouts of cached items. Ireland's climate is equable and wintertime is generally mild. Across continental land masses winter weather is bitter and few species are resident. Among those that are, several store food. Titmice commence gathering seed in autumn and deposit individual items in bark crevices for winter consumption. One species was provisioned with radioactively labelled sunflower hearts, rendering cached seeds visible to specialist detectors. Simultaneously, researchers placed numerous 'control' seeds in identical sites. Which would be found and in what proportion? Hoarded seeds disappeared first, followed gradually by controls. Clearly, the birds remembered the storage sites. Controls, on the other hand, were discovered through random search.

Many feeding stations in Ireland's gardens contain sunflower hearts. With the husk already gone, the food is 'good to go'. Each kernel is similar in size and shape, spool-shaped with a pointed end and is palatable to a wide variety of species, none of which has to go through the time-consuming process of dehusking before reaching the contents. Finches prefer to occupy a feeder perch and dine there. Titmice opt to remove one sunflower heart and fly off to eat in private. Why, therefore, do Coal Tits 'draw and drop' up to three or more identical items before disappearing with the next? Few settle for the first to be picked. Intriguingly, the fate

What explains Coal Tit's seemingly wasteful habit of removing and dropping identical-size seeds from a feeder before flying off with one that is no different?

Jackdaws are partial to the pith below the bark of Ash trees. They strip away smooth fresh wood and hammer the glossy underlying heartwood to expose whitish pulp at its core. Minuscule amounts are nibbled. The quantity derived would hardly feed a fly, yet the birds indulge in the activity throughout the year. Perhaps, to a Jackdaw, pith is snack food on a par with honey?

of almost all that were available in one garden between early September and the beginning of January was burial rather than consumption. They were cached in a variety of locations. Concealment behaviour encompassed tapping or shoving the seed into rotten wood, under leaf litter or among lawn moss. Alternatively, the cargo was spirited away within conifers and evergreen hedges where it was attached to foliage having first been coated with saliva. Both processes require the seed to be held parallel along the axis of the bill. Might seed position account for the discards? Perched briefly at a feeder, a Coal Tit is unable or reluctant to transfer a seed from the bill to its foot, from where it can be manipulated and replaced, facing forwards, inside the bill. Rapidity is a hallmark of mannerisms and the sight of a lottery win of sunflower hearts may further intensify foraging. Rather than fuss over alignment, the bird chucks away ill-fitting seeds until one slots correctly into position. By way of confirmation, fallen seeds that are subsequently removed from below an empty feeder are readied for transportation using bill and foot adjustments. Could it be that there is simply not enough 'floor space' at the feeder port to permit preparations? Impatience may be a factor. If only one seed was available, it would be unlikely to be tossed aside.

Across Ireland, the autumn of 2012 was notable for large numbers of Coal Tits. This was more than likely the result of a successful breeding season rather than the populace being augmented by an influx from Britain or beyond. By observing traffic at a single garden feeder, it was possible to place some figures on the quantity of sunflower hearts that were removed by the species during a four-month period ending at the start of the new year. Although action was frenetic and hoarding activities were elusive, a good fundamental grasp of behaviour was gauged. January ushered in two changes. First, numbers of Coal Tits declined dramatically. The reasons for this are unclear. Perhaps they shifted into breeding habitat or an arrival of feeder-dominating Greenfinches and Siskins intimidated the tiniest tit into looking elsewhere for food? Secondly, a greater proportion of seed was not buried but was carried off and consumed. At times a seed was partially eaten and the remainder hidden. The total number present during the autumn 'Klondike' is not known. A handful of distinguishable individuals made repeated visits. It is likely that many undistinguishable others did the same. In essence, a relay system was in operation involving at least twenty Coal Tits. Over the course of four months they removed approximately 50,000 sunflower hearts, the majority of which were cached. How many cached seeds were retrieved and when? Such questions remain unanswered.

Marsh Tit does not occur in Ireland. Across Britain and Europe the species is sedentary and habitually stores food. Research found that it stored several hundred items of food per day, in separate locations within a territory. In controlled experiments, most items were retrieved within a day of being hidden. On the face of it, such comparatively rapid retrieval is hard to comprehend. In principle, hoarding ought to be insurance against hard times ahead, rather than exploiting a supply before circumstances change. Possibly the activity follows a diurnal pattern with items cached quickly to be revisited and eaten later – at leisure and in comparative safety. Short-term storage intentions are supported by the fact that many items are secreted at ground level. If Coal Tits were laying down a winter larder, snow cover could scupper retrieval. For this reason Scandinavian Marsh Tits tuck away all food items in tree bark (Perrins 1979). In northern North America, chickadees are close cousins of Coal and Marsh Tits. For them snowy winters are standard. They cache food supplies in autumn and revisit them in winter. Does success in rediscovering hidden booty rest on memory or, more prosaically, by conducting random searches within a defined territory? A peculiarity of bird vision is a lack of 'inter-ocular transfer'. Unlike humans, most birds have eyes placed on the side of the head. This greatly restricts forwards-facing binocular vision, although monocular lateral vision is excellent, allowing most of the arc of space surrounding a bird to be kept under constant scrutiny. Certain brain functions are controlled exclusively from either the right or left hemisphere. In birds, the optic nerve divides itself between each hemisphere. Rather bizarrely – to our minds – the memory of what a bird sees with its left eye does not 'read across' and allow its right eye to access the same remembered information. While birds are not inhibited by this configuration – in fact, each eye specialises at scanning different distances – the unique property allowed a test. Researchers attempted to establish if Marsh Tits were using memory to relocate food by covering one eye during storage activities. Afterwards, with only the other 'naïve' eye uncovered, the birds did not return to storage sites. However, when the eye uncovered during storage was again unmasked, they re-found each cache. Neatly, this appears to prove that memory, not chance encounter while foraging, is used. Short-term memory of a cache is one thing, recalling the whereabouts of many hundreds of locations in preparation for a forthcoming winter is a different undertaking that would fox a human mind.

Coal Tits and chickadees look quite alike and their vital statistics are the same. Each weighs a little less than 12 grams and easily fits inside an adult human hand. But it is what happens inside the chickadee's brain that is amazing. For all we know, the same applies to Coal Tit. During an autumn burst of food storing, the hippocampus – the cerebral region responsible for spatial memory in vertebrates, including humans – expands in volume by around 30 per cent. New nerve cells generate. Come the return of spring and a widespread availability of food, feats of memory are no longer needed. So the hippocampus shrinks. Basically, the bird grows an additional hard drive to accommodate a map of winter food depots. By implication, its unique ability to regenerate parts of its brain through hormonal activity could benefit medical research into human neuro-degenerative diseases involving the hippocampus.

9. HOW BLACKBIRDS DETECT WORMS

ONLY EXPONENTS OF YOGA could hold their body as stock-still as a Blackbird peering for worms. The bird draws itself up, leans forwards and adopts a stationary pose with the head tilted to one side. Without warning, it hops, pauses and recasts. This time the head twists left then right and the bill is lowered and steadied at a shallow angle, suggesting final preparations for a bayonet charge. One eye points towards a spot on the ground. A few moments later the head rotates, allowing the other eye to scrutinise the same location. In a stiff breeze the plumage ruffles and shakes, yet the gimlet eye is motionless. Because birds lack the muscles that allow us to swivel our eyes, the eyeball is relatively immobile in its socket. So the bird must move its head to make best use of central vision. But is it watching, listening, smelling or sensing vibrations below its feet? Cocking the head to one side does not give much of a clue, as the action might facilitate both hearing and seeing. Like a patient fisherman it waits for something to happen. Nothing stirs. Periodic shifts in position seem curiously random rather than systematic. Suddenly it covers several metres in a few bounds and without further ado crouches and stabs the ground. The lunge was not a complete success. It pinpointed a burrow but the quarry rumbled the attack and began a hasty retreat. Frantically the Blackbird changes position, hacks the ground and manages to seize the animal's disappearing tip. A tug of war commences but the worm's grip on life slips away. Stepping backwards and pulling, the Blackbird hauls dinner into the open. The hunt was spectacular. But how did it find the worm?

Body language fits the conclusion that Blackbirds are looking for visible clues. Worms are brought close to the surface by moisture in the ground, or at dawn and dusk when they forage near or on the surface. When prey is visible, eyesight is, axiomatically, the means by which quarry is found. However, the technique is also employed among impenetrable long grass or tussocks. The plot thickens when the bird tosses overlying foliage out of the way before nailing a victim. Although its vision is more perceptive than ours, seeing through vegetation beggars

A Blackbird searching the lawn for worms is a familiar sight. Robotic stops and starts imply that predetermined tactics are being used. But what are they – listening, looking, smelling or sensing vibration?

belief. By twisting its head and directing its ears (hidden by feathers and located behind the eye) could it be doing the human equivalent of cupping ears to focus a sound? For years this supposition was believed and books were written that repeated the conjecture. Although worms do produce some sounds when burrowing into soil, the intensity is feeble and masked by the greater level of background sound. On the one hand, it is possible to press an ear against a burrow opening and hear a faint rustle; on the other hand, trying to detect the same sound from as little as a few centimetres away is impossible, especially when wind or traffic noise greatly exceeds the murmur.

During the 1960s researchers in California attempted to get to the bottom of the mystery. American Robins, Blackbird's counterpart in North America, were held in captivity for a year. During this time, individuals were observed in great detail and subjected to trials involving sight, sound and smell. By constructing artificial burrows, only some of which held a worm tip, it emerged that the birds responded to the sight of the end of a worm in a burrow. If the hole was empty, the bird did not peck at the entrance. Detection by hearing was disproved when white noise was played during trials. No difference in foraging success rate was observed between control birds and others exposed to white noise. In other words, if noise drowned out wriggling sound and the birds still located prey, the conclusion was inescapable: sight was the key sense. Smell was discounted when freshly dead worms tainted with various chemical odours were selected from burrows in roughly equal proportion to live, unscented worms.

Like people, birds utilise and process information from several different sense organs simultaneously. Situations are sized up and assessed. If we smell smoke we know there will be fire. We do not have to see flame or hear crackles to support our opinion. Similarly, if the researchers' birds were presented with (albeit barely) visible targets, might not other senses have remained unchallenged? Following the California study, two Canadian scientists put a fresh set of American Robins through different tests in 1994. This time all worms were buried.

Worms that wriggled in the fine tilth used in the experiments might have left a visual clue in the form of disturbed soil particles. Covering the surface with thin cardboard eliminated this possibility. Invoking belt and braces, the cardboard was itself covered with a shallow layer of soil. The scope of the research was widened to ascertain if worm vibrations were being tapped, perhaps through pressure-sensitive pads in the soles of the birds' feet. Researchers working with shorebirds had discovered that elongated probing bills detect buried prey using specialised vibration 'mechanoreceptors' embedded in pits in the bill-tip. Short-billed shorebirds, such as Lapwings, lack the ability but tap the ground with a trembling foot. Allegedly, the action simulates rain and causes worms to draw themselves close to the mouth of burrows (in anticipation of moving around and not drying out, thanks to the high humidity after rain), thereby inadvertently revealing themselves to a stalking plover. While the habit is a striking adaptation in obtaining food, interpretation of the behaviour could be flawed. The Canadians devised a system that, for the American Robins, delivered an unequivocal answer. Trays containing buried worms were attached to a shelf that a bird could not reach, except by perching on a separate ledge. Nonetheless, the invisible worms were found. If the birds found hidden prey and were deprived of any tactile contact with ground containing it then, by a process of elimination, only two options remained. Odour was one. Live and freshly dead worms, with no apparent change in odour, were buried. If smell were used to detect the worms then the birds would not discriminate between dead or alive food. Almost exclusively, the birds struck the ground where live prey was buried. Probes were not random and virtually none were directed at a dead worm.

Collectively, all other experiments suggested that hearing was the most likely method by which buried food was found. Probably like members of an audience baffled by a magician, the Canadians disbelievingly revisited the white-noise experiments that had been conducted in California. First, they recorded worm sound. Noise was only audible during movement and registered at low amplitude in the frequency range 6,400–7,920 Hertz. Although songbirds are most sensitive to sounds between 10,000–50,000 Hertz (1-5 kHz), most species studied can hear sounds below 10,000 Hertz. White noise was generated at 50–20,000 Hertz and played above ground. It had no effect on the birds' worm-finding abilities. However, when a speaker emitting low-frequency white noise was buried alongside worms, the birds were less successful at finding prey. Thus, while the white noise did not completely obscure the sounds made by worms, it impaired hunting significantly. Therefore, Blackbirds (and all thrushes) listen for food. Vision complements hearing and the two senses act in tandem. Head cocking may be an attempt to focus the source of a sound prior to launching a strike. The angle of the head integrates both senses. Still the remarkable truth remains: Blackbirds are searching for prey that they cannot see.

Song Thrushes find snails by sight but hunt worms using a similar technique to a Blackbird.

10. BERRIES AND BIRDS

MANY BIRDS switch from a summer menu of invertebrates to a winter diet based heavily on berries. When cold weather arrives, frozen ground prevents foraging for worms, grubs and fallen seeds, leaving berries as a lifeline. Berries grow on trees, bushes, climbing shrubs and certain ground-level plants. Fleshy pulp contains starchy carbohydrates that conceal and protect the seed within. Moreover, most berries are full of vitamins. Birds eat the produce and spread the seeds over a wide area by dropping them away from the parent plant. However, seed dispersal does not work when tough-billed species crack open berries and eat the seeds. For this reason hawthorn and other shrubs produce kernels enclosed within a rock-hard shell that pass through digestive systems unscathed. For most berry-producing plants, birds are partners. 'Come dine on me' is the message.

Birds and berries are a perfect example of interaction in nature and have 'co-evolved' to meet the needs of both. Across Europe and North America the patterns of ripening fruit trend

Background: bushy woodland in southern Europe in autumn. Berries and fruits abound and their availability is timed to the arrival of birds – such as southbound Irish Blackcaps – that eat and disperse the seed. *Inset (l–r)*: Pokeberries, Elderberries and haws.

with the southward migration of fruit-eating birds. Over continental land masses, winters are hard and all fruit-eaters must either leave or face starvation. For this reason, berried shrubs in Mediterranean lands, the winter home of huge numbers of North European thrushes and Blackcaps, have later fruiting seasons than those at higher latitudes. Upon reflection, this pattern runs counter to the expected rhythm based on climate – the more obvious expectation would be that sunny southern weather would stimulate early flowering, with fruit following in midsummer. Instead, berry-producing plants that occur across songbird wintering grounds come into fruit later, to coincide with the arrival of seed-dispersers. Juniper and olive trees are two examples of plants that ripen in autumn. In North Africa, juniper seedlings sprout from berries digested and spread by visiting winter thrushes, including North European Ring Ouzels that roam hill forest and even Saharan oases seeking out fruiting trees.

In Ireland, more than thirty species of native plants produce berries. Summer marks the start of the fruiting season with the ripening of Wild Cherry in June. All berries are fruits and some of the most popular with birds are more 'fruity' than others. Every flowering plant produces a fruit containing a seed. Succulent fruits develop solely from the flower's ovary and come in two types, the drupe and the berry. Drupes (such as cherry and plum) have a single large stone at their centre, containing a seed. Many hedgerow plants, among them Bramble, Elder and Ivy, bear fruits formed from multiples of drupes, each containing a tiny seed. Irrespective of the reproductive biology, 'berry' passes muster for understanding. By July, Rowan foliage sags under the weight of scarlet clusters; then it is the turn of Bilberry and Yew. Floodgates open in autumn and the cornucopia includes elderberries, blackberries, rosehips, haws and sloes. Luckily, production is staggered. Like the variable pace of emerging willow catkins in spring, brambles containing ripe blackberries can be encountered right up to Christmas. Different sections of the same briar come into fruit asynchronously, with hard unripe green clusters maturing alongside spent black segments. By and large, colours between red and black – from ruby Rowans through cobalt sloes to inky Ivy berries – signify ripeness and good taste. Bird vision is sensitive to colours in the ultraviolet range. To maximise the chances of dispersal, some dark berries stand out in ultraviolet. A waxy bloom, characteristic of sloes and the berries produced by Ivy and Juniper, produces the sheen. If the bloom is rubbed off, the reflectance disappears. Where cultivated fruits occur in white and red forms, birds prefer the coloured varieties. In 1789, Gilbert White noted: 'Birds are much influenced in their choice of food by colour; for though white currants are much sweeter than red, yet they seldom touch the former until they have devoured the latter.' By the same token, Starlings prefer dark grapes to green.

Some autumn-ripening species, such as holly, remain on plants until the spring. During winter Ivy ripens and different strains yield berries over a prolonged period, right up to the end of May. Ivy, Holly and Yew are evergreens. They are not tied to a defined deciduous schedule so the upshot is a boon, since evergreens harbour berries during the leanest time of the year. Cotoneaster trees and bushes, widely planted ornamentals from China and the Himalaya, have become naturalised in some areas. However, simply because foliage is adorned with aesthetically pleasing fistfuls of red berries is no guarantee that the produce is appetising.

The berries of Japanese Rose *Rosa rugosa* are a favourite with Blackbirds in autumn. The plant is tolerant of salty air and may be the first cover and sustenance for migrants along wild western coasts.

Blackbirds, Redwings and Blackcaps generally leave cotoneaster berries until native species are stripped. Indeed, if winter is mild, cotoneaster berries may be ignored. Yew is a coniferous tree that offers a poisonous seed dressed up in a succulent red casing. Greenfinches, by dextrously manipulating their macho bill, manage to remove the toxic casing and get at the nutritious kernel. Other species are not as well endowed. The seed is swallowed but not for long. The flesh contains a strong emetic that causes the bird to regurgitate the kernel. This ensures efficient dispersal without the need for the seed to pass through the digestive system. Ivy would appear to be dispersed by an equivalent method.

For birds, venting seed by regurgitation is important for another reason: it leaves room for the absorption of more nutritious pulp in the digestive system. Food preferences vary and are dictated by a range of factors including berry size, the effort required to wrestle items from the plant, taste and digestibility. Hips are large and cumbersome. Only Mistle Thrushes, Fieldfares, Blackbirds and Greenfinches (which pick out the seeds, Neville McKee pers. comm.) tackle them successfully. Redwings prefer haws and are generally thwarted by the bigger dimensions of sloes, only managing to pierce the skin and pick at the pulp. Song Thrushes prefer soft pulp and small seeds. They avoid hips, haws and Holly, opting instead for elderberries, Guelder Rose

Fieldfare feeding on cotoneaster berries. All thrushes are essentially ground feeders but flocks gather on berry bushes when ground is frozen.

and Yew. The rate at which pulp and seed can be separated during digestion matters greatly. Larger seed can be regurgitated; small seed is defaecated. Captive Blackbirds invariably spat out large seeds of Ivy, haw and sloe but excreted the smaller seeds of hip, Elder and blackberry. Depending on method, their processing time is significantly different. Large seeds were ejected six to ten minutes after swallowing but smaller seeds were passed around thirty minutes later. By comparing digestion time and the choice of seed (based on the nutritive value of the pulp), researchers concluded that birds derived the highest rate of energy by eating fruits whose seeds are regurgitated. By jettisoning the unwanted ballast as quickly as possible, the bird creates space in the gut for more food but also keeps body weight to the minimum needed for fast flight. In many ways the eating habits of birds and jockeys are similar!

The tribe of berry-eating birds is an exclusive club. Finches with specialist or weaker bills are excluded. Chaffinches are at a distinct disadvantage because their bill is pointed and not sufficiently robust to crack tough seeds. Bullfinches, bestowed with a unique, calliper-shaped bill, scissor small berries from stems and are restricted to soft-pulped fruit such as Elder and Privet. Members of the crow family, despite being bestowed with a formidable bill and being partial to nibbling small items, are noticeable absentees. Crows are surprisingly dextrous and agile, adept enough to winkle seed from feeders. Why then, do they shun hedgerows stuffed with Ivy berries, easy pickings eagerly consumed by Woodpigeons and others? The answer may lie in poisons concentrated in the seed, to which Woodpigeons appear to be immune. Because some seeds pass intact through the bird's digestive system and germinate, the plant succeeds in propagating itself. In effect, the plant discriminates against potential seed predators, welcoming helpers but deterring those who might consume the fruit without facilitating germination.

For birds capable of digesting berries, further limitations need to be overcome. The fruit may be difficult to pluck and the bird's physique may not be up to the task. Larger fruits can be tugged free by more powerful species. However, patience rewards those who wait and less athletic foragers – such as Song Thrush – seize their opportunity when berries ripen and become more easily removed later in the season. Operating from a perch, feeding options are restricted to picking or reaching. Leverage is greatly improved in other ways. Blackcaps frequently combine reaching and clasping with a well-timed downward fall. By using the body as a dead weight, the bird turns itself into a crowbar powered by gravity. Robins, Redwings and Waxwings regularly tug berries by fluttering or hovering into a favourable position before apprehending. This method negates reaching; pulling actions may derive added thrust from backward-directed wingbeats. Robins often 'swoop, pluck and go'. Perhaps, like Blackcap, body mass adds momentum to a flying tackle. At other times fluttering seems to be used to preserve balance while reaching or tugging. Starlings, as ever, have to be different. They morph into a pendulous dagger and attenuate themselves to lunge at purple elderberries and squeeze juice from the soft fruit.

Mistle Thrush is the largest thrush. Its deportment says 'Sergeant Major', a persona that is entirely justified during winter. Superior size and a sturdy build equip the bird for removing berries and for driving away would-be foragers. Despite an intimidating presence, the bill is not quite as long as that of Blackbird or Song Thrush. Berries do not come in XXL size, yet no Mistle Thrush is able to handle more than a single fruit at a time. During late summer, at the close of the breeding season, flocks form and parties roam widely. Coastal headlands, upland fields and thinly vegetated mountaintops may harbour troupes consisting of several family parties. Soil invertebrates are a staple at this time. During autumn the wandering flocks break up. Pairs or loners seek out a single source of fruit and set about defending it for the coming winter. Certain trees, when in fruit, are defended every year, probably by the same individuals. Holly trees are highly regarded, especially as the berries do not rot and can be eaten throughout the winter, sometimes right up to the start of the next breeding season. If the supply lasts, the final berries may be included among chick food. To qualify for defence a tree needs to meet a size criterion. Small trees offer an inadequate food supply and are ignored; ironically, a bounteous smorgasbord may constitute a liability if it is too large to protect. For this reason, only 'just right' trees are safeguarded. All others are deemed a fair fight.

Monopolisation of a winter larder does not preclude foraging elsewhere. In many ways, the underlying philosophy appears to be insurance to tide the owner through lean times ahead. Rather than live off the cornered food resource in the short term, owners feed nearby and eke out the supply, diminishing it gradually. All the while, a watchful eye is kept and an exclusion zone is maintained. Trespassers are attacked immediately. The off-duty vigilante may be 100m or more away but returns hurriedly, flying in a fast direct line rather than undulating, the typical flight mode. Vexatious rattling bolsters aggression. Opportunists get the message and flee. By late winter an uneaten crop is a strong clue to protectionism. So long as the winter weather is mild, rival diners can be kept at bay. But severe weather begets no-holds-barred foraging by hungry hordes, including dispossessed Mistle Thrushes. Defenders, no matter how belligerent, can be overwhelmed. Force of numbers results in coveted fruit being stripped. Varying numbers of Waxwings arrive in Ireland during winter. Flocks hail from taiga where, during summer, insects form the mainstay of the diet. Fruit is eaten throughout the rest of the year. Despite being smaller and not much more than one-third of the weight of a Mistle Thrush, a Waxwing's gape is bigger, enabling it to swallow large fruits that are processed quickly in a long, spiralling gut. Mistle Thrushes, no matter how bellicose, are no match for these machine-gunners whose intake is exceptional. They need to part-digest lots of berries in order to extract enough protein, which is relatively scarce in berries (Neville McKee pers. comm.). A Waxwing, watched in England for a day in December, was estimated to have eaten 600–1,000 berries of *Cotoneaster horizontalis*. The weight of fruit stood at about 170 grams, approaching almost three times the bird's weight (Gibb 1951).

11. BANDS OF BROTHERS

UNLESS YOU ARE A PREDATOR suited to the role of a solitary hunter, life is generally easier in company. Outside the breeding season, most small birds band together. Groups may be exclusive brethren or a mixture. The majority come together at different seasons and for different reasons. Few stay united year round. Troupes of Long-tailed Tits are an exception. Ringers have found clusters of individuals present in the same flock over a period of years. Packs roam widely, some covering 100km between ringing locations. The fellowship functions as a single organism. Cold weather is a hazard. Overnight, songbirds are inactive and drop their core temperature to reduce heat loss. A roosting individual balls up by fluffing feathers to create a warm layer of insulating air. The bill is tucked among plumage, thus deriving heated air to breathe. As best it can, the bird stays still to avoid dispersing heat through convection. Any movement will generate a cold airflow around its body and draw warmth away. Despite everything, most songbirds stand to lose almost 10 per cent of their body weight overnight.

Facing page: Illuminated by the light storm of downtown Belfast, Pied Wagtails gather from surrounding habitats to use the city's 'heat island' effect as a dormitory. Tall and densely packed buildings warm during the day; their heat slowly dissipates after sunset, producing local hotspots. Unlike Starlings, roosting wagtails arrive in dribs and drabs.

Like lead filings clouding a blank page, Starlings darken the sky en route to a roost where 250,000 cram together each night among the evergreen foliage of coniferous trees. In cold weather huddling distances shrink, promoting an estimated energy saving of up to 38 per cent per bird (Kelty *et al.* 1977).

Starlings converge from a radius of up to 50km to roost in a favoured spot. Dense stands of conifers and reed beds are favoured. During clement weather, snoozers space themselves 5cm apart. However, in cold conditions they squeeze together in rows. Suitable groves of trees are not in short supply. Nonetheless, winter-visiting Starlings travelling to Ireland from Britain and Europe gather in thousands each evening at one spot. Group flights with their split-second coordination and pulses of directional shift are almost as baffling in behaviour as they are spectacular. While the prize may be a safe roost, the purpose of the convoluted manoeuvring appears to be avoiding predators. Fleet-flying birds of prey and opportunistic Ravens are attracted. Despite the bounty of quarry, most attacks fail. Through sheer force of numbers, danger is dodged. Starling flocks do not do estrangement of members. Cohesion is so tight that any attempt to split a singleton from the pack is foredoomed. Even the superior intellect of a Raven has not discovered an Achilles heel. A tactic of blundering into the midst of circling flocks and hoping to knock a bird for six is pie in the sky.

Cyclists know the value of remaining closely bunched. Except for the leader, everyone has an easier time than if they were riding solo. The explanation has to do with the shelter provided by being in a slipstream, which hardly applies to birds. Or does it? Starlings fly in high-speed formations; their ranks generate wind noise. Flock aerodynamics collectively reduce drag and therefore an individual's energy expenditure. Birds coalesce in all manner of group arrangements, from amorphous undulating lines to rigid V-formations favoured by large birds. Formations seem to epitomise experience leading youth since adults, distinguishable by plumage, are invariably in pole position with juveniles tucked in behind. There is an even greater benefit. Researchers fitted pelicans with heart monitors and trained them to fly behind an aircraft. Performance was compared between flying alone or as part of a squadron. By gliding behind a neighbour, energy was saved through cutting down the number of strenuous flaps needed to maintain momentum. As a result, those in the lee of front-runners had reduced heart rates.

For species that nest in colonies there is safety in numbers. Outside the breeding season flock security generates other benefits. Feeding parties of waterfowl, especially geese, deploy sentries. At least one individual keeps watch while others feed. How the delegation of duties is determined remains unclear. Posting a lookout means that others forage in peace, so less energy is wasted in having to be vigilant and regularly look up or scan for danger. Mixed flocks of small songbirds invoke 'all for one and one for all' tactics. The first to spot danger saves everyone's bacon. Mobbing is another element of collective behaviour. Noisy ostentation deters predators caught off guard and gives all potential prey within earshot a heads-up to the danger. Crows often form the vanguard, pointing out the offender like an agitated linesman flagging offside. A swirling clamour from Swallows or other small birds can attend a scuttling Sparrowhawk, rumbled in the open and harangued. Mobbing appears to be innate. Some of it is learned and knowledge of 'bad guys' is transmitted culturally from one generation to the next. Unfortunately, although for understandable reasons, humans are amongst those blacklisted. Research involving crows has shown that even individual human faces are remembered (Marzlhuff *et al.* 2010).

Despite everyone constantly living on their nerves, foraging success has been found to be twice as high in a group compared to going it alone. The increase in feeding efficiency may arise partly from copycat feeding or information exchange. The location of food resources is learned through becoming a union member. Birds do not keep secrets, although they may squabble over the booty. Roosts bring birds together from a wide feeding range. Many will have fed apart and individual foraging efforts amount to a sweepstake. Next morning, less successful birds follow those privy to better sites. The phenomenon is commonplace at feeders. Within a short space of time, attendance swells once scouts pay a visit. Many questions remain, however. What interpretation can be placed upon a daily twenty-strong conference of Blackbirds that gather in the first blink of a winter's morning? Hopping randomly and contentedly across a lawn bearing food, few are actively feeding. By full daylight most have disappeared. Could it be that an unseen rota is in operation and that all might come and go over the course of the day? In the meantime, they leave the 'committee room' but report back regularly – perhaps with news of better? If they gather only where food is most abundant or easily accessible, concentrated appetites might precipitate starvation, while food elsewhere remains neglected. Blackbird dispersion therefore promotes efficient exploitation.

Birds learn insights and the perception of one individual somehow reaches others. Over the last 150 years, Treecreepers have made a discovery that has changed their sleeping habits for good. Dating mainly from Victorian times, majestic redwoods from North America were planted as ornamental trees in parks and large estates. The bark is soft with a texture like cardboard. For the tree the spongy exterior acts as a fire blanket. Using their toenails,

Treecreeper roosting in purpose-made cavity on Giant Redwood. Researchers who placed a stuffed Treecreeper in another bird's roost site were amazed to see it dislodged by the nook's owner.

Treecreepers began to scratch out a neat, body-sized hollow and flatten themselves against the trunk. Birds from a wide area converge on mature specimens and several may be found clamped on a single tree. Ingenuity does not stop there. Over time, each bird gouges out more cavities. This ensures that, irrespective of wind direction, draught-free overnight accommodation is assured.

Blue Tits' coochie-coo reputation suffered a setback when they began piercing milk bottle tops to drink the cream. In Britain the habit began in Southampton during the 1920s, reached London by 1935 and soon became nationwide. Blue Tits seldom disperse west from Britain. The Irish Sea acts as a barrier to migration. Yet the practice, allegedly spread by copying, reached Ireland. Here and elsewhere the practice stopped only when milk and cream were homogenised before bottling. Perhaps we continue to underestimate birds' ability to learn new tricks? A Jackdaw was trained to open eight boxes, five of which contained food. It quickly mastered the fact that it needed to check every box until it had accumulated all five rewards, some of which were in pairs to test the bird's counting skills. The human researcher was impressed. Fortunately, he was also sharp-eyed enough to notice a small quirk in the bird's manner. As items were gathered, it nodded its head, analogous to the lip movements of someone counting silently. One reward was signalled once; two together received a double nod. When four rewards were placed in the first boxes to be opened, the Jackdaw's nodding arithmetic kept pace until it found the fifth, secreted in the final box.

12. WHO SEES WINS

WHEN A PREDATOR APPEARS out of the blue, the ability to make quick decisions is essential. Reactions are instinctive and imprinted for bêtes noires. Depending on the nature of the threat, potential targets may choose to freeze, flee or mob the attacker. A sudden encounter with potential death elicits panicky calls that serve as a lingua franca to all that hear them. Blue Tits broadcast a Mayday bird-of-prey alert and Hooded Crows harangue passing raptors with guttural swearing. Both show considerable bravery and shadow the danger. House Sparrows, on the other hand, scarper. In the aftermath of an ambush by a Sparrowhawk or Merlin they hide and intone a plaintive Rosary – a nervous parping that is the antithesis of cocky chirruping. Escape speed is accompanied by swerving and, if needs be, rapid changes in direction. Manoeuvrability is a function of size, rate of wingbeats and the shape of wings and tail. How quickly can a potential victim shift? Calculated from camera flashes, a tit was airborne and had changed course within 30 milliseconds. Recording such ultra-fast movement is difficult for a human eye. Blue Tits investigating a nest box provide an insight. When one (usually the female) enters the accommodation, its partner clings at the entrance hole and peeps inside, watching deliberations. The onlooker's body is half in, half out. When the hidden bird emerges, it does so by flying straight out – as though slingshot through the entrance hole. To avoid a collision, the onlooker ducks its head. None of this is down to luck. Reflexes are coordinated with impeccable timing. The two pass each other so quickly that, to our eyes, the outsider's reaction fails to register, even as a blur. Only the streak of the exiting insider is noticed.

Frequent head movements suggest unending watchfulness but are necessary for another reason: compared to human eyes, those of birds are set rigidly in their sockets. We possess several groups of muscles that facilitate swivel-eyed vision. However, we share a retina upon which the lens of the eye casts an image containing two light-sensitive components. Rods register contrast and definition; cones record colour. In larger birds-of-prey, the retina may be physically larger than ours. Comparisons between Starlings and us yield a statistic underpinning vision as birds' dominant sense. Although the weight of the head in both species is about one-tenth of total body weight, the ratio of eye weight to head weight in people is less than 1 per cent; in Starlings it is 15 per cent. The benefit of the large size is more detailed visual information. Kestrels can detect a 2mm-long object at a range of 20m. Even a sharp-eyed human will fail to register the item until less than 4m away. Another reason birds-of-prey see so well is because their retina contains two foveae. The fovea is a pit-shaped hotspot that serves as a focusing point. Rods and especially cones cluster around it and nerve cells connect to the optic nerve. Without a fovea, we could not read. The world would be a blur. Like us, songbirds have only one fovea. Ergo, winged hunters have stolen a march on prey. Their second fovea is slightly convex, a curvature that effectively magnifies the image, just like a telephoto lens. The result is high-powered binocular vision, perfect for assessing the

Clockwise from top left: Kestrel, Long-eared Owl, Meadow Pipit. In daylight, a bird of prey's visual acuity exceeds a human's, threefold. Bird vision discerns ultraviolet (UV), enabling Kestrels to detect small mammals in dim light (rodent urine and faeces reflect in UV). Owls do not deploy UV to hunt. Instead, their eyes contain far more light-sensitive photoreceptors (rods) than diurnal birds of prey. Although owl eyesight is no better than ours, their hearing is superior: even below a carpet of snow, furry movement can be pinpointed. The eyes of Meadow Pipits and other insectivorous birds are set on the side of the head but provide enough forwards-facing binocular vision to lock on to prey. Probably, no fly is safe within an arc of 270 degrees.

swerve of a fleeing target. Swallows and Swifts, because they feed by snatching insects in flight, have their eyes on the side of the head so that they have binocular vision forwards as well as backwards. Woodcock and to an extent, most waders, have their eyes set slightly back of centre so they too have binocular vision both forwards and backwards. All angles are covered, from scanning the sky for danger to studying – even magnifying – the ground immediately in front of a foraging bird.

Songbirds live life on a hair trigger. A fleeting movement could portend death. For this reason false alarms are frequent. Feeding is a nervous activity, especially by a group. While there is safety in numbers through added vigilance, more eyes increase the chance of over-reactions. The sudden appearance of a predator-like silhouette – such as Woodpigeon or Collared Dove – prompts a wave of panic, although tense normality soon returns. By the same token, windy weather that sways branches and foliage in the vicinity of feeding stations deters customers. Despite being fully stocked and bustling with diners on calmer days, blustery conditions often produce a low turnout. Presumably, the difficulty of distinguishing the flash of a hawk among a universe of movement means that small birds feed elsewhere – or roost early.

Prey or predator, all birds have good reason to stay svelte and not put on weight. Research shows that even a slight weight increase during the course of a day reduces lift-off speed. In experiments, Blackcaps were exposed to simulated attacks. As they fled, the heaviest individuals showed a 30 per cent decrease in angle of ascent and were almost 20 per cent slower than the leanest. After a kill, a Sparrowhawk remains inactive for hours until its 'fighting weight' returns. However, for potential victims, there is an alternative to fleeing. Wheatears and Skylarks often put their faith in remaining immobile. Upon seeing a predator, Wheatears have been known to freeze for up to half an hour. While Skylark plumage is cryptic and provides camouflage, a Wheatear's costume is potentially a liability. Its assassin's eyesight may be honed to perfection but all its eggs are in one basket – prey has to move to be detected. Escape may lie in nerve-racking stillness.

Bird colour vision differs from ours in two main ways. First, we have three channels – red, green and blue – that synchronise to produce colour. To these birds add ultraviolet. The fourth channel shows feather tracts in a new light. Indulging in poetic licence, it is tempting to imagine what birds look like to each other: Kingfisher robes turn neon and debutante male Starlings resemble knights shimmering in metallic-blue armour. By using selective filters to cut out particular wavelengths of light, behavioural experiments conducted at the University of Bristol have already shown that the ultraviolet component of plumage colours is important in mate selection in Starlings. Certain berries exude an ultraviolet lustre to attract diners and propagate seeds. A hovering Kestrel can tell where rodents pass because ultraviolet vision highlights urine trails and turn them into dashed dark lines. Secondly, it was formerly believed that humans had amongst the best colour vision of any animal, and that most other vertebrates saw the world within the same visible spectrum as us. This is as flawed as assuming that our sense of smell matches the olfactory range tapped by a dog. In fact, not only are there basic differences between birds and us, there are also distinctions between bird families. Variation is found in all the main parameters: binocular vision, field of view and blind spots. Perching birds have a significantly wider field than most and crows have the widest field of view of all. Forwards-facing binocular vision exists in different configurations and its main function is now believed to provide a three-dimensional 'looking space' within which bill movement can be coordinated (Martin 2014). Birds' density of cone cells greatly exceeds ours; theirs also contain oil droplets that register extra detail. To optimise acuity in both long and short sight, each eye assumes a different task. One specialises in close-up vision, perhaps scrutinising leaf litter for seeds; the other covers distance, a weather eye for danger. Optically, both eyes are identical but each is 'tuned' for a different role by the brain. However, like us, brain function is divided between left and right hemispheres. For example, the left side of the brain controls human speech. 'Sidedness' is determined as the chick develops inside the egg. Asymmetric light levels determine the outcome. One side of the embryo will be exposed to brighter light than the other.

The optical arsenal operates at high speed. Natural history film-makers use slow motion to reveal a hawk's dexterity at steering between branches or the agility of a warbler pursuing a fly. Birds process ultra-fast eye-to-brain information in real time. The synchronous 'sheet lightning' veering of thousands of Starlings is thus achieved in the blink of an eye. Eyes are also used as a badge that indicates the sex and maturity of kin. Iris colour is determined by pigments and, in some cases, refraction of light. Pigmentation can change with age and may differ between sexes. Bare skin that encircles the eye – the orbital ring – often flushes bright with the onset of breeding condition. We can formulate how birds see but it is impossible to look down the barrel of the weaponry. One thing is clear, however. Their identification skills of each other are almost infallible. How, therefore, do hybrids arise? Waterfowl are well known for hybridising, although not through faulty identification. Females with excess eggs dump them in nests of other species and ducklings imprint on foster parents. Species expanding range and finding themselves without a partner invoke 'any port in a storm' morals. All-black Carrion Crows, currently establishing themselves in eastern Ireland but short of kin, hook up with two-tone Hooded Crows and produce dusky offspring. Tall, dark strangers do well in all walks of life.

13. A HAWK'S LIFE

HAVE MERCY ON THE KILLER. A Sparrowhawk is a one-trick pony. It hunts to survive and is incapable of earning a living except as an assassin. Accipiter, the family to which the species belongs, is derived from *accipio*, the Latin verb for taking or seizing. Sparrowhawks are harbingers of havoc. Given that, in Anglo-Saxon Old English, 'hafoc' meant hawk (Yalden 2002), it is not unreasonable to suggest a linguistic link. All birds instinctively recognise the moving silhouette with its longish tail and short neck. Even at

Female Sparrowhawk grasping what began as a Chaffinch. Perversely for a professional killer, Sparrowhawk is small-billed. More importance is attached to catching prey than despatching the victim. Long legs and a gangly central toe are designed to snatch quarry at breakneck speed.

birth, songbird chicks show fear responses if presented with the prototype passing over them as a shadow. Consequently, Sparrowhawks are pariahs. Youngsters are born into an arms race not of their making. Prey is ever vigilant, lookouts are everywhere and voice alarms proclaim warning. Springing an ambush must seem close to Mission Impossible. Yet the hunter does not seek out the weak and indolent. Victims are chosen opportunistically and carrion is, by and large, avoided. A Sparrowhawk has keen eyesight. When it sees airborne prey it registers the target through forwards-facing owlish eyes. A natural assumption is that vision is in stereo, a three-dimensional picture akin to ours: in other words, binocular vision. In fact, where we focus an image a Sparrowhawk has an extra focusing spot, which enhances the ability to track and strike at high speed.

The bird is a highly manoeuvrable guided missile. During normal travel, it is not especially fast. The usual speed is around 30km/h. In combat sorties, round wings cup the air like a sprinter's flailing arms. Acceleration skyrockets and hits 50km/h. Bursts are designed to propel the bird rapidly, rather than sustain momentum. When the red mist is down, the attacker morphs into a projectile. Fuelled by the initial injection of pace, it swerves like a bobsleigh. Although songbirds can jink more acutely, time is not on their side. By vaulting out of the blue at high speed, the pursuer has shaved vital seconds off prey's ability to flee. A common hunting strategy involves making a series of short flights through woodland or along a line of cover, pausing regularly and scanning the surroundings. Actions are furtive and fast; body language accords with operating behind enemy lines. If terrain lacks cover but is undulating, high-speed low-level contour flying is deployed. It is easy to miss a shadow zooming at ground level across an open field and cresting a rising contour. Anything on the blind side of a lee will have no inkling of oncoming death.

Talons are the executioner's chief weapon. The legs are long and the middle toe is elongated. At the moment of impact the feet attempt to snag any part of the target. If purchase is made, toes lock automatically. The hawk quickly lands and squeezes. Puncture wounds and shock despatch most victims. To end struggling the talons are sometimes opened and closed

Clockwise from top: flight silhouettes; carrying male Blackbird; road casualty. A Sparrowhawk's outline, when cut out in cardboard and moved through the air above defenceless birds in captivity, elicits a fright response. A researcher tried a number of shape variations in an attempt to isolate the silhouette's scariest component. This proved to be the short neck (Tinbergen 1948).

to grip more tightly. In fact, Sparrowhawks do not deliver a *coup de grâce*. The bill is small and comparatively weak. Unlike Peregrine Falcon, prey is not rendered lifeless by biting through its spinal chord. Sparrowhawks are only capable of pinning, holding down and then eating. Females occasionally down Woodpigeons. Sometimes the assailant has bitten off more than it can chew. Pigeon plumage consists of an underlay of deep down and broad, powerful wings. Were it not for long 'cattle prod' legs, the hawk's hefty opponent could, if held only in a clench, wrestle free. Crime scenes are littered with feathers. Except for the legs, bill and big bones of large prey, everything else is eaten. Later a pellet of bone fragments and shards of plumage is ejected.

Females outgun males and tackle larger prey. When quarry is scarce, especially in late winter when mortality has whittled down numbers, male Sparrowhawks may themselves become targets. For a butch female, a slim male makes an ideal meal. Sparrowhawks are not long-lived. The average mortality over the first year of life has been estimated at 70 per cent for males and 50 per cent for females. Survival rates improve with age. Old males seldom exceed eight years of age; females reach ten years of age or older. The greater mortality of males is not easily explained. Presumably, smaller size makes them less able to withstand food shortages. Attacks by other predators, among them Peregrines, also render the smaller sex more vulnerable. Across Europe, Goshawks breed alongside Sparrowhawks. The two species grade in size and exploit a range of woodland birds. Goshawk, however, is also the main natural predator of Sparrowhawk. Until Ireland's original deciduous forest disappeared during the reign of Queen Elizabeth I, Goshawks were native. Along with wolves and other wildlife they became extinct once their habitat vanished and a growing human population – farmers, gamekeepers and well-heeled collectors – persecuted top predators for selfish motives. Nowadays, small numbers of Goshawks occur in some parts. Most are escaped or unwanted falconers' birds. Breeding pairs have become established with obvious implications for their small cousin.

After the Second World War agricultural pesticides acquired chemical warfare capabilities. Organochlorine compounds, such as DDT, were developed to improve crop yields by, among other methods, protecting seeds from fungal attack. The chemicals persist in the environment for decades. Furthermore, because they are soluble in fat, they transfer and become part of living tissue. Sparrowhawks are a species at the top of a food chain. As a result, they accumulated multiple doses of chemical residue by eating prey containing sublethal doses. Migrant songbirds – potential Sparrowhawk prey – travelling from areas poisoned by chemicals meant that harm was exported to predators operating in remote areas. Apart from outright paralysis, lethal effects arose through eggshell thinning, leading to egg breakages and embryo death. A massive decline was most marked in intense arable districts. In Britain, the species virtually disappeared from eastern England. Legislation removed the persistent pesticides and Sparrowhawks recovered, demonstrating the worth of the natural world as an early warning system for human tunnel vision. What, over time, might the chemicals have done to us?

At breeding time, each female settles within hunting territory occupied by a male. Throughout the rest of the year females occupy larger territories and overlap with smaller holdings patrolled by males. Females include a greater extent of open areas in their diocese. Males, it seems, feel more at home hunting in confined, well-timbered spaces. Competition for mates is a female prerogative and catfights, rather than dogfights, occur. Pair formation peaks in early spring and fine weather is used for display. Betrothed females warn off others by soaring high, then tipping and descending gracefully in a long glide. The process is repeated in a series of undulations. As the pair bond strengthens, the male joins in. As they age, male Sparrowhawks become orange-eyed. Young males are yellow-eyed. Life expectancy is comparatively short in Sparrowhawks and a mature and reliable orange-orbed hunter is quite a catch. Having become an item, she will be fed by him and will stay at the nest site throughout incubation and chick rearing, refraining from hunting until the family are large enough to be left unattended. To feed his mate the male delivers partially plucked kills. Most pairings do not persist from year to year. Death of first-years occurs mainly in early autumn. By then youngsters are fully independent and prey numbers are at a maximum. Inexperience weeds out the poorest hunters. A Sparrowhawk that succumbs to starvation or is killed by a predator passes unnoticed. However, a whirling dervish that crashes into a window or collides with a moving vehicle will draw attention. Hence ring recoveries are inadvertently skewed and, statistically, the cause of death through collisions is disproportionately high.

Although Ireland's breeding population is non-migratory, post-breeding dispersal does take place. Juveniles travel furthest, particularly young females. Dispersal is an annual event and helps to mix individuals between locations. Adults, once they have bred successfully, tend to travel less. Irrespective of age, most stay put on territory that became familiar during autumn, even when winter becomes severe. However, across northern latitudes migration is a fact of life. In autumn, as many songbirds shift south, their nemesis follows suit. Scandinavian Sparrowhawks track Chaffinches to Ireland. Peak arrivals occur in late October and most hawks are youngsters. Chaffinches are fairly conspicuous and feed in edge habitats, away from cover. Skulking species, such as Wrens, Dunnocks and Song Thrushes, are taken much less. Over a whole year food intake amounts to roughly 16kg of meat for a male and 22kg for a female. A breeding pair probably kills 55kg of prey to raise a typical brood of three offspring. Put another way, this equates to around 2,200 House Sparrows, 600 Blackbirds or 110 Woodpigeons.

With nationwide feeding of garden birds, Sparrowhawks have attracted much attention, some of it unfavourable. Unlike cats and Magpies, Sparrowhawks have no impact on eggs, young or incubating adults, but they are undoubtedly drawn to feeding hotspots. Prey is not naïve and soon learns to avoid the area. In turn, the hunter moves elsewhere and the cycle is repeated. It is a time-honoured ritual. Is it possible to minimise risk to garden birds, such as by placing a predator-proof mesh around a busy feeding station? The answer is no. Songbirds have evolved to flee and not put their trust into trembling behind a screen. To save their skin, they rocket into the nearest cover. For those who do not like to see nature red in tooth and claw, establishing a tall thick hedge within bolting distance of a feeding area is the best you can do.

14. MOULT

AS ANYONE WHO KEEPS HENS WILL KNOW, the birds down tools and stop laying when they moult. At some point during the year their energy is diverted to grow brand-new plumage. Timing is of the utmost importance and periods of greatest food abundance are utilised. Like a human bodybuilder, protein intake is boosted and most seedeaters switch to more nutritious insects during the moult. In plants, we are familiar with the concept of a rose that buds, flowers, matures and then dies back. In many ways feathers are no different. They make up an outer layer embedded in skin and enable birds to do things that defeat us. Flight, temperature regulation and incubating eggs against the brood patch are all made possible by sprouting a coat of feathers that emerges from follicles clustered in well-defined tracts. By leaving corridors of bare skin between tracts, body warmth can be trapped and held among plumage. Conversely, in hot weather, heat escapes efficiently when some tracts are raised. Good maintenance is paramount. Daily preening, scratching, bathing and drying only postpone the inevitable. Ultimately, feathers start to disintegrate and need to be replaced. In preparation for courtship, many males take the opportunity to change appearance by growing feathers of a different colour, pattern or even shape. Once breeding duties are discharged and 'empty nest syndrome' becomes reality, a collective period of moult commences. Recently fledged juveniles moult the gossamer plumes in which they fledged. The virginal cloak was sufficient to get them up and away but the flimsy weave of the vanes will not last. Youngsters become independent at a time of food abundance. The extra nourishment is needed to generate a more robust tunic with a shelf life running to months, not weeks.

Moult saps energy. Depending on progress, the stress of undergoing a makeover can add 20 per cent to the bird's daily calorie demand. Keratin, the raw material from which plumage is

Once formed, feathers receive no nutrients. Pale tips are least resistant and wear off first. New in autumn, the right-hand Robin's pale wing-bar will be gone by the following spring (left).

No Irish bird falls apart as dramatically as Rock Pipit. Living on the coast and shoving aside piles of brittle sun-dried seaweed to find food and raise young, hard-pressed parents 'go to wrack and ruin'. The combination of abrasive sand (especially windblown), salt-laden air and intense UV desiccates feathers.

made, is a protein designed for strength. Its molecules are tough, fibrous and lightweight. Like plastics, the material comes in many textures, degrees of toughness and durability. The same substance is moulded to make human fingernails and hair, as well as animal hooves and horns. However, full-grown feathers are dead material. They cannot be renewed from the feather base. Starting with the growth of a chick's fluffy down, each follicle is under genetic control and over the course of a lifetime produces a range of feather types and colours. Job done, follicles become dormant for up to a year. Each consists of a tiny cylindrical pit, surrounded by muscles and nerves and with a core of living tissue that nourishes the growing feather, known as a pinfeather, which resembles a short matchstick encased in semi-transparent plastic that bleeds if damaged. Ultimately the casing splits and, unfurling from a waxy sheath, vanes flatten out either side of a rigid shaft (the quill). The feather, once fully grown, does not need to be rooted in live tissue. Blood supply is cut off; it is no longer umbilically connected to the living bird. The shaft becomes hollow, although a tiny hole at its base marks the spot where it was once attached.

Feathers fray, bleach, break or are lost. Wear and tear erodes their structure by breaking off or splitting the interlocking filaments that hold the vane together. Because the filaments zip up to form an air-catching surface, the cumulative effect of abrasion will impair flight. The plumage of birds that slide through dense vegetation such as reeds or thorny scrub, or are exposed to sun, sea and sand, take the biggest hit. Island communities of Robins and Dunnocks in western Ireland start to look dishevelled in late spring, a time when their mainland counterparts are dapper. The costume of Rock Pipits, living under the cosh of windblown sand grains, spray and intense levels of reflected sunlight, has an air of dereliction by mid-summer. Normal appearance is restored when adults moult at the end of the breeding season. Unlike most other juvenile songbirds that retain the large feathers of the tail until just after their first birthday, many young Rock Pipits replace the middle pair of tail feathers in their first autumn, a reflection of relentless battering by their environment. This portion is constantly exposed and, except in flight, shields the rest of the tail and protects it from the elements. Many Wheatears spend the winter in windy semi-desert habitats in Africa. Returning to breed or halt on northbound spring migration in Ireland, migrants freshly arrived in our latitude often show signs of bleaching from a searing tropical sun. Fading is not uniform, however. Pale plumage wears more quickly than dark areas. Melanin, produced by the bird as dark granules, is incorporated within the feather structure. Melanin is not only black but is a strong structural protein whose beneficial effect can be seen in the differential rate of wear in the wing-tip pattern of gulls. By late summer, white ovals have perished. The black tip, although somewhat frayed, remains intact. Why, therefore, do the wing tips of gulls breeding in subarctic regions lack melanin? The explanation lies in the lower levels of feather-bleaching ultraviolet light in those parts of the world (Neville McKee pers. comm.).

In addition to physical wear, feathers are chewed and devoured by feather lice and damaged by bacteria and fungi. Even the hardiest, such as the large feathers of the wings and tail that take longest to grow, cannot keep the bird airborne forever. Consequently, deciding how, where and when to schedule moult is a dilemma. Domestic hens do not migrate or live in fear

of being hunted down. They can moult whenever they feel like it. Wild birds need to balance priorities. Certain times of the year are impossible, notably periods of active migration. So, for most, moult takes place over a period of weeks or months, a phased replacement that does not leave any part of the wings or body overly exposed. Life must go on and cannot be interrupted. In particular, the moult of wing and tail has to be staggered. Across both, feathers drop in a precise sequence; normally from the centre of the wing or tail towards the outer margin. Symmetry is important – without it flying ability would be compromised. During summer, moulting crows and gulls passing overhead show gaps in the wings. Moulting feathers leave open windows with some plumage missing completely, whereas others are new but not fully grown. However, a chink on one wing will be mirrored in the other. To save time, waterfowl take precipitous action and moult all flight feathers in one short period by becoming flightless. Corncrakes do the same. A legendary skulker by nature, adults fall silent in July and remain hidden until they regain the powers of flight in August. With that, they leave for Africa.

Feather moult leaves plenty of clues. For birds that replace like with like irrespective of age or season, the contrast between old garb and emerging new attire can be obvious, even to an inexperienced eye. Wren plumage is fundamentally similar at all times yet, in summer, there is a palpable contrast between fresh, gingery-brown juveniles and worn, fawn-coloured adults. Much less obvious is the effect of wear on the bill, which grows continuously. A quality that affects hardiness is colour. Some species change the bill colour depending on the season. And, as with plumage, melanin granules confer strength. Coinciding with the onset of moult at the end of the breeding season, Starling bills change from yellowish to black, due to the deposition of melanin; the entire population becomes dark-billed during winter. The switch may have a mechanical function, reflecting a preference for a more robust bill; black is stronger and dark parts of the bill are more resistant to wear than pale areas (Bonser & Witter 1993). However, any understanding of bill structure, use and function has to take account of aspects such as signalling during courtship (adult male Starlings acquire an azure bill base, see p. 30), the type of feeding technique and the amount of time spent foraging. In this regard, Rock Pipit's bill becomes fascinating. During spring it begins to darken. Furthermore, in many individuals, the girth and length expands. By summer, a few look like Pinocchio! What is going on? Lengthening daylight and the exigencies of foraging required to rear several broods of chicks must place a heavy demand on the bill's serviceability. Presumably for this reason it turns black – thereby becoming harder wearing. Who knows? It is possible that in terms of 'bill hardiness' Rock Pipit could be a world leader? Based on the excessive attrition sustained by its plumage, a sturdy bill would seem essential.

Facing page: Rock Pipit in July (above) and November (below). By incorporating melanin in bill growth – which increases abrasion resistance and can be synthesised by the bird from its own diet – the schnozzle becomes blacker, longer and thicker when feeding needs peak during the breeding season.

15. LONGEVITY

G EORGE MACKENZIE DUNNET was a well-known Scottish ornithologist who passed away in 1995, aged sixty-seven. The photograph that accompanied his obituary shows a timeworn face with threadbare grey locks clinging to temples. However, his sense of fun shines through. Throughout his life George studied seabirds on Eynhallow in the Orkney Islands. He had his picture taken in 1951 holding a ringed Fulmar. By pure coincidence he caught and posed beside the same bird thirty years later. Personal vanity was brushed aside in his admiration for the bird's unchanged looks. Other seabirds, notably two Manx Shearwaters, have reached fifty years of age. In all three cases, the birds were already mature adults when first ringed, so their true ages are a mystery. Both Manx Shearwaters were alive in the new millennium; perhaps the Fulmar is, too.

Unlike humans, birds do not go grey or develop wrinkles. In captivity, Ravens have reached the ripe old age of seventy and not altered appearance. If looks do not change, how can we tell age? In most cases ringing provides data on lifespan and longevity. Natural clues to the precise age of a bird only chart survival into adulthood. Small birds replace distinctive juvenile plumage with that of an adult within months of being born. After this, outward appearance cannot be used as a guide to their age past their first birthday, even though over subsequent years many species change appearance as they moult into – and then out of – courtship plumage. Larger birds take several years to reach maturity during which time they grow progressively more adult-like feathers. Over a four-year period the offspring of Herring Gulls moult and replace a brown adolescent coat for overall grey and white plumage, the badge of maturity. In eagles, gannets and albatrosses, age based on plumage features can be established up to around five years of age, but no further. In captivity, where an individual is not subject to predation, starvation or other natural threats, geriatrics live longer and may manifest incapacity that would make them easy targets in the wild, such as gout, swollen toes and a lengthened bill tip that needs clipping like human toenails.

Certain species are predisposed to live longer than others. The BTO maintains longevity records based on ringing recoveries. Millions of birds have been processed. Ironically in seabirds, consistently the longest-lived group, individuals can outlive metal rings because, over time, the metal corrodes and perishes in seawater. So, in truth, estimation of lifespan in marine species is largely guesswork. At the other extreme, only one Goldcrest has made it past four years of age and, on average, Stonechats, Wrens and Robins seldom live for more than five years. In all birds, inexperienced juveniles bear the greatest mortality. As a species, Great Tits usually lose around 80 per cent of all young in their first year of life. Such heavy losses probably also occur in less well-studied songbirds. Thereafter, survivors can expect to fulfil a standard life expectancy according to species. Death rates do not decrease with age. It seems as though all age groups are equally fated; all face similar threats. Disease, predators, food shortages and other hardships take a universal toll and do not discriminate. Curiously, a

Ireland's smallest bird, the Goldcrest, is preordained to a brief life. To ensure that some young survive the winter, short-lived adults produce two broods, each containing up to a dozen eggs.

study of captive birds showed that while they lived longer than wild counterparts, they did so by only 30 per cent when direct comparisons were made. In other words, there was a parallel in the intrinsic life expectancy, irrespective of a mollycoddled existence in captivity.

Is it possible to define factors that confer longevity in some species but impose a shorter term on others? Aristotle pondered the same questions. He discerned a link between life expectancy and the time spent as an embryo. Small mammals live short lives and take only a few weeks to develop in the womb. And so it is with bird incubation times. The more protracted the breeding cycle, the greater the life expectancy. Clutch size is also significant. Seabirds lay a single egg and the only child can remain in its nest burrow for six weeks or more before fledging. It becomes possible, therefore, to distinguish two lifestyles. For small songbirds, in which the reproductive cycle is tightly timed and often double-brooded, the clutch is large and lifespan is short. On the other hand, larger species such as birds of prey raise just one brood and lay a small clutch. Their choice is modest reproduction and extended life. However, as a determining factor of lifespan, size is a red herring.

Storm Petrels are sparrow-sized seabirds that lay a single egg and do not reach breeding maturity until they are around five years of age. But they are long-lived. The current record holder was a minimum of thirty-one years of age in 1992, having been ringed as a mature adult in 1962. Ferrying food from far out at sea to feed young is much easier if there is only one hungry mouth waiting at home. By fledging in the relative safety of a burrow, emerging under the cover of darkness and disappearing straight out to sea – where predators are few – the juvenile's chances of survival are good and mortality rates in the first year of life are remarkably low, around 10 per cent. Rearing more than one chick would be disproportionately demanding. Investment in a single, long-lived descendant makes sense. Each generation can weather caprice, particularly food shortages, that may preclude breeding. By living longer, good times balance out lean spells. Regrettably, honing breeding strategy to a low – but protracted – reproductive output from a core of long-lived individuals is undone by unanticipated precipitous declines wrought by humans: from long-line fishing techniques that decimate seabirds to wind turbines that annihilate bats. For songbirds living life in the fast lane, losses to predators and the seasonal nature of food supplies needed to rear a family large enough to produce heirs mean that life expectancy is shorter. The good news is that, in compensation for a live-fast-but-die-young philosophy, the species survives through sheer strength of numbers.

Stonechats. (Left) adult male in breeding plumage; (right) juvenile. Recent severe winters decimated Ireland's Stonechat population, most of which is resident. By producing up to three broods in a breeding season, survivors fuelled a fairly complete recovery.

16. SPEED OF FLIGHT

IN 1938 AN AMERICAN NEWSPAPER published a report from a pilot who was nose-diving at 240km/h. The speed of his plane was not exceptional. What was remarkable was the fact that he was passed by a Peregrine stooping on some ducks 'as though the plane was standing still'. In 1955 another observer used a stopwatch to record the speed of White-throated Needletail Swifts crossing a valley in India. The birds traversed a ravine 3km wide in times that ranged from 32.8 to 41.8 seconds. Thus the fastest speed was around 350km/h.

Why are these claims difficult to accept? Chiefly because the speeds are so much in excess of the known speeds of such fast fliers as the racing pigeon. A careful experiment was conducted with Royal Air Force pigeons during the Second World War. The speed calculated was the average of a two-way flight. The fastest individual travelled at 90km/h. Interestingly, this almost matches the maximum-recorded speed for a Common Swift. Furthermore, although they cannot fly, Ostriches can trot at speeds of up to 70km/h. Naturally the pace of a bird running on land is much easier to measure accurately as its speed is due entirely to its own efforts, without help from gravity or wind. This is why contradictory figures are arrived at for birds in flight. A species diving in a strong tailwind may well reach 160km/h. Climbing against the wind the same bird may clock only 20km/h. A crude estimate of the top speeds of birds flying parallel to a car indicate that most, in slack wind, fly at around 60km/h. More accurate determinations have been obtained in wind tunnels, where air velocity is controlled. During tests, a sparrow flew with an average speed of around 25km/h. To maintain a constant position at differing wind strengths it varied its air speed, sometimes more than doubling it and, when forced to battle against a stiff headwind, made no progress. Although still flying, it was effectively treading air. Had the bird been a migrant overpowered by a headwind, it would have been travelling backwards.

Nearly all birds have several gears – for cruising, emergencies and migration. The smaller the bird the faster it seems to be travelling. A House Sparrow beats its wings almost thirteen times a second in fast flight, a Grey Heron just two or three. Take off requires most energy. If a bird is made to rise and fall several times in quick succession it will eventually stay panting on the ground. Larger birds like geese are among the quickest, sometimes maintaining a speed of a mile a minute. Formation flying, whether in a V-configuration or in an ad hoc group, saves energy. By synchronising wingbeats, turbulence is harnessed. Slipstreaming is beneficial provided the wake of displaced air is tapped as it rises. Airborne 'group sync' of large birds can be seen in a burst of digital images – the wing positions conform to a follow-my-leader pattern with each in phase but subtly different from the one in front. A surprising aspect of bird flight is that attaining a burst of top speed bears little relation to overall size. In panic, everything from a warbler to a swan can hit a maximum escape momentum of around 75–90km/h. The most impressive statistics are those charting distances covered by birds in short periods of time. Lapwings are known to have crossed the Atlantic from Britain to Newfoundland in

Muscular yet smoothly streamlined, Peregrines are capable of speeds up to 389km/h (242 mph) when stooping on prey. Baffles in the nostrils protect the lungs and air sacs from excessive air pressure.

about twenty-four hours. Forced west by a big freeze and unable to feed, flocks pushed out across the North Atlantic, desperate to find unfrozen terra firma. They had to travel 4,000km and the average speed was, therefore, close to 140km/h. But this does not mean that they flew at this speed. At the time, an 85km/h easterly tailwind was blowing across the ocean, accounting for over half the birds' speed.

In athletics and motorsport we tend to regard short sprints and fast acceleration as the measure of swiftness. How quickly can someone run 100m or how many seconds does it take for a Formula 1 driver to reach a blurring high speed? Some of the quickest birds are shorebirds and wildfowl. Teal are the smallest duck and, unlike most wildfowl, do not need to taxi to take off. They spring into flight and twist and turn at speeds of up to 90km/h. Lapwings, whose broad-ended wings cup and displace a large pillow of air, are capable of outflying a pursuing Peregrine in level flight. However, if the falcon can gain height and keep its quarry below, then the added speed derived from gravity in a stoop will enable it to overhaul prey. When a Peregrine attacks from high above, its velocity rockets to a staggering 70–90m per second (252–324km/h). The G-force encountered when pulling out of a stoop would cause a human pilot to black out. The rush of air through nostrils is also pressurised. For a captive, performing Peregrine wearing a small 15g falconer's bell, 25 G-force in a 300km/h stoop effectively increases the bell's 'drag weight' to 350g – equivalent to a full jar of marmalade. Inside the Peregrine's head, the air cavities leading from its nostrils are spiralled. In this way the incoming air is buffered.

The name Peregrine Falcon was coined because of the bird's migratory habits (peregrinations). In North America, a ringed bird covered 1,600km in twenty-one days: an average of 76km per day.

There is little point in rising to a great height unless an advantage can be derived. Moreover, wind velocity increases considerably with altitude. Provided that a bird's meteorological sensitivities are accurate and weather patterns conducive to migration can be anticipated, a migrant can avail of strong winds blowing at heights in excess of 1,000m. Fast-moving tailwinds circulating in the wake of active depressions are not tapped exclusively by large-bodied fliers such as wildfowl: songbirds migrating in autumn from subarctic regions to wintering areas in the tropics also hitch a ride. The return leg in spring is aided by riding northbound airflows, this time zephyrs directed around the flanks of anticyclones. Probably all birds are able to detect alterations in barometric pressure that presage a change in weather. However, being a savvy weather forecaster is not good enough because other physiological challenges need to be met if high flight is used. The steeper a bird climbs, the greater the energy demand. Air temperature drops, as does the level of oxygen.

Adaptations made by some trans-hemisphere migrants have been studied. Like long-distance runners training at altitude, the birds prepare for a spectacular 'slingshot' in thin air by reconstituting their blood. Red corpuscles are multiplied, increasing the bird's ability to absorb oxygen. High-energy deposits of fat provide fuel for the journey. To cram in as much fatty fuel as possible, non-essential organs such as the stomach and digestive tract are shrunk for a flight whose duration may last 100 hours. How does the bird drink? As stored fat is metabolised it yields water. Furthermore, in cool air, liquid is captured in each outgoing warm breath because water vapour condenses in the nasal passages at the base of the bill. In most autumns a few

American 'astronauts' err and arrive in gardens along remote western fringes of Munster and Connacht. Contrary to mass media speculation, no migrating bird is ever lost. But a few finish up in the wrong place. Off the Atlantic seaboard of North America, the pull of crosswinds associated with the aftermath of hurricanes whips southbound high-fliers eastwards. While some meet a watery grave, others are accelerated towards Ireland. Pushed along by tailwinds that produce groundspeeds of 90km/h or more, they make landfall in around forty-eight hours.

Shaped like frying pans, Lapwing's outer wings whump more air than most fliers. Hugely efficient in travelling quickly and over great distances, migrants crossing 3,800km of open Atlantic were estimated to have expended less than one-tenth of the fuel needed by a small plane to make the same journey.

Mourning Dove, a North American migrant that arrived in westerly winds on Inishbofin, County Galway, in October 2007. Based on the bird's unique 'fingerprint' of plumage spots, it was established that the same individual flew on to Germany.

17. MIGRATION

MIGRATION IS, for the most part, a way of following the seasonal ebb and flow in food supply. The onset of winter across the Northern Hemisphere displaces millions of birds southwards. Routes evolved since the world's climate changed after the last Ice Age provide true Olympians with a map and compass for twice-yearly journeys that, on average, span a third of the earth's circumference. Heredity plays a key part in determining the onset of migratory behaviour; evolution's handiwork is pressed into every fibre. These are troops ordained in the hope that some will complete a cycle ensuring that the species, rather than every individual, survives. Juveniles, unguided by parents, undergo a far-reaching metamorphosis. Despite a frail build, Willow Warblers perform one of the longest and most arduous migrations. Ireland's summer visitors head for sunny scrubby woodland in Africa's southern savannahs. Before autumn departure they increase muscle mass by almost 85 per cent. Of those trapped for ringing purposes in northern Nigeria after crossing the Sahara, most had lost one-third of their body weight.

Acceptance of Swallow's flight from northwest Europe to southern Africa was only grudgingly admitted as fact 100 years ago. In the opening years of the last century bird ringing was in its infancy and activities were centred in Europe, chiefly along the southeast coast of the Baltic. Initial recoveries confirmed a sweep of autumn migration connecting Finland to France,

Swallows use the same nest site over several summers. Youngsters park close to home – often a dark rafter inside a barn – and wait for a parent to deliver small food balls of compacted insects.

Young Swallows have a ginger face. Autumn gatherings bring all ages together before departure for North Africa and a twice-yearly crossing of the Sahara. As in all epic migrations, young troops sustain the heaviest casualties.

although earlier evidence hinted at much greater odysseys. In May 1822, a German nobleman – Count Christian Ludwig von Bothmer – shot a White Stork that attracted attention due to the presence of a projectile among its plumage. When the object was identified the specimen was christened *Pfeilstorch* – arrow stork. The missile was of central-African construction, a startling disclosure. Realisation that birds from Ireland's proximity penetrated deep into the Dark Continent came from a Swallow ringed in Staffordshire on 6 May 1911 and recovered on 23 December in Natal in the far southeast of South Africa (*British Birds* 1913). The editorial note that accompanied the report expressed scepticism: 'Unfortunately the few records we have as yet of ringed Swallows recovered during migration do not afford a clue to the routes taken and it seems unreasonable to suppose that [British and Irish] Swallows proceed southwards down the east side of Africa as *might* be inferred from this Natal record.'

As with a good detective story, we are still short of discovering quite how birds manage to navigate accurately over vast distances. Like unseen rivers in the sky, daytime migrants orientate above landscape features such as shorelines, valleys and mountain chains. The advantage of an aerial view is considerable, especially for finding feeding habitat. Yet visual orientation is practically useless over featureless desert or large stretches of ocean, especially when the sun cannot be seen and used as a rough guide to latitude. Nocturnally, topography is largely ignored. Radar studies show migration on a broad front and in a standard direction. In radar's early days human operators were baffled by the occasional 'meteor showers' of multitudinous pinpricks of light. Endearingly, they named them angels.

Aloft in the dark, travel is purposeful, but how do birds find the way? Researchers captured migrating Robins and kept them in specially designed 'orientation cages' with a view of the night sky. Restless and keen to continue migrating, their hopping movements were recorded as footprints scratched into inked paper. Upon examination, they aligned with the preferred migratory path. To begin with, the researchers concluded that the Robins were navigating by the stars. When the cages were covered (with white Plexiglass or paper) so that the occupants received light but could not observe stars, they were not disorientated and continued to hop in the correct direction. They had to be using another method of guidance. Next, when the cages were subjected to an artificial magnetic field, it emerged that the guests possessed a magnetic compass because, when the polarity was altered, they shifted position accordingly. The conclusion seemed inescapable. The behaviour fitted any adjustment made in the direction of the magnetic field. Not just Robins, but all birds as well as insects, fish, reptiles and some mammals possess the same ability. In short, our planet has an iron heart comprised of alternating shells of solid and molten material that determine its magnetic behaviour. Although human bodies cannot feel the force, we see the evidence of its existence in the pull of a compass needle.

To a bird, is the earth's magnetic field visible or might it be sensed? The intensity of the field is often measured in gauss (G) and it ranges from 0.25 to 0.65 G. By comparison, a refrigerator magnet has a field of around 100 G. Much as imaginary lines of latitude and longitude girdle the planet, invisible meridians of magnetism loop from pole to pole. The lines arc steeply from each pole and effectively point downwards (southerly) in the northern hemisphere and upwards (northerly) in the southern hemisphere. Importantly – and crucially for any living thing that can measure magnetic intensity – inclination steadily tapers until the lines become parallel to the earth's surface at the equator. Unlike arbitrary lines of longitude that wreath the globe in great circles, the bent meridians that trace the strength of the earth's magnetic field indicate latitude and direction (toward the equator or pole) within each hemisphere. Eureka, they can be used for orientation! Of course, latitude can be ascertained by the length of the day, or by the height of the sun or known guide stars above the horizon. However, travelling migrants, because they need to orientate correctly at all times, achieve better guidance by using the strength and direction of the magnetic field as an unerring touchstone.

Current understanding indicates that multiple clues are used as guidance systems. As well as the sun, stars and the earth's magnetic field, polarised light patterns in the sky are tapped (Muheim, Phillips & Akesson 2006, orn-lab.ekol.lu.se/~rachel/). Much like a rainbow, polarised light results when air molecules scatter light particles. Unlike a rainbow, polarised light is not ephemeral and is a permanent component in the atmosphere. Daily, it moves as a band and maintains a constant position at 90 degrees to the sun. Each day, when the sun is low on the horizon at sunrise and sunset, polarised light forms a discernable halo that bisects the sky's zenith. The ends of the halo dip and meet the horizon at 90 degrees left and right of the

Scientists used to believe that migratory birds, just like human navigators, used star patterns as a compass. In particular, by observing the rotation of constellations around the Pole Star, geographic direction can be gauged. Such an assertion loses weight when migrants set off on starless, cloudy nights. Moreover, birds born at high latitudes never have a chance to see a starry sky before they depart – because of the midnight sun. Fledglings reared indoors with no exposure to the sun, stars or other landmarks still orientate in the correct direction. Senses that detect the Earth's magnetic field and the pattern of celestial polarised light are, in fact, key in determining position. Nonetheless, experimental evidence shows that birds also possess a 'star compass'. However, the window of time during which birds can learn to calibrate star formations means that, for the most part, star maps serve as a backup and not a vital guide.

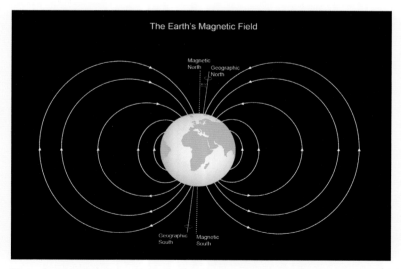

Lines of magnetic force encircle the Earth and run through its heart from pole to pole. In simplified terms, the field lines sprout from the magnetic South Pole at a 90-degree angle and then curve back – like segments of an orange – and are drawn into the magnetic North Pole, again at a 90-degree angle. When the lines reach the equator, they are parallel (horizontal) to the Earth's surface. Birds sense the change in the angle of the field lines at different latitudes (called the inclination angle) and use it to navigate. Basically, they interpret inclination angles to tell which direction is pole-ward and which is equator-ward.

sun's position. Irrespective of the sun's visibility, the polarisation band is detectable, except during heavy, overcast conditions. Research shows that birds use it as a marker indicating position along the north–south 'grain' of the magnetic field. In fact, during the earth's twice-yearly equinoxes when the plane of the equator faces the centre of the sun and daylight and darkness are of equal length (around 20 March and 22 September), the polarisation band is perfectly aligned with north–south meridians of longitude (Phillips & Waldvogel 1982).

Bees, ants, marine life and various other animals can distinguish polarised light as easily as we distinguish colours. Octopus, squid and cuttlefish have the most acute polarisation sensitivity of all. Alas, we are not one of the in-crowd. Birds also possess the ability, the extent of which is not fully understood, although they are certainly able to discern it at sunrise and sunset, when it is most prominent. Other than polarised lenses in sunglasses that remove glare and make the sky a deeper blue, most people know nothing about polarised light, and scientific apparatus is needed to demonstrate how light travels and how some of it becomes polarised. How best to describe it? In science classes at school we learn that light comes in waves (or planes) and that ordinary light wiggles in all directions. Polarised light is light in which all the waves vibrate on one fixed – polarised – plane. Most waves (except sound waves) involve a vibration at right angles to their path. Think of an ocean wave that only goes up or down as it travels forwards. But the waves made by wiggling a rope can be made to wobble up, down or in any sideways direction. Polarisation simply consists of forcing the waves to vibrate in a single, constant direction.

Imagine trying to wiggle a rope in such a way that it will pass through a vertical gap in a fence. Vertical wiggles get through but wiggles in any other plane fail to penetrate and are bounced back along the line of the rope – scattered. Funnily enough, this kind of effect explains why the sky is blue. The sun's light is a mix of wavelengths (mainly red, green, blue and ultraviolet) but as the rays hit earth's gaseous atmosphere (15km deep) not all pass through simultaneously. In basic terms, blue rays 'hit the fence' and are scattered, turning the sky blue. With the sun hidden at night, no rays fill the heavens above us and we see stars in a black firmament. Hence, polarised light comes from the blue sky and its intensity and vibrations depend on the position of the sun, according to its height in the heavens. Probably, the Vikings were aware of the significance of sky polarisation as a means of navigating in cloudy weather at sea. They are believed to have used a crystal, coined a 'sunstone', as a polarising filter that glinted blue when pointed to the invisible sun.

What, precisely, do birds look for in the polarised aurora that they behold? Remember, sunrise and sunset mark the two times of day when the band of maximum polarisation is vertically aligned on the horizon and arcs across the zenith like a blue seam. Moreover, because of the sun's position on the horizon, the band inevitably sits at a right angle to the sun. Thus, in contrast to other times of the day, the polarisation pattern at sunrise and sunset is relatively simple and its intensity is at its strongest. During spring and autumn the polarisation axis is aligned approximately north–south and coincides with the migratory directions of many birds (Muheim 2011). Imagine that you were taken blindfolded to Belfast and told that, upon the mask being removed, you had to travel to Cork without the aid of a map. For a bird, the

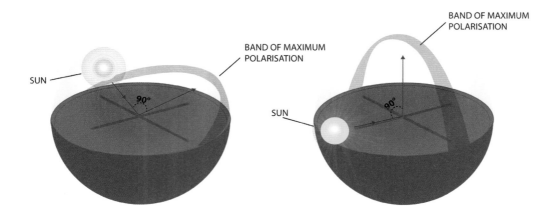

Sunshine reaching Earth comprises light of different wavelengths. Earth's atmosphere scatters the light particles – called photons – and creates a band of strongly polarised light at 90 degrees to the sun. Although invisible to us, birds and many life forms detect the band's pattern, which follows the movement of the sun across the sky. By observing the band's position, birds are able to use its end points as a navigation reference, even when the sun is obscured.

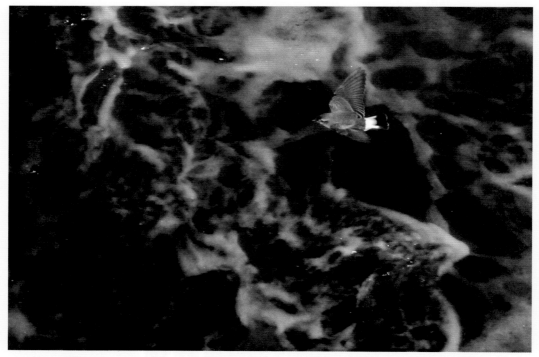

Wheatear, 300km west of Kerry. Caught in the lights of a research vessel on a wet August night, the Robin-sized songbird battled against a prevailing headwind but never alighted. Many Wheatears fly from Greenland to Morocco in one hop.

challenge would be easy, provided it was given the coordinates of Cork, expressed in longitude and earth magnetism. First, it would take a bead at sunrise or sunset from the sky's polarisation pattern. Although the band of maximum polarisation extends from one end of the horizon to the other, it may be that the band's end-points are used as compass bearings – like lining up a sentinel tree or telegraph pole in the distance. Departing south, the bird switches to sensing the change in gradient (analogous to the strength) of the earth's magnetic field until Cork's target value is met. Indeed, according to current theory, birds may perceive the magnetic field as a three-dimensional pattern superimposed on their visual field (Phillips, Muheim & Jorge 2010). In concert, polarised light and magnetism provide a compound compass. The concept, although simple, is mind-bending.

Ironically, although the prominence overhead of the polarisation band is a constant reference, it transpires that a sunset or sunrise view of its position vis-à-vis the horizon is crucial. Few birds migrate in a single, straight geographic direction. Most routes are curved and their trajectories are genetically imprinted. New generations obey an inherited Sat Nav that has been fashioned by evolution. To take account of latitudinal changes encountered in the course of a journey that may carry a migrant diagonally across vast distances (timed to derive advantage from seasonal tailwinds and deflected to avoid barren terrain such as mountain ranges or deserts) periodic updating is needed. The horizon is likely to play an important role in averaging the alignments of the polarisation band at sunset and sunrise, because a migrant bird must compare – and compensate for – minor differences in the two observations if its internal clock is to remain accurate. Failure to do so would result, over time, in an uncorrected course. Think of it this way: as the bird migrates it is not simply following the sun as a compass, it is following a unique path. During migration, it could land at a stopover site where it can view the polarisation pattern at sunrise and then again before departing at sunset. Once the alignments of the polarisation band at both times are split, position is pinpointed. The calculation allows the traveller, by measuring the variation from place to place, to resolve position over featureless, unknown terrain. Intriguing parallels are suspected within birds' physiology that may, in future, reveal a common receptor system that processes polarised light in tandem with 'earth strength' magnetism. Logic suggests that eyes might be best suited to detecting such stimuli, although in several species iron-rich magnetic material has been found in the bill's nasal cavity. Recent insights based on Robins have established the existence of two senses by which birds register the earth's magnetic field. Having found evidence that birds' brains process magnetic information, researchers are now attempting to understand the sensory pathways that convey the information. For example, can the retina visualise magnetism? The quest for birds' magnetic senses is fast becoming a Holy Grail to which science is inching ever closer: 'We are no longer searching for a needle in a haystack.' (Mouritsen 2012).

New generations are programmed with an innate directional migration and are not intended to be an end-of-era elite. Rather, they are seed corn, launched to reach winter quarters and return home. If they manage to make it back, they will enter the breeding ranks. Tried and tested genes will be passed on. Nonetheless, things sometimes go wrong. Before

Downed by heavy rain in late March, a migrant Chiffchaff surveys its surroundings on an island in the Irish Sea. The bird's forehead and chin are uncharacteristically dark – still sticky from pollen gleaned from blossoms in Iberia.

youngsters migrate in earnest, they disperse in haphazard directions. Even for species that are long-distance migrants, 'off-piste' explorations may be beneficial in helping to familiarise them with the vicinity of their birthplace. If mistakes are to be made, autumn is the time to make them. Migration at this season is a more relaxed affair and birds tend to wait for optimum weather before starting a long journey. After all, there is no urgency to find a breeding territory and attract a mate. Starling is hardly the first species that springs to mind when epic flights are considered but results from an intensive ringing programme involving 11,000 individuals in the 1950s produced some of the most important information ever gathered on bird migration. Perdeck (1958) captured and ringed adults and juveniles during autumn in northern Holland and transported some to Switzerland, where they were released. After several months, information on recovery locations began to trickle in. Most of the youngsters flew southwest from Switzerland and finished up in southern France and northern Spain. They had continued migrating in the same direction as other rookies released in the Netherlands. In so doing, they overshot their intended destination, which was southern Britain and northern France. Adults, on the other hand, corrected their course by 90 degrees and arrived in winter quarters remembered from the year before. This proved that, by successfully completing its first migration, a bird refines a rudimentary map.

Some birds live sedentary lives. A local universe may supply all needs. For those that choose a parochial existence, intimate familiarity with their surroundings is essential. House Sparrows eke out a year-round existence by following a catholic diet. A menu of nectar, insects, buds, seeds, and fruit reads like a lesson in nutrition, but savants exploit them all and then mine human activities for a hidden wealth of crumbs or animal feed. The chief spanners in the works are environmental change wrought by man or a prolonged big freeze spelling starvation and a shivery grave. Starlings, Rooks and Pied Wagtails make longer everyday movements. Feeding grounds are separate from roosting quarters and may be miles apart. Overnight gatherings serve as information exchanges. Meeting the neighbours for gossip, tips and the possibility of romance are not exclusive to our society. Movements in search of seasonally available foods are among the most spectacular. Insectivorous Swifts commute from the Congo to breed among inaccessible nooks and crannies in Ireland's built environment, where they trawl the sky for its summer bounty of (increasingly diminishing) insects. Species departing from northern climes in autumn direct movements towards milder lower latitudes. Tailwinds provide optimum flying conditions. Bramblings quitting Fenno-Scandia may be carried west on easterly airflows to Ireland – or coast south on a fair wind to the Low Countries. Periodic 'food flights' bring them to our shores. Each autumn, their Viking armies set off in search of beech mast. A heavy crop in one year is invariably followed by a mediocre yield. The tree is 'tired' after the previous year's production. Likewise, Siskins, Lesser Redpolls, Crossbills and Waxwings all depend on sporadic crops of berries and tree seed. It is not far-fetched to regard their wanderings as nomadism, rather than migration.

Waxwings live in taiga and dine on the forest's numberless insects during summer. In autumn they switch diet. Rowan berries become a new staple. A bounteous crop ensures winter survival and boosts breeding numbers for the following summer. Then, because berry production is cyclical, bust follows boom. When prolific breeding success coincides with crop failure the imbalance between population and food supply reaches a flashpoint and migration is instigated. Hungry hordes irrupt west and south. Some movements appear to have a directional trend; others seem random. Basically, the species is cold-searching Europe as far west as Ireland for food.

Swallows are harbingers of spring and the sight of the first to return is an affirmation that migration has, once again, delivered an annual miracle. They are among the most faithful of migrants and make return movements at around the same time and often to the same destination. Punctuality and site fidelity apply equally to the winter quarters in South Africa. Irish and British Swallows retrapped over successive winters had all returned, dartboard style, to within a radius of 100km of where they were first ringed. They arrive in late November having flown more or less directly from Ireland. Most depart in early autumn and aim to pass through the northern tropics before the rains finish and reach the southern tropics as the rains begin. Rather than laying down extra fat as fuel, they feed as they go. An exception occurs when, southbound, they reach the Mediterranean. Ahead lies the scorching wilderness of the Sahara. Before steeling themselves for the ordeal, they linger and fatten.

In their daily lives, all birds utilise water and are able to obtain it from their own metabolic processes. So how do Swallows manage to cross the Sahara without dying of thirst? To complicate matters further, waifs found dying in the Libyan Desert showed normal water levels, but had run out of fat. Fuel depletion rather than dehydration appeared to have been their downfall (Biebach 1991). A balance needs to be struck between energy requirements and water supply. Depending on whether fat, protein or carbohydrate is metabolised, water is derived in different proportions. Up to a point, a properly conditioned migrant could meet its needs as a by-product of burning an ample supply of fuel and muscle. Into the equation come ambient temperature and the direction of the prevailing wind. In autumn, southbound Swallows flying at low altitude could be assisted by tailwinds. However, rather than fly in the dehydrating heat of the day, many travel at night and climb to a moderate altitude. High flight, although tapping cooler air, risks water loss through a change in humidity, requiring greater energy expenditure which, in turn, depletes the bird's output of metabolic water. Talk about the horns of a dilemma! A different problem occurs in spring. At this season northbound Swallows crossing the Sahara are likely to encounter headwinds. To avoid them high altitude travel is essential, despite the strain on water and energy budgets. At around 2km elevation 'anti-trade winds' blow northeast, the opposite of surface headwinds, thus constituting tailwinds. Radar studies show that many migrants opt for these higher flight altitudes in spring (Newton 2010).

Even so, fatalities are considerable. Swallows and legions of other songbirds face dangers that simply do not exist in Ireland. Eleanora's Falcons patrol promontories along the North African coast, waiting to pounce on small migrants that have just completed a long sea crossing. Inland, across vast stretches of desert devoid of all vegetation, Sooty Falcons breed under the harshest conditions of searing heat and raise young by hunting at dawn and dusk for autumn migrants crossing bleak terrain. Sandstorms are another hurdle, downing weakened fliers, and are most prevalent along the southern margins of the desert, benighting migrants almost within range of verdant habitat and salvation. Perhaps not surprisingly, Swallows are the most frequently found bird corpses in Saharan oases. Life expectancy is short. While the oldest ringed bird lived for sixteen years, average annual mortality is nearly 80 per cent for juveniles and around 40 per cent for adults. In total, around one-quarter of each year is spent migrating. Swallows reared in Russia and northeast Europe spend the winter closer to the equator. Unwittingly, at roosts in Nigeria, they have sailed straight into the rapids – in excess of a quarter of a million are caught and sold for food.

Why do Swallows and many other European songbirds launch themselves so intrepidly over the Mediterranean and disappear into the heart of Africa? Earth history has unquestionably moulded these wild excursions. As a class of living being, birds have been in existence for 145 million years and 'modern' species have been around for the last 80 million years. In that enormous time frame whole continents have moved, ice ages have caused massive evacuations towards warmer climes and climate itself has alternated. Even the magnetic poles have occasionally switched alignment. The timeline of Swallow migration has, through the millennia, known days when the trip to Africa did not include crossing the Mediterranean – it did not exist – and routes were over lush land the whole way. Probably, in ancient aeons,

Not all migrants depart with a fixed destination in mind. Bramblings head south in autumn and roam across Europe until they locate beech forest that set seed (mast) during summer.

Irish Swallows found the journey fairly straightforward. Ten thousand years ago the Sahara was green and consisted of many large wetlands, much like Botswana today. Not even the Irish Sea or English Channel lay in their path. In other words, today's generations are the toughest yet. They have been forced to lengthen their stride to take account of tectonic 'road works'. In light of the annual trek's sheer adversity, might it change? Increasingly, small numbers of Swallows remain around the Mediterranean. In the New World, some North American Swallows wintering in Argentina now breed there and have evolved a novel migration involving a round trip north to the Amazon (Alex Lees pers. comm.).

How does a bird that weighs little more than a slice of buttered toast manage to fly so far? Each round trip clocks up 30,000km. Flight demands that weight is reduced to a minimum. Like all birds, Swallow bones are hollow and the wings are powered by massive pectoral muscles, aligned either side of the wishbone. The wing action involved in a long flight is the most sustained effort by any group of muscles in an animal. At 30 per cent of total body mass, the muscle tissues consist of fast-contracting fibres – an attribute of the quickest human sprinters – enabling the wings to beat without let-up. Unlike the inhale/exhale action of human lungs, a bird's respiratory system extracts oxygen from air using air sacs as well as lungs. Sacs are located throughout the body, such as within abdominal cavities and between the skin and body walls. Ironically, the lungs themselves hold almost no used air. Each intake of breath travels a continuous path around various parts of the anatomy where sacs extract oxygen from the passing stream of air. A comparison to the journey made by the Flying Scotsman from Edinburgh to London is not unreasonable. Like the steam locomotive, powered by non-stop shovelling of coal into the engine's furnace, a Swallow's wing action is sustained by the automatic action of its heart that pumps blood continuously. For this purpose the heart of a Swallow is, relatively speaking, four times as big as ours.

18. BLACKCAP'S BELLE ÉPOQUE

NAÏVETY CATCHES OUT all of us some of the time. Until the turn of the millennium, birdwatchers laboured under the delusion that the distribution of wintering Blackcaps across Ireland was linked to the geographical spread of observers and that the species' whereabouts had been pinned down thanks to eagle-eyed observers who knew what a Blackcap looked like and were alert to out-of-season appearances: on a par with seeing a Swallow at Christmas. Hark back to 1913. The erudite pages of *British Birds* published a letter stating: 'The occurrence of the Blackcap during winter in Britain and Ireland is sufficiently unusual to deserve notice. On December 29th 1912 I saw a male near Bourne End in Buckinghamshire' (Baynes 1913). During 1953, Ireland mustered just two winter records, both in County Antrim. Over the next decade, sightings among leafy retreats increased steadily and the 1963 *Irish Bird Report* noted a change in status: 'Now recorded in January and February in south Dublin suburbs'.

Over successive post-1980s winters, there came repeated requests to identify a 'mystery bird' that was slipping through backyard shrubbery and, more often than not, coming to a feeder and driving away all-comers. The feisty newcomer was becoming universal. A winter bird survey conducted by the BTO in 2004 found that, in those where food was provided, one in three English gardens held a Blackcap. A similar statistic would probably have applied to Ireland. A childhood rarity was becoming commonplace. Almost simultaneously, breeding numbers started to explode. Recently a different question has surfaced: could the species become resident? Wintering individuals are still around in March when the first bars of song are heard. Sightings and song continue throughout the spring, followed by glimpses of scruffy moulting adults in summer and the emergence of a new generation. The explanation – two discrete populations, one spending the winter and departing before being replaced by a separate breeding contingent – seems hard to credit. But, for the present, this is what is happening.

Blackcaps breed from Ireland across the whole of northern Europe with the overall population estimated at around 20 million. Migrants head south. Winter quarters lie in a huge arc encompassing West Africa, the Mediterranean and the Middle East, and south through East Africa's rift valley. Like any bird that travels a considerable distance to reach a defined goal, departing migrants ready themselves for a twice-yearly odyssey. Preparations come under genetic control, and restlessness, born out of willingness to migrate, grips the bird. A French ornithologist recognised the condition, coined *Zugunruhe* by German researchers. Telltale signs are an urge to eat voraciously and convert food to fat. Soon the pilgrim is off and flies relentlessly for a given period until it has covered a predetermined distance in a set time to a specified location. For first-time migrants, journey's end will be brand new. Once there, like a patient snapped out of hypnosis, the bird reverts to routine behaviour. As with all migratory birds, the routes taken by Europe's Blackcaps have been honed by evolution.

Food is an immediate priority for migrant Blackcaps in spring. Ivy berries ripen and are widely accessible in late March and are available well into June. Few birds eat them but Blackcap is a major diner.

Painstaking research, involving detaining migrants to ascertain standard direction by monitoring *Zugunruhe*, has established that the species varies its migratory behaviour across Europe. Populations breeding in Ireland and Western Europe travel southwest to the western Mediterranean and West Africa. However, at some point across central Europe a migratory divide exists. East of this line, the preferred direction is around the eastern edge of the Mediterranean to East Africa. Although autumn migrants are born with the wherewithal to sense the correct route, inexperienced first-timers often disperse off-piste, probably wooed by ideal meteorological conditions such as high pressure and a favourable tailwind. In most cases false starts (or deliberate youthful explorations?) are corrected, but a comparatively small number persist in travelling in an erroneous direction. They continue to miscue either due to the persistence of lulling tailwinds drifting them ever more off-course, or because their genetic compass is at fault. Whatever the reason, some arrive in areas off the beaten track. For wayward East European fliers that cross the North Sea and make landfall in northwest Europe, *Zugunruhe* seems to have run its course and tyros find themselves in Britain or Ireland sometime in late autumn. Less fortunate others presumably meet a watery grave. Occasional strays reach the south coast of Iceland where, around Reykjavik, gardens save their skin and increasing numbers spend a long, dark winter.

Suburban gardens have become the winter home for Blackcaps, except those well inland. Ousting other birds from fruit, fat balls or feeders, this small guy punches well above his weight. Females are brown-capped and equally pugnacious.

Winter survival is less of a problem for troops marooned in Ireland's climate. Many return eastwards to breed during the following spring. If still alive in autumn, where will they travel to spend the next winter? Based on the maxim 'if it ain't broke, don't fix it', the bird will return to Ireland, effectively overwriting its inborn migratory roadmap. Moreover, subsequent offspring are likely to follow parental footsteps. Captive breeding, which paired individuals from differing migratory populations, proved that, when cross-bred, the next generation showed route preferences that were intermediate between those of their parents. This crucial discovery led to the realisation that, in the wild, migratory direction could be changed by natural selection. The situation is not without irony. Because 'lost' Blackcaps wintering in

Ireland survived, their genes became a template for a novel migration route. Mild weather and garden bird feeding may have acted as a tipping point. While much larger numbers of Eastern Europe's core population return safely from winter quarters stretching from the Middle East to Ethiopia, Irish troops gain a further advantage because the return leg of their journey is shorter. Of greater significance, after the spring equinox, Blackcaps wintering in our latitude experience longer days than those wintering further south. Lengthening daylight stimulates reproductive development. Males from Ireland are in mating condition and able to establish a breeding territory ahead of returning migrants from the traditional winter range. Before departing from our back gardens in spring, some mumble song, usually in late March. Whether delivered by adults or young, the early attempts are rehearsals for overseas performances. Ringing data confirms that, in most cases, home lies in west-central Europe, mainly southern Germany and western Austria. Research there confirms that returning Irish Blackcaps are increasing. Another factor driving the process and producing exclusively Irish heirs is breeding partnerships with females that also travelled northwest and overwintered in Ireland.

Hot on the heels of our departing winter visitors, immigrants arrive via Iberia. April has become a grey area. Song in the early part of the month probably hails from outgoing Blackcaps, emigrants bound for Europe. However, by month's end, summer visitors are ensconced on nesting habitat and broadcasting for all they are worth. Suitable habitat was never in short supply, yet the bird was, until the 1990s, fairly local in distribution. Perhaps, like Collared Dove, colonists discovered an under-utilised niche? In Ireland, no other warbler champions the tangled, virtually impenetrable undergrowth that flourishes within well-lit woodland. The 'Plantation of Ireland' has been matched in Scotland. Meanwhile in Britain, where the species has been common for centuries, breeding stock is estimated to have increased by 102 per cent between 1995 and 2010. In Ireland, the increase is a staggering 439 per cent over the same period. A check of putative reasons fuelling expansion in Britain suggests parallels with Ireland. On both sides of the Irish Sea, summer visitors arrive at least a fortnight earlier than they did in the 1980s. Because early arrival is not an impediment to breeding, 'time saved' can be used to generate a previously rare second brood, thereby boosting productivity. A domino effect of changing climate leading to earlier migration and an extra brood could be driving a Blackcap baby boom.

Not all European Blackcaps are migratory. The species is sedentary on Tenerife and the Canaries and breeding populations in Iberia and elsewhere around the Mediterranean perform much shorter migrations than those making mammoth treks to East Africa from countries such as Finland. The circumstances that formerly suppressed a migratory urge in some regions might echo ongoing events in Ireland, especially the 'unnecessary' exodus of a wintering population. Given that migratory traits fall under genetic control, an option that favours some birds becoming partially resident is a possibility. In Britain, a confirmed British-bred Blackcap was recently discovered during midwinter. Could this be the start of a new habit?

19. THE GREAT DETECTIVE

GAZING UPON the misty black-and-white image of Richard Manliffe Barrington that accompanies his obituary (Moffat 1916) you are struck by a neat appearance and intellectual poise. His side profile is illuminated from the front and dust-speckled rays of sunlight pick out the hem of a long nose and piercing pale eyes anchored by a grey beard whose tapered point suggests years of ruminative stroking. An aloof academic he was not. Moffat writes: 'No adequate idea can be given of the loss inflicted on Irish Natural History … the love of nature grew up with him like an instinct.' Barrington, a land-valuer and farmer-cum-naturalist, was obsessed with migration. Unlike today, nobody really knew where migrant birds came from or where they went. Passage periods were grasped but full itineraries were a mystery. For example, where did the Great Shearwaters that passed south off the west coast each autumn, actually breed? The answer is the remote archipelago of Tristan da Cunha in the Roaring Forties of the Southern Hemisphere. Barrington's guess was a bit closer to home – Rockall. He decided to check and sailed to the remote outcrop in 1896. The expedition's hopes that the island might prove to be the Great Shearwaters' nesting home were groundless but, in this era, negative results were as important in filling gaps in knowledge as positive ones.

Born at Fassaroe, County Wicklow, in May 1849, Barrington was accumulating personal observations on the natural world by the age of thirteen and had his first note published – about the quantity of beechnuts eaten by a Woodpigeon – in *The Zoologist* when just seventeen. By 1882 he was involved in a systematic correspondence with Irish lighthouse keepers on the matter of the birds they encountered at their stations. The effort was streamlined by the issuing of recording forms and then became, under the auspices of the British Association

The foundation blocks of our understanding of bird migration across Ireland were laid when Richard Barrington organised the nation's lighthouse keepers to forward the remains of birds 'killed striking'.

for the Advancement of Science, part of a wider data-gathering network. Barrington (1900) summed up the scope of the endeavour: 'The brilliant lights attract thousands upon thousands of winged voyagers, numbers of whom, when bewildered by the glare on dark nights, fly oftentimes against the lanterns with great speed, and are killed striking. It is hoped that the light-keepers will not think it too much trouble to cut off and label the wing and leg of every common bird which is killed.' By the end of 1887 the official scheme had come to an end, mainly due to the cost of printing the keepers' voluminous correspondence. Barrington felt that this was premature because the results were beginning to show real promise. He sensed that hard evidence was starting to replace inexact opinions and resolved that, for Ireland, the inquiry should go on. Hence, from 1888 until the publication of *The Migration of Birds as Observed at Irish Lighthouses and Lightships* (1900) the whole expense was borne by him.

It is easy to imagine his enthusiasm. With each postal delivery he was receiving the ornithological equivalent of uncut diamonds. Gathering information from lonely lighthouses, whose beams intercepted avian pilots and revealed their identity, was tantamount to exploring a new frontier. He was meticulous in looking for both cause and effect. Assisted by C. B. Moffat, he managed to marshal a far-flung team of keepers to gauge migration in tooth and claw, notably the mixture of species and scale of numbers during great 'rushes'. In short, if a keeper had anything to say about birds, Barrington wanted to know. For over two decades, 30,000 observations were submitted and 2,000 remains were collected, posted, identified, measured, weighed and labelled. As well as issuing standardised paperwork, specially designed envelopes formed part of the operation's attention to detail. What did he discover?

Until the coastline was plunged into a nocturnal light-storm in the late twentieth century, the only commanding man-made illumination came from strategically placed lighthouses. Birds were drawn to them like moths to a flame. In gloomy conditions, such as rain, drizzle and fog, whirling flocks became disorientated with inevitable casualties. Moonlight also plays a role and its presence, particularly when shining in a clear sky, dramatically reduces collisions with dazzling lanterns. Barrington credits Moffat for noticing this relationship, which was extrapolated from the data: 'The influence of the lunar phases on the number of birds killed striking was first detected by him [C.B.Moffat].' Typically, he then goes on to quantify things: 'At least 80 per cent of the Song Thrushes striking were killed in the fourth and first quarters of the moon, and this rule holds good with other birds, apparently without any distinction between species … during these seven years, out of a total of 673 Song Thrushes received, only 106, or less than 16 per cent, were killed when the moon was more than half full.'

Barrington deduced that, *mirabile dictu*, not all Wrens were sedentary and that migrants crossed at least the Irish Sea. This paradigm shift in understanding proved hard to substantiate. Despite most lighthouses being located on islands off the coast, Wrens bred and were resident on all but the bleakest outposts. Mr E. McCarron, light-keeper at the Tearaght, the most westerly sea-girt shard of Kerry's Blasket Islands, reported that 'between 60 and 100 Wrens may always be found … however, its numbers vary, for example, an increase [was] noted in the autumn of 1890'. The autumnal spike in numbers might have been explained by the addition of locally fledged young. Support for overseas migration came from east coast occurrences

Lighthouse on Tory, County Donegal. In the past, lighthouse beams were the only artificial light seen by night-flying birds. In bad visibility, disorientated migrants were dazzled and struck the glass.

on barren rocks such as The Maidens, off County Antrim (three reports, two of which were in November) and Tuskar, off County Wexford (one report in October). On the basis of the Antrim records, he concluded: 'This may mean that the Wren chooses the route between Antrim and the southwest of Scotland as the shortest passage from Ireland to Britain.' Probably, he was mistaken in assuming that the Wrens were emigrating from Ireland. The reverse is much more likely. His conjecture for two Wrens that struck Fastnet, off County Cork, on 30 October 1897, admits a more extraordinary (yet still likely) origin: 'The two Wrens … did so during a rush of many species and may have been blown out of their course during a local migration to some of the southern islands. If, on the contrary, they had crossed from Britain, we have an instance of a flight of some 200 miles [330 km], performed by a bird which might be thought one of the worst adapted for long migratory journeys.' Ringing has expanded our appreciation of the mite's at-sea flight endurance. One trapped on the Northumberland coast on 24 September 1998 had flown 900 km across the North Sea from Sweden (see further discussion in McGeehan & Wyllie 2012).

Goldcrests are even smaller than the Wren. The tiny bird is entirely insectivorous and populations breeding in cold latitudes cannot survive the winter. Countless numbers migrate south. Keepers were familiar with the species at migration seasons but Barrington's perusal of its occurrence patterns fell short of grasping their full gist. Autumn immigration from mid September to mid November peaked along the east coast stations during the first ten days of October. A much reduced but more tightly timed emigration – during late March and early April – occurred in spring. This piqued him because it was concentrated along the north coast, a feature that he found surprising. We now comprehend that immigrants are whittled down during winter, especially during hard weather when insect food all but disappears. Many perish but any that successfully overwinter exit Ireland predominantly through the northeast. On an international stage, Barrington's tallies helped chart the broad-front evacuation of the 'flying fairy-light' right across Britain and Ireland. In 1882 a major rush, probably involving Goldcrests from northern Russia as well as from Scandinavia, crossed the North Sea. The conveyor poured migrants along the entire eastern seaboard of Scotland and northern England. The vanguard made landfall on 7–8 October and reached western Scotland two days later. He explains what happened next:

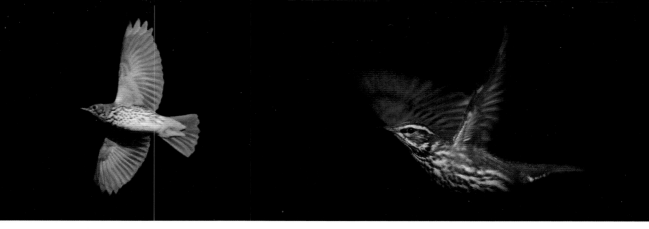

At night, flocks of Redwings (right) and Song Thrushes (left) travel like rivers in the sky. Ireland lies at a crossroads for migrant bands incoming from Iceland to Scandinavia.

It was during this period of its maximum density [around 10 October] that the swarm extended to Ireland, where, previous to 9th October, no Goldcrests had been noted … On 9th, five struck at Howth Baily [County Dublin] and two at Rathlin [County Antrim]; on 12th, a dozen at the Tuskar [County Wexford] … on 13th, Tuskar reports them 'continually striking all night'; while five struck on the same date on Rathlin; the following night the west coast was reached, 14 striking at South Aran Island [County Galway]; on 15th they were noted about the lantern on Inishtrahull [County Donegal]; and after this no more were reported, except a few isolated instances on November 30th and December 17th.

The statistics bring the action alive. His dream was being realised: 'The detailed results … are based on facts, for we have had enough migration theories. Some results may be new, and if so, to have placed them before other students of this most fascinating subject, ornithology, is a more than sufficient reward.'

Wheatears breed on islands and headlands that also contain lighthouses. Keepers forwarded specimens regularly but Barrington sensed peculiarities in the pattern of occurrences. Migrants arrived during March and the first half of April, among them the core of birds destined to breed in the general vicinity. Only along the south coast, particularly at Tuskar, a sentinel rock off the County Wexford coast, did any significant numbers strike a lantern. These, he conjectured, were incoming migrants. The western and northern stations, located within breeding habitat, produced remarkably few references to birds striking. In other words, once ensconced and not on active migration, lanterns were no longer a hazard. Yet, during the latter half of April and May, fatalities from strikes increased at all Atlantic stations from County Kerry northwards; a sign that migrants were again in transit. His meticulous measurements rumbled a difference in the later birds' longer wing length. He concluded: 'It appears unlikely that any Irish-breeding Wheatears would be seeking their summer homes at so late a date as 28th April, to say nothing [of the middle of May]. This being so, it would seem to follow that the birds striking our west coast lanterns at the end of April are passing northward.' Barrington also extended his argument to embrace late movements on all coasts, which he felt referred equally to the same subset of northbound Wheatears. He was right. Effectively, he had distinguished the discrete population of longer-winged and heavier-bodied 'Greenland'

Wheatears that pass through Ireland in late spring bound for Iceland, Greenland and northeast Canada. His wing-length criterion, used as a geographic marker, led him to surmise that 'the birds which strike in autumn are largely composed of individuals breeding farther north.' Alas, his speculation was ultra-conservative: 'Having regard to the general tenor of the evidence … the conclusion seems to be warranted that this island is a main point of arrival and departure for birds migrating between Ireland and some more northern region, not necessarily farther away than the Outer Hebrides.'

Of all migratory families, thrushes absorbed Barrington most. Song Thrush was, he believed, Ireland's commonest immigrant but he freely admitted that, because light-keepers regularly confused Song Thrush with Redwing, his data was difficult to sift. His writing, while analytical, still captured the breathtaking scale of movements:

> This species [Song Thrush] arrives in immense numbers on our southeast coast during October and November … it is seen passing the lighthouses in considerable flocks by day, but occurs far more numerously at night, and in cloudy or foggy seasons numbers are frequently killed striking. In October 1897 the keeper at Tuskar reports 'from 500–600 Blackbirds and thrushes killed each night from 20th to 23rd,' and this represents only a small proportion of the great wave of migration then in progress, which can be traced during some of the same nights at the Fastnet, Mine Head, Coningbeg, Blackwater Bank and Rockabill lights – that is, from the coast of Cork to that of Dublin.

Half a century later, observations made in Dublin, principally over Dun Laoghaire, established that, in the autumn of 1952, ratios of the various species of thrush were different from those noted by Barrington. On the basis of nocturnal flight calls, the overwhelming majority of migrants were Redwings, not Song Thrushes. Did he get it wrong, as some suggested: 'I have always thought it hard to believe that Barrington's conclusion was correct … I find it … incredible to think that there are more Song Thrush immigrants in autumn and winter than the hordes of Redwings one sees, even allowing for the more secretive and less gregarious habits of the former' (Major R.F. Ruttledge, quoted in Browne, 1953), In fact, Barrington was well aware of the need for accuracy and, as best he could, he cross-referenced remains against observations. Today, what are we to make of the debate? After two recent severe winters, the flood of Redwing migration that had become a marked feature of late autumn has considerably diminished. So a bird's status can change, even if only temporarily. The frequency of calling may also differ between species. Redwings typically migrate in loose flocks whose members call as they go. Song Thrushes are less sociable and their calls are more sporadic – and harder to hear. Real-world distribution patterns are, of course, the best measure. While such quantification defies reliable enumeration, it is safe to say that, despite its shrinking-violet nature, Song Thrush is common and widespread during winter, especially in the west of Ireland where, except during hard-weather influxes, they outnumber Redwings.

Barrington was active in all walks of ornithology, not just migration. He visited many of the islands off the west coast and was unstinting in promoting the work of the Irish Society for Protection of Birds, of which he was a leading member. Due to the engrossing nature of his correspondence with lighthouse keepers and personal time spent on data analysis, never mind the responsibilities of his Land Commission work and running a farm, most of his other zoological writings were short notes. Nevertheless, he made himself clear when it came to the subject of introducing species to Ireland, as quoted by the editors of *British Birds* (1912):

> Mr R.M.Barrington announces (*Irish Nat.*, 1911, p. 220) that he is informed that two or three dozen Marsh Tits and a pair of Nuthatches have within the past two years been liberated in County Tipperary. We have recently remarked on the iniquity of introductions of this kind, and we need not repeat our views upon the matter, except to say that we are more than ever convinced that such proceedings are contrary to the best interests of science. Mr Barrington rightly says that it will now be impossible to decide with certainty the origin of any example of either of these species which may be found in Ireland.

Roughly translated, Barrington championed the principle of 'down with introductions'. He is probably spinning in his grave at the recent introduction of Red Kites, despite a lack of 100 per cent proof of the bird's former existence on this side of the Irish Sea. Even if the species had Irish credentials, such schemes put the cart before the horse. The birds themselves best assess suitable conditions for recolonisation: witness the return of Buzzards, Hen Harriers and Great Spotted Woodpeckers.

20. ONE-BIRD WONDER

T HANKS TO Ireland's position off the edge of Europe and beside an ocean, we are ideally situated to receive capricious migrants from middle latitudes stretching east to Siberia and west to America. Migration is music for the soul. Its troops are not lost. Most are children feeling their way. Like all members of a younger generation they sometimes miscue out of youthful exuberance. Seductive tailwinds entice first-time fliers to set off in the wrong direction. Rookies born in Eastern Europe and packed for winter in East Africa may be fooled by warm zephyrs and follow them west to Ireland. The account that follows was dispatched as a letter to a friend in Canada, telling the story of swivel-eyed surprise and delight in discovering an exotic straggler:

> I got back late last night from Donegal. The previous day, 4 September, a weather front crossed Ireland. Overnight the temperature fell and a light breeze set in from the northeast. It felt like a lottery win was on the cards. A ridge of high pressure extended all the way from Central Europe to Rossan Point, the western tip of Ulster. The conditions seemed perfect. Gerard, John and

I went to Malin Beg, followed by the best parts of Malin More before breakfast, scheduled as late as possible in our B&B. Everywhere was, wait for it, birdless. In ideal finding weather there clearly was nothing to find. I did best with a Grasshopper Warbler and a Willow Warbler. Apart from that, there were Meadow Pipits and Grey Wagtails – daytime migrants moving south. So I guess the overnight chill had triggered an exodus rather than an influx, even though the wind direction seemed likely to down a Scandinavian deluge.

After breakfast we tramped out over the point, refocused for New World delights – Bairds' Sandpiper from Newfoundland being just the starter. Yet another duff prediction from you! We eventually found two Dunlins. Also Whimbrels coming down from Iceland and juvenile Turnstones from the Arctic, standard at this time of the year. By now the 0500hrs start was catching up with me. Having run out of birds and now also out of Ireland (next land was your house) I started to lapse into somnambulism and spread-eagled myself over a rock for a doze. The ground was too wet to lie on. I was so knackered that, had I been in the Himalaya, I would probably have been in danger of being picked clean by Lammergeiers. As it was, John spotted me from a distance and, when he worked out that I was simply asleep and not feeding mealworms to an exhausted American Robin, he succumbed to the same drowsiness.

Sometime around two o'clock there was a yell. John's forty winks had scarcely reached double digits before the local midges bit him awake. At least his Whirling Dervish impression ensured we were all suddenly compos, although bereft of vagrancy theories that might yet save the day. Convincing ourselves that a re-check of the morning's habitats might deliver something that had arrived in the meantime (ha, ha) we set off to retrace our steps. With two Kazakh Booted Warblers elsewhere in Ireland over recent days I kept looking longingly at the crappiest habitats in the district, thinking that another would love it here. We have nettle patches to sting the you-know-what off Mike Tyson. While driving back up the road I felt a force wrenching my right foot off the accelerator and onto the brake. Look at that – a field crammed with weeds! John and Gerard amused themselves watching Jackdaws unearthing spuds while I yomped up the road with a Booted Warbler fixation about to be fulfilled just a few footsteps away – or so I fantasised. At least I was still thinking big, although inwardly it felt like I was just going through the motions.

There was nothing in the weeds, nothing in windblown sycamores just beyond the weedy field, and nothing in the jungle of fuchsia bushes running down a ditch. Fuchsia may be a pretty shrub with blossoms designed for hummingbirds, but coming from the southern end of the Andes it never, in my experience, holds a dickie-bird in Ireland. One of the bizarre elements of bird watching in a place were there are next-to-no-birds is that you learn quite a bit about avian absenteeism. Such as? Well, local breeding populations of Blackbirds, Song Thrushes and even the season's crop of juvenile House Sparrows vacate Rossan Point's threadbare gardens at the end of summer, thereby contributing to the *Mary Celeste* atmosphere.

As I was about to pack in the Bootless Warbler flog, I saw two things that did not add up. First, there was, apparently, a bird in the fuchsia. Second, the half-hidden silhouette looked like a House Sparrow. The fact that I found these facts interesting is worrying, maybe a sign that a new hobby is needed? Okay, it was just a stupid, out-of-place House Sparrow.

Definitely time to leave and get an ice cream to bring me around. Mmmm, but it had a funny square-headed look. Probably the light and lack of blood sugar. Something urged me to look harder. Why was a House Sparrow sitting near the top of a fuchsia bush in a traditionally House Sparrow-free part of the Malin More valley and looking block-headed? The answer was thunderous. Because it was a juvenile Red-backed Shrike. Eastern treasure at last – Allahu Akbar!

We all saw it well, although it was unbelievably skulky. It took to perching completely out of sight inside bushes for long periods. But oh, what a beauty when it came out (once with a beetle in its mouth). Everyone felt cured after that. A Chiffchaff appeared in the bush beside it. John missed the Chiffchaff. It meant that he did not see a single migrant warbler, proving that all it takes is one good bird for eternal happiness. Well, for yesterday's happiness at least.

Red-backed Shrike: the discovery of a *rara avis* unlocks emotions in which surprise is surpassed by delight.

21. VOICES OF BLUE, GREAT AND COAL TIT

I F BLUE TIT, Great Tit and Coal Tit were Irish citizens they would be James Joyce, Samuel Beckett and Oscar Wilde. Because the birds possess such a varied and complicated vocabulary, they tend to be shoehorned into a 'don't know' category. The troika may sound similar but they can tell each other apart. By paying attention and lending a curious ear, we can do likewise. Although some fog never clears, trademark notes can be learned that help to cut through the ambiguity. During June, caterpillar-hunting fledglings shoulder through foliage and babble high-pitched, lisping calls. Members of the new generation are furtive and their sounds are the last hurrahs of begging behaviour used during infancy. However, as early as July, coherent stanzas are produced. The more you listen, the more a 'linguistic nationality' emerges; a bit like overhearing fragments of German, French or Polish and knowing which language is being spoken. Each species has something of a stereotype. In all the sounds they make, certain constants apply: Coal Tits are sharp and piercing; Blue Tits come closest to constructing a sweet aria and Great Tits are cheerfully outspoken. With a bit of imagination,

Blue Tit's purring churr has a revving quality. As momentum stalls the pitch rises subtly. In life, the sound is easy to learn. Memorise it by looking at its pattern on a graph (called a sonogram). See p. 13 for instructions on how to hear the bird sounds described in this book online.

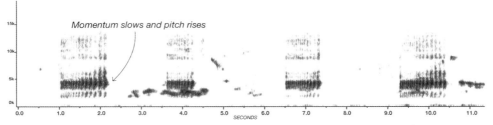

Momentum slows and pitch rises

SECONDS

picture and sound gel in your mind's eye and you begin to get into the bird's skin. What follows is a phrasebook, not a thesaurus. Titmice are talkative and sociable, a combination that quickly exhausts phonetic representations.

Blue Tit and Great Tit share a cheeky conversational churr that suggests the revving of a miniature motorcycle. The sound serves mainly as a marker denoting the caller's position and is also used as an auditory finger-pointer, such as when shadowing a human passer-by or cat. If the bird were human, an alerting whistle would replace the revving. For Blue Tit, the sound is a rolling, burry '*turr'r'r'r'lit*'. Listen carefully to the conclusion. Like a spinning coin losing momentum, the reverberation peters out and is often accompanied by a subtle 'last gasp' rise in pitch. In contrast, the revving of Great Tit is homogeneous. The burst is uniform from start to finish – individual notes do not space out towards the end – and the sound has a fuzzy 'castanets' quality or the cowboy-movie sound of a rattlesnake's vibrating tail. Revving in both Blue Tit and Great Tit expresses mood so, while there are minor variations in tone, fundamental differences in the pattern are unaffected. Moreover, Great Tit's sequence comes to a sudden halt, as though its engine cut out. A further clue to Great Tit is the ad hoc insertion of one or more prefix notes before revving. Alternatively, the same prefix is uttered just after revving. Great Tits are skilled mimics. Often prefixes are, to human hearing, perfect copies of a Chaffinch's *pink*, a Dunnock's *peep*, a Coal Tit's *pete* or the several short syllables in the shuttled call of a Long-tailed Tit. The renditions are good enough to spur any one of those species into responding. Probably, this is the impersonator's intention. But what are the Great Tit's motives? On the one hand, it may be altruistically alerting all songbird peers to

Coal Tit has a thin nasal twang and delivers prissy utterances. In most cases notes are paired; at times the pairings are repeated in reverse order. If renamed 'Binary Tit', identifying the species on sound would be a no-brainer.

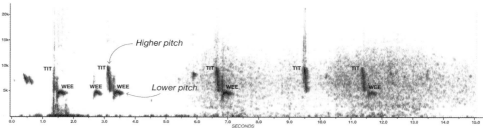

its discovery of a potential danger. On the other hand, the tactic may be entirely selfish and designed to rally recruits – analogous to a human shield – should the Great Tit find itself at risk. By matching its neighbours' own anxiety notes, it cons them into unwittingly showing support. Moreover, the selected calls belong only to those species that the Great Tit knows to be within earshot. Perhaps not surprisingly, in the exigencies of kicking up a fuss, Great Tit occasionally mimics Blue Tit (but not vice versa).

Coal Tit does not include revving as a regular theme, although a rapid chiding trill is sometimes interjected. A frequent note is a rising *pete*. Often the note is doubled and becomes *paid pete*. Other regular utterances include *twee* and *t-twee* – coining *tit wee* as a transcription, a useful label that serves as a 'putting two and two together' mnemonic tabbing Coal Tit's voice to its wee size (the smallest of the trio). As a general rule, all elements of Coal Tit's vocabulary are quick-fire repetitions in a binary language. Typical variations include *pitchew-pitchew-pitchew* or *per-chee, per-chee, per-chee*. The songster uses a limited range of motifs. Indeed, in the course of a performance, the same phrases crop up but are used in reverse. Hence, a sequence comprising repetitions of *wee-**chew*** may be followed by ***chew**-wee*, an inverse of the same notes. The same applies to *tit wee* (that becomes *wee tit*). As a general rule, couplets are symmetrical – suggesting inhalation keeping pace with exhalation – and an inherent squeakiness 'blurs' the acoustic: the equivalent of smudged handwriting. To a lesser extent than Great Tit, Coal Tit also imitates. However, the mimicry involves copying the song of another Coal Tit. When the original bird switches to a different composition, the copyist continues reprising the initial track.

Great Tit is a master mimic but sticks to a unique pattern when 'giving out' or shadowing a trespasser. Its narky sound is flat and homogenous: no change in pace or pitch (unlike Blue Tit). An audible sulk.

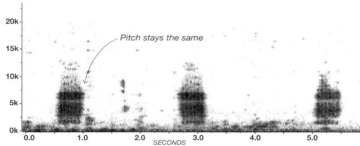

Pitch stays the same

Lone Coal Tits or Great Tits, when investigating a source of unease, sometimes employ a tactic that may be based on psychology. The singleton stays hidden but issues contrasting alarms: first, a sharp couplet, next, a low churr. The two sounds are completely different; the first is hard to pin down and almost ventriloquial. Is the bird trying to hint that more than one agitator is present? For a predator, the implication is that it has been rumbled and will be subjected to mobbing, spoiling its hunting chances. Furthermore, the feigned increase in the number of vigilantes often serves as a tom-tom that quickly rallies the avian equivalent of a rent-a-mob.

A common denominator in much of Blue Tit vocabulary is a tremble or oscillation. Neither Great Tit nor Coal Tit wobble like this. Blue Tit song consists of one or more *see* syllables swept along rapidly until, as though emerging from a chrysalis, a winnowing *hoohoohoohoo* develops. Remarkably and somewhat incongruously, the same basic pattern is used as an alarm. Alarm versions are more strident and up-tempo and tend to consist of a single shrill *see* melded to a *hoohoohoo* crescendo. The phonetic combination of 'See who?' suggests the call's underlying purpose. A perched Sparrowhawk elicits revving. But when the hawk flies a watchful Blue

Tit erupts into a fusillade of *see see see* notes. To maintain heightened vigilance in the general vicinity, the notes are repeated after the hunter appears to depart. An intriguing possibility is that the high register of Blue Tit's notes may be inaudible to the predator, thereby conferring an 'invisible ink' warning to songbird listeners. Research has shown that Sparrowhawk hearing is 30dB less sensitive in the 7–8 kHz frequency band used by songbirds to broadcast shrill alarm calls (Klump, Kretzschmar and Curio 1986). Another Blue Tit song variant is close to three notes. Hot on the heels of an opening pair of high pure pipes, a third teeters into a trill – *sweet, sweet, Hannah.* Grey Wagtail song follows a broadly similar style.

Trying to pigeonhole the song of the Great Tit is challenging. Males have many tunes and can vary the tempo of each. As a common theme, bonhomie radiates from a caroller. Telling a songster from a Blue Tit is not difficult. Distinguishing Great Tit from Coal Tit is a different matter. Great Tit often produces paired combinations, as Coal Tit habitually does. Keep listening. The caller will soon switch to an unequivocal combination with a typical twang. Coal Tit is high and shrill, the tit whose voice failed to break. While Coal Tit and Great Tit vocalisations can be likened to a bicycle pump, the impression for Coal Tit is that more gusto is being used: Coal Tit seems driven; Great Tit exudes panache.

Titmice are the Sparrowhawk's favourite meal and they often band together in order that many eyes can watch for danger. Coalition troops utter a selection of calls, sometimes overlapping simultaneously. In this situation it is best to concentrate on one vocalist. To secure a view of the cheerleader and link picture with sound, you can employ a trick. Remain hidden and simulate the *kish-kish-kish* sound of a child pretending to fire a gun. Repeat the salvo several times and watch what happens. With any luck one or more piqued callers will approach and can be identified.

22. ATTRACTING BIRDS AROUND HOME

TABLE MANNERS

FEEDING BIRDS has come a long way since Mary Poppins fed London's House Sparrows for tuppence a bag. In younger days maternal intuition put me and other siblings to work laboriously knotting together unshelled peanuts. Strung up like a rope ladder, they provided great entertainment. The amount of energy used by Blue Tits hacking them open was only surpassed by the minutes of peace enjoyed by a mother whilst her children were busily engaged. Nowadays an industry has sprung up and a wide cross-section of the public is as hooked as the birds. Much food comes ready made and it is easier to fill a feeder or hang up a fat-ball rather than scatter food on to a home-made bird table. What seems like a humble feeding station will, almost certainly, attract far more customers than imagined. Ringers visited a garden that produced a maximum of nine Blue Tits at any one time. In a single day, they caught 148 individuals. Numbers of Greenfinches are even more misleading.

Blue Tits are lively, aggressive and approachable. Mother superior is quivering her wings and shooing away the human builder of her nest box so she can feed her young.

One garden's daily maximum winter count of forty was eclipsed when over 1,000 were ringed over the course of a month. Among a nexus of lawns frequented during winter by what seemed to be no more than a few Blackbirds, a single garden emerged as hallowed turf and hosted a morning twilight assembly of around thirty, most of which dispersed at dawn but then rotated during the course of the day.

Birds, irrespective of the benefit of supplementary rations, are independently minded. In severe weather, food will undoubtedly prolong many lives. Furthermore, having access to a well-stocked supply, especially if replenished on a daily basis, is bound to make a difference. Knowing that grub is regularly available in one or more places ensures that energy is not frittered away. In time, winter visitors leave and local residents change diet to take account of seasonal changes in naturally available food, especially when it comes to feeding invertebrate prey to growing chicks. Hence, diners may vote with their wings and move. Different concerns arise about keeping food, or indeed certain types of food, on the menu during the nesting season. Conventional thinking holds that nestlings find nut particles indigestible and may choke to death. The natural nutriment for most songbird chicks is insects. Egg-laying by all

When snow falls or ground freezes hard, worm-eating birds are in trouble. Garden offerings of food attract new faces desperate for grub, such as the normally shy Fieldfare.

members of the tit family is timed in response to unknown environmental factors that portend the emergence of caterpillars in June. Nestlings hatch at the peak of caterpillar abundance. Given such a correlation, the hazard of adults feeding nuts to youngsters may be real. But does this happen? In my experience, adults recognise the need to feed young appropriately. Although grown-ups may nibble nuts, they have the wit to supply nestlings with caterpillars. However, if supplying some nut content, portion size is small and is scaled down by a savvy parent that trims the kernel to suit.

Is it best to confine feeding to winter when vegetation and insect life is dormant and birds are hard-pressed to find enough food in the shorter hours of daylight? Observing the rhythm of garden bird activity throughout the year is revealing. During the dark days of winter many roost early, some by mid-afternoon. It is a fallacy to suggest that all available daylight is utilised for feeding. Seed-eating finches, as well as Woodpigeons and Collared Doves that hoover up a variety of offerings, are able to forage and stockpile what they collect in a large storage chamber – the crop – attached to the oesophagus. In addition, many finches have pouches that serve as storage sacs, either in the mouth cavity or on the sides of the oesophagus. Food is gathered in a hurry to reduce exposure to enemies; the cud can be digested at leisure in a safe place. Jays and Coal Tits hoard food. During autumn Jays lay down a larder of acorns that provide the bird with a basic wintertime 'five a day'. Coal Tits visit feeders but remove and bury more than they eat. Quite when buried supplies are retrieved is unclear, although lengthening daylight in the new year significantly reduces hoarding. Insectivorous species are at a disadvantage. Deciduous branches are bare and insect life is, for the most part, dormant. Goldcrests, because they cannot accumulate food for processing later, are obliged to forage until their calorie intake has been met. Every winter day is a marathon and the mite can be seen hovering and shouldering among coniferous foliage right up to dusk. Robins and Dunnocks, because their bills are weak, are limited to small, soft prey items. They too are active from dawn to dusk, times when Robins' large light-sensitive eyes come into play.

In terms of calories burned, getting through a day in winter is – counter-intuitively – less onerous than most other times of the year. Breeding preparations require much more energy. Females boost food intake to produce a clutch of eggs and paired males busy themselves supplying partners with extra provisions. When chicks hatch, parenting duties skyrocket, as does the family's metaphoric food bill. Once the family is reared, the new generation and surviving adults go separate ways and look to their own needs. Juvenile body plumage is soft and delicate and has a short shelf life. Adult plumage, although more robust, comes up for annual renewal once young fledge. Late summer, when wild food is plentiful, is an ideal time to moult. Of all events in a bird's yearly cycle, moult exerts the greatest drain. Chaffinches increase daily energy consumption by almost 35 per cent, House Sparrows by 25 per cent. Lesser Redpolls, Ireland's smallest migratory finch, face an even greater hike in calorie expenditure – a staggering 45 per cent. Given the scale of each season's activity, should you continue to provide food throughout the year? The answer is a resounding yes. Nuts, especially the manna of dehusked sunflower hearts, can be ground up to last longer. Smaller size also makes them palatable to a wider range of species. Porridge oats, because they are a mainstream staple in our diet, are a bargain. Why bother with expensive seed mixes when a flurry of oat flakes is just as appealing and wholesome? Alternative foods, especially live food such as mealworms, are a bonus for a growing family and moulting threadbare adults. Mealworms can be purchased online or, with minimal effort, propagated for free.

Who could have envisaged a day when the range of commercially available wild-bird food was extensive enough to warrant the publication of sales catalogues? Garden centres have also entered the fray and guidebooks large and small compete to tell you 'everything you need to know to attract, feed and shelter wild birds in your garden.' Several titles cover the subject admirably: *Ireland's Garden Birds* (O'Sullivan & Wilson 2008), *The Garden Bird Book* (Glue 1982) and *The Garden Bird Handbook* (Moss 2003) are among the best.

Facing page: Siskins: females (top) and males. Siskins nest mainly in conifer forests, some as far away as Russia. Once rare, they now occur in Irish plantations and swarm around feeders in late winter, fattening up before returning to breeding haunts.

Putting up a nest box and attracting tenants is a big thrill. To reach a higher level, think about making the box and – entering legacy territory – planting the tree that supports it.

NEST BOXES

Nest boxes, bought or homemade, bring birds closer to our world. Artificial lodgings partly offset a lack of ancient woodland whose cavities once served as natural homes. Contemporary lifestyles favour postage stamp backyards, and sites developed for housing are usually purged of trees beforehand. Although ground cover and hedges can be established fairly rapidly, time is needed to produce a tree with sufficient girth to develop a nook or cranny. Most gardens are not large enough to hold aged, gnarled timber. For hole-nesting birds, a perfect alternative is the provision of a nest box. The act of installing one brings a sense of redemption. You have done something good, a charitable act that shows you care. In fact, our three native titmice, Ireland's chief cavity-nesters, may take to a new upgrade almost immediately. How come? When breeding sites abounded, a hole vacated at the end of one breeding season was unlikely to be used again. Young will have trampled the bedding and even though parents are scrupulous and remove droppings (enclosed in a handy gelatinous bag), sanitation and hygiene eventually deteriorate. Additional aftermath may consist of an infertile egg or dead chick. The birds' burden of parasites infiltrates the old nest and remains among detritus in the hope that fresh hosts might arrive. Fleas are smart and position themselves around the entrance waiting for victims to enter. Blowflies enter nest boxes and attempt to lay eggs directly on nestlings or among nest material. Blowfly eggs are tiny, less than 2mm and are laid shortly after chicks hatch. Blood-sucking larvae emerge within a couple of days and feed immediately by burrowing into skin, attaching to legs and feet and occasionally entering ear cavities and nostrils. As they grow they consume more blood. Over 1,000 larvae have been found in a Raven nest.

Baby birds are born with a full set of wits. Instinctively, they react to sights and sounds that equate with danger. For these Wrens, youthful peering was instantly cut short when a Magpie was heard.

In North America, an examination of cavity nests for Bluebirds recorded blowfly larvae in 94 per cent, whilst for various species of wrens the figure was around 60 per cent. The effect on nestlings is unclear. Despite the presumed heavy blood loss most nestlings survive. Studies show that the larval populations are usually too small to kill or seriously injure most nestlings (Whitworth & Bennett 1992). Moreover, healthy growing young are able to regenerate blood, thereby compensating for loss to parasites. While some level of adverse effect can be anticipated, no parasite sets out to kill its host; to do so would be evolutionary suicide. It appears that, although in some situations blowfly larvae overwhelm, weaken and cause death, in most cases a state of equilibrium exists between the parasite and its host. In a trial in North America, nests of Bank Swallows (Sand Martins) were deliberately infested with larvae. Although blood levels were reduced among infested chicks, all fledged successfully. Not all species are so resilient and little is known about post-fledging survival rates. The young of Pearly-eyed Thrashers *Margarops fuscatus* (a Caribbean species distantly related to thrushes) infested with blowflies experienced 80 per cent mortality after fledging (Arendt 1985). In Holland, it is believed that many parasitised nestlings may be so weakened that they are more likely to die soon after leaving the nest than are unparasitised young (Perrins 1979).

Luckily, birds are not stupid. They like to start each season with a clean slate. Begin, therefore, by removing an old nest. This eradicates parasites. Also ensure that the box interior is clean and dry. By clearing out a nest box in summer, as soon as breeding finishes, there is a chance that the inglenook might provide roosting quarters. The argy-bargy of territorial behaviour may be over until the spring, but adult and new generations of tits and Wrens need somewhere suitable to spend the night. Nonetheless, there is still a need to check the inside in late winter because mess and debris from other visitors can easily accumulate.

Blue Tits lay a single clutch of eggs that hatch to coincide with the peak abundance of small nutritious caterpillars. We can help by ensuring that their nest box is up to scratch.

Male titmice locate possible breeding accommodation and attract a female by displaying, entering the potential abode and beckoning her to follow. The decision to settle is hers. Soft wood, indicative of unsound walls and floor, is singled out and chiselled away. One mouldy floor was chipped away until daylight shone through. A plywood base was installed but the artisans had seen enough and moved. However, following the renovation, Wrens settled (see photograph on p. 120). Machinations by female tits are prolonged and the mother-to-be assesses the dimensions of the nursery to determine the size of her clutch. Without ample space, the brood will be cramped. Overheating of nestlings can cause death, so temperature regulation is important. Chilling is an equal worry. Infants are bare-skinned for a week. During this time they are constantly brooded by the female. Even in warm weather, vulnerable young could die if not swaddled overnight.

An experiment performed by Lohrl (1973) in Germany established a correlation between nest-box dimensions, internal temperature and clutch size. Boxes were erected of two different diameters: 9cm and 20cm. Over the course of two years, Great Tits laid and hatched more eggs per nest in the larger boxes. To test for significance, nest boxes of each size were switched once egg-laying commenced. A link was discovered. The birds reduced the number of eggs in the clutch when the size of their nest box was downgraded. Lohrl concluded that the highest fledging rates were achieved by a brood of eight to ten young accommodated in a space of around 20cm diameter. Therefore all nest boxes should be at least 10–12cm in diameter. More room is created if the box is rectangular, such as 12 by 15cm. Depth should be even greater. A wide, deep and dark home is important for other reasons. Given adequate space, a female tit situates her nest towards the corner. The reasons for the off-centre position are not fully understood, but here are two possibilities. First, the angle might be advantageous when it comes to flying directly out of the nest hole from a resting position. Second, songbirds have relatively poor binocular vision and use one eye for close-range viewing and the other for distance (see WHO SEES WINS, p. 59). An incubating tit may prefer a one-sided view of the opening. Wrens do things differently. Despite having a nest-box roof, they construct a mossy sphere with an overhead dome. Snuggled deep inside, they are able to peer out.

Hole size is equally important. Female Blue Tits spend considerable amounts of time tapping and pecking the hole circumference from inside and out. Is she gauging size or testing the firmness of the wood lest a predator enlarge the opening and gain access? Perhaps both concerns occupy her mind. Diameters from 28–32mm are acceptable, although successful pairs still manage to squeeze through a gap 26mm wide. Design and construction fall strictly under female control, although some materials passed by the male are accepted. To begin with, efforts are fitful and a week or more may pass with no activity, prompting worries that the builder has abandoned the job. For Blue Tit, a cargo of white feathers is a sure sign that completion is near. Great Tits and Coal Tits furnish the lining with hair or fur. An egg is laid each day. Before facing the big sit of around a fortnight, the female enhances her brood patch by shedding some feathers; the flow of blood close to the surface of her body is now able to generate maximum heat. The male cannot provide equivalent care. The loss of a female at this critical stage foredooms the brood. As young grow both parents become increasingly excited. Wing quivering, used initially by the female during courtship to elicit extra food from her partner, infects both parents.

Thanks to nest-box cameras busy lives can be observed without intruding. But not everyone has the benefit of technology and many sagas are viewed from kitchen windows. As fledging day approaches a peep inside seems harmless. Desist! By doing so, you place the youngsters in great danger. Your sudden appearance, especially accompanied by a flood of light entering the chamber from a prised-back lid, spooks the fledglings and instinct takes over. At around fifteen days old they are able to flutter up to the hole and jump. The reaction is innate. Evolution has programmed them to flee from danger, which is the interpretation they place upon a benign inspection. In the wild a predator will attempt to devour them *in situ*. In the hope that not all are killed, the entire brood attempts to escape. Once – or if – they hit the ground they scatter and hide in the nearest undergrowth. Contact calls, established from hatching, guide distraught parents to their whereabouts. The commotion is considerable and virtually guaranteed to invite trouble. Frantically gathering them up and feeling their trembling heartbeat before placing them back in the nest box is pointless. They will immediately make another dash for freedom. Rather than, in a few days' time, witnessing an explosion of airborne new recruits, you are confronted with a kamikaze brood of homeless, helpless and flightless infants. Assuming calamity is avoided, the juveniles whirr into the comparative safety of dense foliage. The wing feathers are not yet fully grown but rookies manage to fly and perch out of sight. Indeed, they are born clever and have the knack of quietly remaining within leafy canopy and not exposing themselves. They 'park up' and the parents continue to feed them. Later they follow the adults and gradually learn to feed themselves.

ROOT AND BRANCH

One summer evening in 1982 I stood and grappled with the challenge of owning a back garden. It was not much bigger than a penalty box. The previous owner appeared to have been a fan of *The Good Life*. There was a greenhouse, vegetable plot and a pen for rabbits. Incipient hedges were a combination of conifers and, to borrow from Radiohead, stuff that looked like green plastic trees. I yearned for deciduous canopy and four seasons peppered with birdlife. At this embryonic stage some views were uninterrupted and revealed the contents of neighbouring gardens. Everything I saw smacked of pound notes: conservatories, decking and obedient shrubberies, statements rather than a place where nature is invited. Conferred with Book of Genesis powers of creation, I realised that glasnost did not entirely underpin my thoughts. I was fine with a few basic commandments: no peat, pesticides or fertiliser and no dead fences but living hedge boundaries. Choice of trees was less principled. I am not a green zealot. Much as I would have preferred to use exclusively native trees, the rules were bent to include cotoneasters, several varieties of which score highly for berries and whose tiny flowers bees love. Nectar for butterflies and moths could come from honeysuckle and tree understorey would be left to run wild and nurture caterpillars and insects during winter dormancy. Clover would be left to flower in the lawn and dance with bees. Furthermore, Woodpigeons love the plant's shamrock arrangement of leaves which they pare down, snip by snip, like a barber trimming the sides of a moustache. Ivy was a 'must have' native. Plants evolved to Ireland's climate generally have a longer flowering period and are hardier than cultivated varieties. Ivy provides cover for nesting and roosting, as well as abundant insects attracted to its tiny flowers in autumn and early winter, a bonanza for insectivorous birds when days shorten. A bounty of black berries lasting from March to June completes a glittering curriculum vitae. However, for some, my green postage stamp would not be an open house. Cats, domestic and feral, are the bane of wildlife the world over. Instead of maligning a natural-born hunter, I blame 'owners' for the carnage wreaked by their pets. So I expected to be plagued by the furry menace. Rather than construct a ground-level iron curtain, I decided on a trees and nest-boxes policy.

A useful adage to remember when setting bare-rooted trees is to plant only when there is a letter 'r' in the month, although in truth, April should be excluded, especially for willows that unfurl blossom early in spring. Most willows can be established from cuttings. An arm's-length piece of green wood stuck securely in the ground (roughly 30 per cent buried) will sprout a tree for free. It took just one St Patrick's Day to complete the work. I chose alders as infantry, birch for stature and colour, and posted rowans as sentries on the margins. Once the company had endured a few winter campaigns I added a seedling Grey Willow. Like a little drummer boy, it was given pole position and all the limelight. Sheltered by serried sylvan ranks, it became a jewel. A decade later, the wall of green suggested that a wilderness stretched beyond the lawn all the way to the shores of the North Atlantic. If only! However, the fragment resounds with birdsong in spring, carries cool breezes in summer and pulsates with autumn colour. During winter its many more inhabitants are sustained by just one feeder that migrates from branch to branch, keeping the guests guessing but healthy, thanks to no spillage concentrations that

Because of its tolerance to salty winds, New Zealand Flax *Phormium tenax* is widely planted in coastal districts of Ireland. In New Zealand it is pollinated by a Tui, whose bill is quite similar to a Starling's (photo shows a juvenile Starling). Nectar at the base of the tubular flower entices the bird to drink. In the process, yellow pollen attaches to plumage.

harbour disease. If I lived in a windy outpost in the west, or near the shores of the Irish Sea, the task would have been far more difficult. Probably, salt-laden winds would have desiccated my wannabe oasis and I would have been forced to establish a battlement to protect it. Several shrubs make ideal praetorian guards. Although not native, escallonia, fuchsia and New Zealand Flax *Phormium tenax* have redeeming worth for birds and insects. In my book, their provision of nectar and pollen, along with their gift of lee (allowing other plants to flourish rather than be hammered by an unforgiving wind), constitute grounds for 'botanical asylum'.

DRINKING HABITS

When it comes to providing sustenance, books dealing with garden birds tend to dish out stereotyped advice about water. A standard mantra proclaims that, as well as the obvious need for drinking, birds need water for bathing. How true are both parts of this statement? Feather maintenance is undoubtedly important. Preening is a daily activity and is complemented by scratching, sunbathing with feathers raised (probably, as in humans, to boost the synthesis of vitamin D by exposing skin to the rays of the sun), dust bathing or vigorous dowsing in water.

Birds also expose plumage to ants and other insects and allow them to walk among feathers. The live ants eat or repel feather mites, possibly because the insect's glands produce secretions that are known to inhibit fungi and bacteria. By 'anting', birds may be anointing themselves. Comparative studies prove that anting reduces the loading of mites among plumage (Kelso & Nice 1963). Hygiene rather than cleanliness probably lies at the heart of bathing activities. Exposing feathers and underlying areas of bare skin and agitating them with water or particles of dust is probably an effort to shake loose parasites, or an attempt by the bird to rid itself of old skin and feather tissue. The procedure appears to be innate. Most species immerse the head, jerk it skywards and then begin beating the wings. Preening follows bathing. Dipper, a songbird that lives by submerging in streams to forage for aquatic insects and their larvae, still ruffles its feathers and has a customary bathe every day. In terms of essential external maintenance, water is just one of several means to an end.

What about drinking? Thompson (1849–52) quoted an excerpt from the diary of John Templeton who lived at Cranmore, Belfast, and kept two Cuckoos, one of which lived for eighteen months:

January 10th, 1822. Last night the Cuckoo which E got on 26th July 1820, died in consequence of C having hurt it with her foot. It was fed generally on hard-boiled eggs, and occasionally with caterpillars: it would sometimes eat 40 or 50 at a time. It was never known to take a drink; though when presented with a drop of water at the end of a finger or straw, it would sip it and seemed to delight, when seated on its mistress's or other person's hand, to put its bill to their mouths and sip saliva.

Let's face it, any bird that lives in Ireland is unlikely to die of thirst. Like other vertebrates, land birds have three main sources of water: free water from streams, pools, raindrops or dew; pre-formed water contained in the contents of their diet; and water that arises when their body metabolises fat or works muscles. In the context of water conservation, birds have a further advantage: their waste products are uric acid, not urea. Uric acid can be vented as a virtually dry powder, whereas urea must be excreted in an aqueous solution. The saving in water is huge. Mammals require approximately 20ml of water to excrete 320mg of urea, whereas an equivalent amount of uric acid can be excreted in less than 1mg of water (Bartholomew & Cade 1963). Many seabirds never drink freshwater and possess a salt gland located above the eye that extrudes brine solution through special external 'tubenose' nostrils. How, therefore, do seabirds obtain water? The answer lies in how they process food. In most pelagic species, oily fishy prey is stored in a digestive tract that operates as a separating funnel. A tapering chamber – called a proventriculus – allows the less-dense oily component to settle above its water content. The watery residue is periodically siphoned off, satisfying bodily needs for both a meal and water.

Ironically, most birds that live sedentary lives in arid deserts are also able to derive sufficient water from their food, by hiding from the hot sun, recycling moisture exhaled in breath (captured in the nasal cavity) and by functioning at a lower metabolic rate. Compared

By beating water into a froth, bathing starlings dislodge plumage mites and skin parasites, as well as other unwanted detritus. Vocalisations suggest that the activity is enjoyed by the birds.

to birdlife living in a temperate climate, the basic metabolic rate of desert-dwelling species is 40 per cent less and their rate of evaporative loss through the skin is 26 per cent lower, due to differences in the strata of fats and oils within the structure of the skin (Tieleman 2002). Moreover, when you think about it, moisture contained in food is the only source of water for nestlings of all avian species. That said, it has yet to be shown that any normally active bird can satisfy its water requirements by metabolic processes alone. Based on what they eat, food consumed by raptors, insectivores and species that consume green vegetation, provides birds with sufficient water. Mostly, freely available water amounts to a treat rather than a necessity, even in high temperatures. A study (Irwin 1956) of drinking habits by all birds, including many wintering European migrants living in the vicinity of a water hole in a hot and arid region of Botswana, found that no species of warbler, flycatcher or chat came to drink. Significantly, members of these families live on insects and probably obtain all the water they need from the body fluids of their quarry. Swallows were an exception and showed a strong attraction to surface water and drank frequently. Presumably, because of their expenditure of energy in frequent flying, they lose more water by evaporation and metabolic exertion than their less energetic counterparts, and drink to make up the deficit. However, when migration beckons, internal rhythms switch and fat accumulates in preparation for the journey ahead. Neatly, water needs will be eased once the fat is burned.

It could be argued that, when water is available, birds exploit it. For most, it is no more than a Happy Hour opportunity. Both Zebra Finches and Budgerigars, native to Australia's parched interior, survive in the wild on a diet of seeds without drinking. Captive individuals, if deprived of water and therefore exposed to real-world conditions, undergo some initial weight loss and then 'thrive indefinitely and at a normal level of activity if given supplementary apple, celery or lettuce' (Bartholomew & Cade 1956). Among Irish species, some appear to be fonder of a drink than others. Collared Dove and Woodpigeon are among the greatest tipplers. Both were among the top ten most frequent drinkers in two annual surveys conducted in Devon (Glue 1982). Uniquely among birds, pigeons and doves drink by sucking up a continuous draught of water. Perhaps this indicates a diet heavily biased towards grains – dry fodder that yields minimal amounts of water, thereby explaining the birds' drinking habit? Wrens, inveterate insect hunters, were noticeable absentees from the Devon survey's list of drinkers, despite being regular bathers. Accordingly, while an absolute need of water is probably not fundamental, a supply is welcome.

PARASITES AND DISEASE

We live such a sheltered antiseptic existence that we shudder at the concept of disease. Yet any bird selected at random will be infected with one or more forms of parasite or pathogen. The battle between David and Goliath is an endless competition in which one branch of the animal kingdom attempts to exploit another. Many parasites are evolved to specific bird families and may be intimately adapted to their host's life cycle. One study demonstrated that lice found on migrant warblers tied their reproduction to that of the host. Lice in the bloodstream detected high levels of hormones linked to the onset of warbler courtship and nesting, resulting in the parasite synchronising reproduction.

Parasitic infestation is a fact of life for birds and falls into two categories: ectoparasites (external-living) and endoparasites (internal-living). Ectoparasites include lice, fleas, ticks, mites and leeches. Sometimes it is possible to see a bird with a parasite *in situ*. Ticks often

Disease and predators take their toll. *Left*: Chaffinch with *Trichomonosis*; *right*: Chiffchaff with tick on eye.

attack the soft tissue around the eye. Close views of warblers, particularly youngsters in autumn that may have been reared in infested nests, sometimes reveal the affliction. Death may result through blindness or visual impairment, making the sufferer an easy target for predators. Among the commoner internal parasites are flukes, tapeworms, roundworms and spiny-headed worms. Several sorts of parasitic worms may be transmitted from one bird to another. More typically, one or more alternate hosts are involved in a worm's life cycle. A bird can acquire an adult stage of a parasite by eating a smaller animal that contains the parasite's larval form, although the unwanted cargo may not necessarily be fatal or adversely affect the bird's health. Whatever the parasite, avoiding infested male birds brings several benefits to females. They escape contagious parasites, the risk to offspring is lower and the health of the male is dubious and therefore he is best avoided. Looks, behaviour, vehemence of courtship display and vocalisations are obvious tests of a suitor's suitability. Only healthy males score highly. In species where the male constructs the nest even before a breeding partner has been found, the female can determine the male's parasite load from the amount of parasites that she discovers squatting in the potential habitation. An Austro-Slovakian study confirmed that nests rejected by females had mite densities up to three times higher than nests that attracted a female (Darolova, Hoi & Sleicher 1996). Moult provides a further insight into state of wellness. Birds parasitised by an excess of mites develop dull plumage. Plumage colouration plays a significant role in female choice of mate in several species. Blue Tit, Great Tit and Greenfinch all assess male breeding fitness from plumage lustre.

Microscopic organisms – viruses, protozoa and fungi – also infect birds. Several studies have shown that around 30 per cent of all wild birds have blood parasites. *Trichomonas gallinae*, a protozoan, infects the throat of pigeons, doves, domestic fowl and several songbirds, notably Greenfinch and Chaffinch. First noticed in Greenfinches in Britain in 2005 and later detected in Ireland, it has become an ongoing killer. It stimulates a growth that obstructs the oesophagus and causes a slow, lingering death through starvation. Victims appear lethargic and bloated with fluffed-out plumage, suggesting that the bird is trying to keep warm. Food may be lodged in the mouth with particles dribbling from the corners of the bill. Fleshy lesions, often yellowish in colour, progressively block the mouth. The swellings extend into the throat and oesophagus, causing death through starvation. The sickness blights healthy individuals when infected, discarded food drops to the ground and is consumed. Because a bird in the throes of the disease repeatedly ingests but then regurgitates food that it is unable to swallow, it sows a bitter harvest and the scourge blights healthy peers when they consume abandoned, soiled food. Water becomes contaminated either by contact with the bill and mouth or from any food particles that may be transported to drinking sources by infected birds. Due to the gregarious nature of Greenfinches at feeders and drinking pools, the outbreak can become rife. Prevention of transmission is difficult. Obvious steps include a cessation of feeding and the removal of water. Surfaces where uneaten food collects, including ground under feeders, should be decontaminated with a 10 per cent solution of domestic bleach in water. Best of all, feeders should be moved regularly to enable potentially soiled ground to dry out. *Trichomonas* does not persist for long away from its host. Moist conditions prolong it and mouldy grains can maintain its viability for at least five days. If exposed to a dry environment, the parasite quickly becomes impoverished and disappears in a single day. Contamination vectors appear to be limited to saliva and crop secretions but not faeces. There are no reports of *Trichomonosis* affecting humans.

Bacteria cause relatively few diseases in bird populations, possibly because many of the micro-organisms cannot reproduce at birds' high body temperatures (Welty & Baptista 1988). Avian botulism is a complicated disease and although many birds have died from its effects, it is not infectious in the normal sense. Symptoms often suggest a damaged wing rather than an internal ailment. Gulls are regular victims. The illness debilitates the nervous system and paralysis sets in. As powers of flight fail, the bird flaps lopsidedly but cannot fly. In a matter of days the condition worsens, the head droops and the wretch becomes immobile. Botulism results from eating decaying vegetation or by consuming flies and their larvae that have visited dead victims. For this reason, corpses and dying birds should be removed. The species responsible is *Clostridium botulinum*, whose spores thrive in water or juicy food waste that lacks oxygen. Still pools of water that contain rotting vegetable or animal matter attract bacteria whose actions absorb all the diffused oxygen. Such conditions suit C. *botulinum*, which proliferates and exudes a powerful neurotoxin into the stagnant water. Although the bacteria are not poisonous and cannot spread infection, the toxin they release causes paralysis. For a more detailed discussion, see a summary prepared by N.D. McKee (reported by McGeehan & Wyllie 2012).

Many parasites hone their life cycle to a small range of avian hosts. When closely related birds share parasites, disproportionate harm can occur if one species proves to be less robust when exposed to a loading that is within the tolerance limits of another. In our species, a corollary is the common cold. When spread among people with no resistance – such as Inuit tribes – it can cause death. In birds, pheasants, partridges and crakes form a discrete cadre. *Heterakis gallinarum*, a gastro-intestinal nematode worm, is found abundantly in Pheasants. Research in Britain showed that, where Pheasants and native Grey Partridges occupy the same habitat, usually as a consequence of large numbers of Pheasants being released for 'sport', the parasite spreads and its infective egg stage can act as a carrier for pathogenic protozoans that cause disease in only the Grey Partridges, which are more vulnerable. In Ireland a quite different species is at risk. Corncrakes on several Irish islands are being forced to share habitat with released Pheasants. On islands where this has happened, such as on Inishbofin, County Galway, and Tory Island, County Donegal, the Pheasant population has increased whereas Corncrakes have declined sharply. On others, such as Sherkin, County Cork, the Corncrake population vanished completely during the 1970s, a decade in which the local population of Pheasants was on the rise. There would appear to be a prima facie connection and, post haste, a need to eradicate Pheasants from all habitats occupied by Corncrakes. In large measure this has already happened on Inishbofin, County Galway, where Corncrake numbers increased in line with the removal of Pheasants.

23. ON OUR WATCH

LONG AFTER the ongoing obsession about climate change has subsided – possibly because debate is academic, the polar ice caps having melted and changed human lifestyles irrevocably – most of the species that conservationists claim are threatened by global warming will have survived. For those that can live elsewhere, range shifts will have occurred: the edges of present-day distributions are coalfaces mined by the birds themselves. The lucky ones chip away and expand range when conditions allow. In this regard our birds are fairly fortunate. In the tropics, forest-dependent species are usually sedentary. When their home goes up in smoke or finishes up as a piece of furniture in a shopping mall then habitat loss means extinction. Because everyone loves a winner we are delighted to discover novel faces: Collared Dove, Siskin, Little Egret and – the new kid on the block – Great Spotted Woodpecker. Pioneering youngsters seeking *Lebensraum* arrive first. They are scouts. Should they prosper, a new frontier is established. Habitat is the key to success, just as habitat loss is the biggest single cause of species extinction. Human activity, because of its almost global reach, affects the fortunes of many birds and the natural world in general.

Within Ireland the impact of humankind takes many forms, both today and as it has done in the past. Persecution or over-exploitation of wildlife for food, sporting quarry, plumage or as cage-birds has largely receded. Relieved of such pressure, populations recover, provided their survival needs are met. These days, Goldfinches are a common sight in just about any garden that contains a feeder. Colourful and fizzing with energy, they bring sunshine to the dark days

Stonechat among clover. Eighty per cent of human Vitamin A comes from plants pollinated by bees. Silage grass has replaced hayfields and fertilisers promote growth but destroy wildflowers and insects, including bumblebees. When did you last scrape a residue of bug life off the car windscreen?

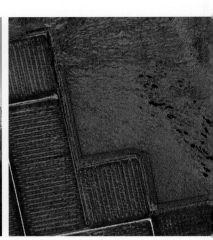

Gardens are places of green retreat that help us reboot. Oases of calm, they allow us to put worries to one side. To hold back unwanted vegetation, we spread peat. As a nation, we know all about the resource – because we have used most of it. Less well known is the destruction of other countries' peat bogs in order that we can prettify our gardens. In Estonia, almost a million tons of peat are mined and exported annually for use in gardens and horticulture (R. Savisaar pers. comm.) Offloaded and then bagged in Belfast (left image) the scale of the exploitation is shocking. Because a small proportion of Irish peat is added to each bag, the product is dubiously marketed as 'Irish Peat Moss'. Some Estonian bogs are protected but even at Laukasoo (centre image) mining still removes the habitat beyond a radius of 100m (right image). Because we, as consumers, are unaware of how we destroy habitats, the effrontery to the natural world continues. Meanwhile, concerned but powerless Estonians watch their countryside being trashed to keep our flowerbeds tidy.

of winter. Previous generations found their attractiveness more appropriate in a cage and they were trapped extensively; hence they became rare. Ussher and Warren (1900) reported that Irish bird-catchers had eliminated Goldfinches 'for miles around our larger towns, and even in many country districts the species has sensibly diminished.' Fashion changed and legislation reflected public displeasure. Trapping was prohibited and the bird rolled a six when bird feeding went viral around the turn of the millennium. Herein lies a fundamental truth – we can exercise a caretaker role over wildlife within our dominion.

For many of Ireland's farmland birds the news is not good. Since 1970, Corn Bunting has become extinct, Corncrake has been marginalised to offshore islands and Grey Partridge was saved from outright oblivion in the nick of time – although its prospects for a return in a changed rural landscape are bleak. Repeated surveys, published in a series of Atlases and conducted by the BTO and BirdWatch Ireland, provide the statistical evidence of a calamity. The roll call of disappearing souls gets longer year on year. The rot set in when Ireland and Britain joined the European Union and were obliged to participate in its Common Agricultural Policy. Lucrative subsidies backed by government policies encouraged farmers to convert fields into factories. The EU sponsored intensification, conversion to monocultures and chemical

Armageddon and is now poised to follow the American superfarm system – 'farmageddon'? Natural cycles have been changed. Crops are sown in autumn and cuts of non-native fodder grass commence in spring, the nesting season of ground-nesting birds. No longer are farms a patchwork of root crops, cereals, livestock and permanent pasture. Specialisation in the name of achieving economy of scale – either to make more money or pay off agricultural investment loans – has combined to shrink the amount of seed, insects and mosaic of natural habitats such as wide hedgerows, ponds, scrub and wildflower meadows. Like riff-raff following in the wake of a gold rush, Magpies, Hooded Crows, Ravens and foxes have flourished. Except they are not really riff-raff, just intelligent omnivores freed from a formerly heavy predation risk. Animal feed, carcasses and roadkill victims suit these natural scavengers and undertakers and inflate their numbers. Regrettably but understandably, some turn their attention to increasingly isolated and beleaguered birdlife. In the wider countryside comparatively little is done by way of predator control. Moreover, new human tolerance has allowed Magpies to proliferate in suburbia where they continue to cull songbirds' breeding attempts. BirdWatch Ireland, voluntary bodies, government departments and concerned, sympathetic farmers are making great efforts to understand and correct mistakes made during the post-Second World War intensification of agriculture and to restore important wildlife habitats. But it is an uphill battle. The chief tool has been through agri-environmental schemes that fund measures directed at providing birds with The Big Three: nesting habitat, chick food and winter food on farmland. Throw in predator control and you have a winning combination. So there is hope.

Apart from extracting turf for fuel from formerly extensive bogland – the scale of which is evidenced on Google Earth – human use of Ireland's land mass has chiefly been to produce food. In Northern Ireland, over three-quarters of the land is used for agriculture. Untouched natural habitat that survived through an accident of being too steep, rocky or high to cultivate, has a new potential. The buzzwords are 'renewable energy'. In something akin to a marriage made in heaven, government and business have embraced the conservation ethos of harnessing energy from the wind rather than depleting fossil fuels. After years of effort to protect habitats with various national and international designations, little more than a polite cough is heard when bird and bat mincing machines are erected across the last sanctuaries of wilderness. Curlews, once the national soundtrack of wild landscapes, are having their homelands blighted with shiningly visible tombstones, even though the mere presence of turbines is known to displace vulnerable – and nominally protected – breeding birds. Rather than a future lit by genuinely benign power, it is being illuminated by burning bridges, with the country's wildlife fuelling the pyre. While there is no denying that future human energy demands are holding the planet to hostage, the switch in mindset to renewables – and away from exploiting fossil fuels in the last remaining great wildernesses – is welcome.

But conservation of wildlife and habitat needs to be more than tokenism. Informed whistleblowers are suggesting that, in their present forms, renewables pose a greater threat to wildlife than climate change (Hambler & Canney 2013). Yet environmentalists, such as the Green Party, are urging that we adopt the technology. Every year in Spain, according to SEO, the Spanish equivalent of BirdWatch Ireland, between 6 million and 18 million birds and bats are killed by wind farms. Twice as many bats die as birds. Per installed turbine, this equates to between 100 and 300 birds. Such figures may be conservative when set against estimates published in December 2002 by the California Energy Commission: 'In a summary of avian impacts at wind turbines by Benner *et al.* (1993) bird deaths per turbine per year were as high as 309 in Germany and 895 in Sweden.' Bat populations reproduce at a slow rate and the animals are long lived; their nocturnal lifestyle means they are not exposed to predators. This strategy becomes unstuck when confronted with turbines, whose very percussive vibrations inflict harm. A recent study in Germany by the Leibniz Institute for Zoo and Wildlife research showed that bats killed by German turbines may have come from as far as 1,500km away. This would suggest that German turbines, which a previous study claims kill more than 200,000 bats per annum, may be depressing populations across a wide area of Europe.

Awareness can be a powerful weapon. During the twentieth century, opposition rallied by women to the wholesale slaughter of wild birds for hat plumes and other adornments ushered in a new era of bird conservation. Today, for different reasons, birds face challenging times. In the course of a year, some populations cross hemispheres to get here and many regard Ireland as home. As a biological group, they are a spectacular phenomenon. They enhance our part of the planet and enrich it – and us.

24. BINOCULARS, TELESCOPES AND TRIPODS, FIELDCRAFT FOR PHOTOGRAPHY

BINOCULARS

FOR MOST PEOPLE, binoculars are not a vital purchase. They are hardly the stuff of big decisions. And why not? Because the casual user does not regard them as a primary tool in the way that Rory McIlroy rates a set of golf clubs or a violinist cherishes a Stradivarius. All the same, anyone who wants to look at nature in close up will need a pair. Because one of my greatest thrills in life is watching birds I will stop at nothing to get the best image that glass can magnify. A bit like the reasons given in *Moby Dick* for going to sea, the magic in birds exerts a draw 'where each man, as in a mirror, finds himself'. Cost is a consideration but top-notch optics are attainable for a judicious purchaser. It saddens and infuriates me to see many interested spectators using binoculars that are massively inferior to my own – a travesty on a par with being handed a ticket to the opera and finding you are sitting behind a pillar. For a ten-year-old boy, especially one fervently hoping for his first binoculars, the present of the best his cash-strapped parents could afford should have been a joyful moment. My folks, not knowing any better, had been conned. Outwardly, the present looked amazing. After that, on

An unforeseen effect of affordable binoculars is that quality suffers. Well-meaning elders purchasing a present for young enthusiasts assume that cheapness does not compromise the image filtered through glass. It does. Moreover, for 'glass' read plastic.

several levels, things went dark. I had to wait another seven years before I saved enough for a working pair – a long time to endure an itch.

'Field glasses' started to become widely available after the Second World War. *British Birds*, the only serious amateur monthly ornithological publication of the era, pinpointed the chief source of the supply. 'Captured German Stores' was a regular advertising masthead near the back page. Beneath it, German Army and Navy products were lionised as waterproof and shockproof. The spiel turned purple when it came to Zeiss, including the use of capital letters when the hallowed brand was mentioned: 'In common with other types of ZEISS instruments, these binoculars are engraved with the manufacturer's code.' To boot, '*almost* mint condition' was even more of an inducement to want to own them. The imagination ran riot. The 1960s price (£5), benchmarked against a workingman's weekly wage, equated to roughly the same amount. No wonder credit terms were available. Curiously, former British Admiralty instruments could be bought for a fraction of the price. By 1970 Zeiss had virtually become a synonym for swanky binoculars. John Gooders, one of the leading ornithologists of the time, was pictured looking lovingly into the distance (allegedly at Tawny Eagles circling in cerulean skies over Thebes) beside the by-line: 'the 10x40B meets all my needs ... superb resolution for feather-by-feather examination, and wide field of view. With no external moving parts they stand the rough treatment that studying birds in marsh, snow and desert involves. Zeiss are not cheap – but they are recognised as the best by every ornithologist I know.'

During the late 1960s German engineers pioneered the development of 'roof prisms'. Housed in an innovative two parallel barrels design, they sidestepped the traditional tiered arrangement of wide front lenses refracting light through angled prisms clamped inside heavy bodywork to small lenses used by the viewer. The maths of specification is a constant, however. The first figure refers to magnification (usually 7, 8 or 10) and the second indicates the glass diameter in millimetres of the front 'objective' lens. By and large, only magnification needs to be borne in mind. Stronger magnification can be alluring but a steadier hand is needed to enjoy the view. For a generation of young and impoverished Irish birdwatchers, post-war German partition was a blessing. Zeiss had factories in both East Germany (DDR) and West Germany (FDR). Roof prisms were manufactured in the Free World and cost a fortune. But from behind the Iron Curtain the original Zeiss factory kept churning out affordable pre-war stock. Like Chairman Mao's *Little Red Book*, Zeiss Jenoptem 8x30 binoculars were ubiquitous. They were not waterproof and an inadvertent thump could knock out the prism alignment and result in 'double vision'. When this happens, two overlapping images are not necessarily seen, more commonly the fault manifests itself in a massive pull to the user's vision that can be tolerated until looking away, at which point pupils swim sickeningly. Overall, the clarity was superb. More importantly, they still are. Herein lies irony. The light-transmitting quality of glass does not have an expiry date. Zeiss Jenoptem 8x30 binoculars (and other models from the same stable, such as 10x50) are still available. The prices are peanuts. Check out Ebay. Would I be disappointed if I accidentally left my costly waterproof, shockproof and bombproof Swarovski 10x42s at home and had to revert to a geriatric pair of DDR vintage? Not in the slightest.

Today, do we inhabit an optical Arcadia? Binoculars have proliferated and camera manufacturers have joined the fray and issued their own brands. Although I do not scrutinise the market – Swarovski and I live in happy monogamy – I am exposed to the choices of others and sometimes asked the difficult question: what would I recommend? Because I lead birdwatching tours I gain insights. No one would stump up for several days of hotel accommodation and dawn-to-dusk birdwatching and *knowingly* come along with substandard optics. The lady with the pocket binoculars was having obvious and predictable difficulty. Frustration was written all over her face. I took a look. Not out of alignment, individual eyepiece setting fine and clean lenses (for which she used a lens pen, highly recommended). Although full marks, the gear is junk. Reluctantly, I hand her mine. She lifts them for a peep and immediately exclaims: 'Oh my goodness!' What can I say? I know that, for just about everyone in the group of a dozen enthusiasts, the reaction would be the same. The truth is that people spend money on instruments that are far from cheap and are, in many cases, rubbish. The worst are garbage and should be made illegal. Take zoom binoculars, happily no longer in vogue. The sales patter runs: 'these let you change magnification with the throw of a lever. You can find the bird on low power, then zoom in for a detailed look. Easy!' Codswallop – the glass is plastic, the field of view tiny and the resolution is foggy.

Some conservation charities endorse particular brands, which is helpful: these are the ones to avoid. Because they are a thousand miles away from even the Zeiss of my youth, they should be cheap and cheerful as junk jewellery but they can cost well in excess of €300. How many of us buy cameras that are not Canon or Nikon? While there are, of course, other quality cameras, the top names are trusted for a simple reason – they are good. It should be the same with binoculars. Yet inferior and pricey products have elbowed their way into the ranks of prospective purchasers conned by advertising and unaware of pitfalls. A common failing is the rigidity of the spacing between each barrel. In no time, a high proportion of mid-price models start to sag together instead of staying a steadfast distance apart that suits an observer's eyes. On the other hand, tastes are personal and satisfaction cannot be overlooked. So, for the record, this is my advice: Swarovski, Zeiss and Leica are all superb. New models are expensive but reputable optical companies carry guaranteed second-hand stock. The instruments do not dull with age or become obsolete. Moreover, the maker will stand over and fix any repair that may have arisen through a manufacturing fault. Any such requirement is free of charge from Swarovski. If you cannot afford second-hand, you should at least try out a top-flight pair and use the experience as a baseline for comparisons with what you can afford. Sales personnel are not optical tailors and unless steeped in practical knowledge their advice carries little weight. Rather than being presented with a glittering galaxy of sparkling optics, much on offer today is mutton dressed as lamb. Because the joy of viewing birds is so uplifting, it is sinful to see natural vision dumbed down by fashion, hype and quackery.

TELESCOPES AND TRIPODS

Think carefully. Do you really need a telescope to look at birds around home? Telescopes come with baggage. To use one, you will need a tripod. The relationship is so umbilical that the term 'telepod' should be invented to cover it. Those who succumb to temptation are usually wooed by a superlative view enjoyed through someone else's equipment. On a par with enjoying grandchildren, the experience is sublime because you do not have to do the work. Telescopes are much bigger than binoculars and tripods add weight. Ah – but carbon-fibre tripods ease the freight-load. Well, they do but they tend to cost more and in windy weather their stability is compromised. A widespread misconception is that an expensive telescope will function adequately on a cheap, rickety tripod. Such a mismatch generates wobble, undermining the worth of the image. Another vogue is a quick-release plate that, in place of a sturdy screw mount, is attached to the base of the telescope, allowing it to be popped on and off a tripod. Seldom are these as stable as claimed and, in any kind of wind, some kind of wobble is imparted. Time after time users who compare the distortion-free, rock solid panning of a properly affixed, screw-mounted telescope enjoy a Damascene moment in which basic mechanics miraculously enhance optical performance. Most modern telescopes come with an angled body, although many makes offer a straight-bodied alternative. Angled is my choice. By looking down, the tripod height can be lowered, making the telescope more stable. Equally, the viewing eye does not face into wind, rain or glaring sun. A neat trick, although only mastered through persistence, is to keep both eyes open. This substantially improves the view through your 'telescope eye'. Those few optical companies that manufacture the best binoculars also produce telescopes. For their outstanding telescopes, Kowa and Nikon also deserve podium places in the art of telescope manufacture. Most companies offer models in conventional glass or highly expensive material that, depending on brand, is termed ED or fluorite. Not only do I use regular glass, I prefer it. Eyepieces range from relatively low power x20 set magnification to zoom eyepieces that hit x80 magnification. On top models with a large, light-gathering front objective lens, zoom eyepieces are excellent. However, lower power is still, for most users, power enough. Moreover, some eyepieces of x20 or x30 are available in wide angle that 'feels like' viewing through binoculars rather than peering down a telescope. The image is bright, sharp and – depending on both telescope and tripod – magnificent.

FIELDCRAFT FOR PHOTOGRAPHY

The march of technology is inexorable. Not so long ago, photographing birds required expensive equipment and, because the results could not be looked at with the press of a button, a lot of patience. Film was not cheap and, unlike memory cards, not reusable. Also film had to be developed. For Kodak transparencies, the choice for most enthusiastic amateurs, a fortnight wait was standard. Digital has changed the practice of photography but not the theory. From mobile phones to point-and-shoot cameras, any piece of kit with a lens will resolve an acceptable image and can be pressed against binoculars or a telescope to record a picture magnified by the Mother Superior instrument. Indeed, digiscoping has developed as a photographic technique in its own right. The results can be surprisingly good but considerable practice is needed and ownership of a telescope is obligatory. For users of conventional equipment the formula for capturing a pleasing image has not changed. In place of a spool of exposed film, a sensor stores the end product as a digital negative on a memory card. A sharp lens is paramount and the photographer needs to prefigure a certain amount of camera information to ensure that exposure and shutter speed will yield a satisfactory result. Although the playing field is more level than ever, old hands who produced the best images using film still turn out top work using digital equipment. As with so many things, a good product only takes you so far. It is pointless owning a Porsche if you do not know how to change gear.

For most budding photographers the main challenge is gaining access to the subject. This means getting close enough to take a photograph. Downloading the result onto a computer and tweaking it for desired effect are something of a black art. However, unless the raw material is good, no amount of processing will produce a masterpiece. What is in this for the bird? The answer is nothing. Photography is, by its very nature, a selfish activity. It should be harmless and not lead to disturbance from a feeding area or deliberate flushing to get a flight shot. Nest photography is best avoided. Many eyes will be watching, especially those of predators. Even if no visible sign of the photographer's visit remains, a scent trail will pique the curiosity of passing four-legged opportunists. Because the bird, out of a need to incubate eggs or feed chicks, is drawn to the location, the imposition of being snapped is below the

belt and reduces photography to the level of shooting fish in a barrel. Depending on species, some parents freak completely and abandon the breeding attempt.

Entering the realm of birds is a privilege that should not cause them stress. Garden birds coming to feeders, or to food presented in ways that favour a photo opportunity, is a great way to hone technique and discover the personality of each species. While opportunities for a striking pose may be fleeting, time spent observing routines and mannerisms will pay long-term dividends. Robins, Blackbirds and thrushes hop and then remain stock still for brief interludes. By anticipating this behaviour, a chance for a crisp, unblurred photograph is feasible. In contrast, ground-feeding Starlings and finches rarely stay still – but will be much less fidgety when perched above terra firma. No portrait photographer fails to put a human subject at ease before assessing the sitter's best side. Get-to-know-you time reveals the full spectrum of artistic angles and intimate expressions. Birds are no different. Yet when it comes to them, zealous firing of whirring shutters seems to count as part of the action. Little wonder that so many images show nervous beings in pre-flight attitudes.

Clichés attesting to the sharp-eyed vision of birds ought to alert a stalking photographer to the certainty that every stealthy step will be seen. We stand out like a tomato in a sugar bowl. Nestlings have inborn survival techniques and parents teach them to recognise and avoid human silhouettes. There are ways around this, however. A vehicle can be used for a judicious approach, a partly opened house window may allow a lens wriggle room to train on an unsuspecting target, a garden shed with a viewing port facilitates access to a feeding station or a cheap pop-up tent can be converted into a portable hide. So long as you cannot be seen, birds do not take evasive action. For this reason 'guerrilla warfare' camouflage is unnecessary. In the same way that a charging elephant does not flatten a tent – because it assumes that it is a solid object – your presence will not register if you are out of sight and motionless. Movement is your Achilles heel. Bird vision reacts ultra-fast. An expensive camouflaged hide counts for nothing once a protruding lens moves, even fractionally. Because optical glass glints, the effect on the bird is akin to shining a mirror in its direction. Slow gradual panning movements can pass unnoticed. Moreover, aligning the lens beforehand in roughly the right direction will place it close

Great Spotted Woodpecker, photographed with a standard lens. Sometimes composition beats lens magnification.

Stability is everything. A tripod – even an expensive one – can be fool's gold and out-performed by a cheap sand-filled beanbag.

to the expected picture-taking zone. Failing that, the golden rule is: 'no jerky movements.' What if you are in the open? It is exasperating to see birds feeding contentedly among livestock. Skylarks, Pied Wagtails, Wheatears and Lapwings do not bat an eyelid when surrounded by sheep or cattle. Over millennia, they have learned to trust a four-legged, mainly horizontal silhouette. Along the coast, seals are also afforded similar benign status. The recommended option is 'if you cannot beat them, join them'. By lying down, staying still and – if needs be – crawling carefully, it is possible to slip under a bird's natural radar. Into the bargain, a low angle generates a better aesthetic composition. But how will you manage to hold the camera steady, especially as you need to remain prone? The secret is a beanbag. These can be bought empty or pre-filled. Empty is best as you can fill them with sand or grains – even bird seed. Sufficient is needed to absorb the camera and lens and cushion any movement when pressing the shutter. A beanbag can be used in place of a tripod. Used properly, it is actually more stable. Should you adopt the troika of camera, lens and beanbag, your photography will almost certainly improve.

Patience, knowledge of behaviour and a degree of sleuthing mean that you do not need a paparazzi lens to take bird photographs. Very few of the photographs in this book were taken using a lens of more than 300mm magnification. Large lenses are frighteningly expensive. And, as if locked in a compulsory symbiotic relationship, their owners feel obliged to use them to portray feathered targets in dental record close-up. Machismo and bare-knuckle male competitiveness fuelled by bird news websites decants 'lens men' to locations where a newsworthy, usually rare, bird can be found. Pack mentality ensues with no thought given to the bird's desire to feed, preen or rest. Beauty is in the eye of the beholder and 'a bird in a picture' may trump 'a picture of a bird'. The choice is yours but the subject's needs should come first.

25. LABELS TO KNOW

FEATHERS ARE DRESSES. They provide warmth, which was probably the main reason they evolved. If, as seems to be the case, birds were descended from creatures that have a dinosaur lineage, then their ancestors would have been cold-blooded – a fact that limited any kind of activity until warmed by the heat of the day. By growing feathers, birds broke free.

Feathers hug the body's underlying contours. They grow in tracts, each with a unique shape and, as with Meadow Pipit, also a different pattern.

Over time, manifold functions became possible. Feathers prettify males. In most birds, men strut the catwalk and are inspected by females. The feminine flip side is camouflage, another gift of feathers. Body form underpins all plumage arrangements. Few human males understand the relationship between clothing and underlying silhouette. They regard garments as purely functional, attached to the body and secured by fastenings such as belts, buttons and zips. Birds have none of these. Their plumage is aligned in tracts. Flesh is hidden and tracts follow contours. In fact, birds are not uniformly feathered, although the costume is so well designed that it creates this impression. Every undulation is tightly draped in a corset, nipped and tucked and totally aerodynamic. Watch a Robin sing or a Blackbird stop and start while foraging. Global shape and posture alter simultaneously in actions that are sinuous and supple; plumage gaps never appear. So it is not true to say that feathers create the various shapes of birds. Bone, muscle and fat work together and harmonise with external visage. Think jeans. Female readers will be familiar with the concept of the Galaxy dress. Designed by Frenchman Roland Mouret, its key to world renown was a cut that hugged curvature by means of a mesh 'inner tube'. The outcome was a sartorial sensation. In the same way, birds are perfectly streamlined. Feathers do not hang on a frame like baggy trousers or a loose-fitting T-shirt. The wearer is, at all times, fit to walk the red carpet.

From such understanding, empathy springs. Birds and people share many features and by employing a basic vernacular (forehead, crown, cheeks, throat, chest and so on) a detailed picture can be constructed. By and large, plumage patterns follow the contours of feather groups. Species that have a bright stripe over the eye (corresponding to an eyebrow and labelled 'supercilium') restrict the feature to just this tract. Hence, feather groups represent a universal framework. Learning the basis of common markings can be tried out on any bird, pets included. Wings complicate matters. Here a different lexicon applies. At rest most of the wing is folded out of sight, like an outfit carefully stowed away when not needed. Similarly, the tail shuts like a fan. Once airborne – or when preening or stretching at rest – the wings and tail reveal true patterns and colours. Several species reserve a block of white near the base of the tail, on the rump. Examples include Bullfinch, Wheatear and Jay. Concealed beneath overlapping wings at rest, the rump flashes upon take-off and is a signal, sometimes a visual alarm, to others. Rabbits and deer show the same pattern.

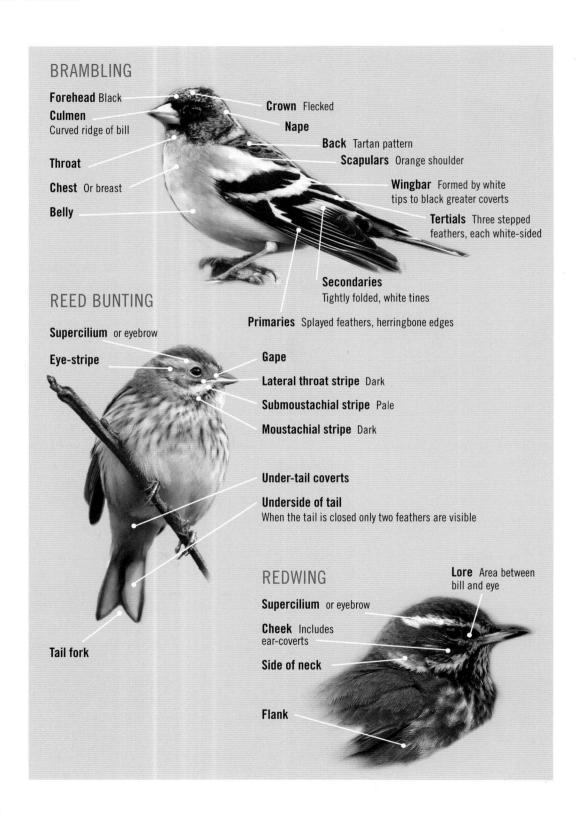

BRAMBLING

Forehead Black

Culmen
Curved ridge of bill

Crown Flecked

Nape

Back Tartan pattern

Scapulars Orange shoulder

Throat

Chest Or breast

Belly

Wingbar Formed by white
tips to black greater coverts

Tertials Three stepped
feathers, each white-sided

Secondaries
Tightly folded, white tines

Primaries Splayed feathers, herringbone edges

REED BUNTING

Supercilium or eyebrow

Eye-stripe

Gape

Lateral throat stripe Dark

Submoustachial stripe Pale

Moustachial stripe Dark

Under-tail coverts

Underside of tail
When the tail is closed only two feathers are visible

Tail fork

REDWING

Lore Area between
bill and eye

Supercilium or eyebrow

Cheek Includes
ear-coverts

Side of neck

Flank

FIELDFARE

Back Brown

Scapulars Brown with grey edgings

Tertials Two parallel sets of three feathers, each with black inner vane and grey outer vane (or web)

Rump Plain grey

Tail Black, straight-edged

PIED WAGTAIL

Eyering Narrow white orbital circle

Median coverts
White fringes, scallop pattern

Greater coverts
Outlined in white, Venetian blind pattern

Outer tail feathers

WILLOW WARBLER

Secondaries
Bunched between primaries and tertials

Tertials

Primaries

Rump Yellowish area

Greater coverts
Partially concealed by overlap of scapulars

First primary
Tiny, always reduced in size

Primary coverts

Upper-tail coverts
Worn, located between rump and tail

133

SPECIES ACCOUNTS

GREY HERON *Ardea cinerea*

Grey Herons demonstrate Walter Mitty mood swings. Skinny as a beanpole when staring forwards and straining to pounce, off-duty they resemble prayerful monks, hunched against the world like a cleric lost in reverie. Stately wingbeats have the spring-sprong rhythm of an 'intellectual gait'. Both at rest and in flight, the bird is of such unadulterated greyness that it would be hard to locate on a foggy morning. Nevertheless, small birds fear the grandee's silhouette. Grey Herons are omnivorous and have no scruples when it comes to snatching ducklings, Little Grebes or unsuspecting shorebirds that amble past a motionless – and seemingly inattentive – fisherman. Deterring a garden-pond plunderer is best achieved by criss-crossing the attraction and its shorelines with a few loose wires or ropes set about a metre high. These cause difficulties both for landing and, especially, taking off. Passing overhead, the retracted neck forms a keel, gangly toes on trailing feet are neatly folded and cavernous wings are blunt-tipped and not splay-fingered, as might befit something so large. The underwings are plain and smoky. Grey across the back extends outwards and forms a panel, hemmed in by dark slate flight feathers. Roughly midway along the wing's forward edge, at the wrist, two pale patches wink like white knuckles. Viewed head-on, the effect is akin to landing lights. At rest, the same part of the wing catches the eye and is reminiscent of a pom-pom or tassel, an effect enhanced by black body plumage displaced by the cusp of the folded wing. Adults are badger-headed. The face and forehead are white and a black stripe along the side of the crown attenuates into a ponytail plume that hangs against the nape and flutters in wind. Young birds have a grey crown. As they reach their first birthday the ghost of the adult pattern starts to emerge. Their bill is greenish; adult bills are banana-coloured. In early spring, a hormonal surge linked to the onset of breeding flushes the colour and briefly transforms it to reddish pink. Hunters are primarily solitary. If disturbed (and sometimes when flying to roost) a loud *Frank!* explodes silence like the crack of a gunshot. Most breeding colonies are in tall trees and sited within reach of a feeding wetland or coast. Several heronries are as old as the trees that support the bulky nest. The structure is renovated at the end of winter. Early in spring Trappist vows are abandoned and established pairs renew annual trysts and greet each other with audible bill snapping and a range of bizarre sounds, from clicking and clacking to burps and popping. Couples entwine necks and are as affectionate as swans. Chicks are fed regurgitated food. Adults are resident but young disperse in random directions to find their own demesne; some emigrate overseas. One British nestling was recovered in Morocco.

LITTLE EGRET *Egretta garzetta*

As recently as 1980 this small, pure white heron was a rarity. On a handful of previous occasions vagrants strayed north from breeding haunts in southern Europe and graced an estuary or freshwater wetland. Since then, Ireland has been colonised. Key to establishment

GREY HERON Top left: adult; **top right:** one-year-old in flight; **middle left:** adult breeding plumage; **middle right:** juvenile in autumn. **LITTLE EGRET Middle left:** first-winter (bi-coloured legs); **middle right:** adult acquiring breeding plumes; **bottom pair:** adults in flight (dipped-in-custard feet contrast with all-black legs).

was a recovery from past persecution at breeding colonies in Mediterranean countries and the propensity for new arrivals to linger and become resident. Eventually settlers opted to breed among existing Grey Heron citadels. The pioneering spirit that brought colonists to Ireland has not dimmed: youngsters born in County Galway have reached both Iceland and the Azores. Unlike its sauntering, leaden-footed cousin, Little Egret is a silent swashbuckler and dashes after finny prey. Adults in breeding plumage sprout lacy 'bridal train' back plumage and wispy head plumes. Vivid yellow unfeathered skin between the eye and bill becomes florid and turns tangerine at the height of courtship. Throughout the year, yellow feet on black legs resemble ankle socks. The legs and feet of youngsters are greenish. In winter, farmland ditches and ponds in urban parks suffice as foraging habitat. The once implausible spectacle of a diminutive snow-white egret flapping over suburban skylines and dropping into an adjoining wetland is no longer the stuff of dreams, but delightful reality.

SPARROWHAWK *Accipiter nisus*

Solitary, swerving and secretive, Sparrowhawks present a songbird's worst nightmare. Garden feeders are often in the saboteur's crosshairs. Surprise is the key; unless a target is taken unawares the hunter will go hungry (see A HAWK'S LIFE, p. 62). Perched raiders are soon rumbled and mobbed, so 'wait-and-see' ambush tactics are usually impractical. Most sorties are fairly random and serendipitous. In open country the sleuth flies low and close to the ground before breasting a bank, hedge or drystone wall. At times, both predator and startled prey seem equally surprised to encounter each other. Duels are short-lived but if the quarry pitches high and out of reach from a first strike, it usually escapes. Unlike falcons, Sparrowhawks are not fast-paced rugby backs; they thunder into victims like a crushing front-row forward. Among woodland the shadowy shape is not in view for long as it slips along edges and through glades. Short bursts of three or four wing beats are followed by a glide. When prey is sighted, the wings shut and the bird morphs into a missile, slewing like a bobsleigh. When the red mist is down mistakes can occur; crashes with windows and traffic exact a regular toll. Males are smaller and more brightly coloured than females. He is bluish-grey above with rufous bars across light underparts. Females and youngsters are brown-backed and more distinctly patterned below; barring resembles a concentric ribcage. Young birds retain coppery edges to the upperparts throughout their first winter. Unlike Kestrels, Sparrowhawks like to bathe and, regardless of whether they are loved or loathed, will frequent garden birdbaths. A variable – often absent – feature shown by all ages is a 'dusting' of a few pale spots across the upperparts, the result of random whitish bases to scapulars. Normally silent, half-hidden juveniles in tree canopy simper to be fed, even when parental ties have been cut off. The source of the sound – an abstract intermittent squeak akin to squeezing a bath toy – is hard to pin down. Its incongruity belies the caller's identity.

KESTREL *Falco tinnunculus*

Kestrel is the hawk that hovers. In truth it is a falcon but many class the stationary icon, parked in the sky with downcast eyes transmitting pin-sharp images, as 'the hawk'. Wind assists hovering by providing lift. On calm days hunting is conducted from vantage points such as telegraph poles. Distracted by the chances of spotting a rodent, the bird sometimes obliges and affords grandstand views. Terracotta-backed adult males have a blue-grey head and tail (unbarred, with a broad blackish tip). Females are browner, including the tail, which is laddered with several slate-coloured crossbars as well as being dark-tipped. The upperparts are more profusely barred, although older females show a greyer, more male-like head. Young resemble females; some are distinctive and look almost 'sandy' due to light edges to the upperparts and wing feathers. When not hovering, flight is direct with a fairly shallow, rapid rhythm. Sparrowhawk is a different matter. Apart from minor differences in shape, a

KESTREL Top and middle right: juvenile female (profuse tail barring indicates female, less profuse on juvenile male); middle left: adult male. **SPARROWHAWK** Bottom left: adult male; bottom right: young female (rufous fringes at the edge of the folded wing are unmoulted juvenile feathers).

key distinction is Sparrowhawk's repetitive mechanical flap-and-glide momentum. Kestrels employ long phases of shallow wingbeats interspersed with infrequent glides. Numbers have declined sharply across eastern districts. Intensive agriculture in lowland areas is intolerant of 'untidy' margins where shrews and mice live a subterranean existence but emerge regularly and forage along grassy trails. Kestrels spot prey using UV vision, which picks up urine spots and pinpoints active latrines. Although live prey is preferred, sluggish sickly rodents are also nabbed. Little does the Kestrel realise that it has, quite literally, caught a poisoned chalice. Through 'secondary poisoning' rodenticides kill not only Kestrels, but also owls. Urgent action is needed to address the shameful practice of dispensing death in chuck-and-forget sachets, which is banned elsewhere in the EU. When it was outlawed in Holland, Kestrels recovered and had reached 7,000 pairs by 2012. Many now breed in nest boxes and are regarded by Dutch farmers as a cheap, safe and efficient way of controlling unwanted rodents (see McGeehan & Wyllie 2012).

MERLIN *Falco columbarius*

Merlin is a small falcon that specialises in catching small prey. Meadow Pipits and Skylarks are favourites. To a certain extent the species is Sparrowhawk's equivalent in open habitats. Upland and coast are its bailiwick. Unless your home is among such wild places you are unlikely to encounter this pocket-sized hunter. Built for speed, the wings are sharply angled and the tail is ample and square-tipped. Kestrels hover and are slowcoaches with a fulsome, less raked wing tip; their slightly longer tail has a vaguely swollen tip. Merlin flight is low and fast with a telltale tripping action maintained by quick, shallow wingbeats. The flier seems to be constantly changing gear. Prey is grabbed in a lightning-fast low-angle stoop but many targets spot the assailant and 'tower' (fly or circle steeply) immediately. What follows is a protracted aerial

game of cat-and-mouse with predator and prey swirling around as the potential victim tries to stay above its pursuer and deny it a gravity-assisted strike. Females are larger than males and are roughly the size of a Mistle Thrush. Adult males are Blackbird size with blue-grey upperparts and rust-coloured underparts. Females and young are 'ploughed earth' brown with distinctive hooped tails: four or five regularly spaced light bars look like pale guides on a dark ruler. On adult males, the tail is blue-grey with little or no barring but a prominent, dark subterminal band and a narrow white tip.

BUZZARD Top three: probably all are youngsters due to pale eye (adults are dark eyed). PEREGRINE Middle left: juvenile; centre and middle right: adult. MERLIN Lower left: adult male; bottom right: adult female chasing Meadow Pipit.

PEREGRINE *Falco peregrinus*

At rest imperious and granitic, Peregrines are capable of hitting over 250km/h in a near-vertical stoop. Ironically for a denizen of wild crags and windswept headlands, hunters regularly fly out to sea to catch unsuspecting shearwaters and petrels. Urban life has attractions in the form of Feral Pigeons and nocturnal migrants – such as Woodcock – that are illuminated from below by city lights. In overhead profile a stocky neck, bodybuilder chest and heavy hips complete a gladiatorial physique. Cruising or circling, the silhouette suggests a crossbow. When things get serious the assassin cups the air and accelerates effortlessly. Often the first clue to a Peregrine's presence is panic among other birds. When one slingshots among them, Starling flocks assembling at roosts divide instantaneously, like fish shoals pursued by a shark. Perched adult Peregrines are blue-grey above. Slate-coloured barring on the breast and flanks blurs to smoke-grey at a distance, leaving the relatively unmarked white chest to stand out against a cowled face. Young are dark brown above and extensively streaked below, including the chest, which is not as clean and bright as an adult. Until juvenile head plumage moults and is replaced, around one year after fledging, by a black balaclava, youngsters have a thinner moustache and a striated brown crown.

BUZZARD *Buteo buteo*

Buzzards have repopulated all but western districts of Ireland. Once common in northeast Ulster (Thompson 1849–52) they were exterminated by gamekeepers in the late nineteenth century. Commencing in the 1950s, colonists from Scotland provided the seed corn for a natural comeback. By 2012, the population had reached an estimated 2,000 pairs and was breeding in all four provinces. In general dark brown, the underwings are lighter, although variable. Airborne, a dark patch at the wing's 'wrist' is a constant feature, as is a pale cummerbund, bounded by a dark bib and barred belly. Perched birds, often parked atop a telegraph pole, look dumpy and owlish. At closer range, large yellow feet are noticeable. In some areas, grassy motorway banks and adjacent overgrown farmland ditches have become popular hunting grounds. Nationally, rats make up almost 15 per cent of prey; rabbits account for 45 per cent. Hovering hunters are ungainly and conjure an image of an overweight American attempting to skip. Surprising, therefore, is an ability to catch crows that taunt and pursue the big slowcoach. The Buzzard waits until only one flight follower remains. Unexpectedly, it flips and catches its persecutor off guard. Because no other crow witnessed the incident, the Buzzard's secret is safe (N.D. McKee). Mewing calls are broadcast in flight, yet often the bird appears to be solo. In reality the caller is probably interacting with another far beyond the range of human vision. Walls (1942) stated that, with around a million cones per square millimetre in its retina, a Buzzard's visual acuity must be 'at least eight times that of man.'

CORNCRAKE *Crex crex*

When hay was cultivated throughout rural Ireland, Corncrakes were in heaven. 'Haycrake' would be more apt. Calamity struck when farm operations entailed the use of mechanical reapers. Hand scything allowed the handler to spare nests. A nationwide switch to silage production, where grass is cut earlier and repeatedly, was the final straw. Pockets survived in areas where traditional agriculture remained or where alternative habitat consisting of nettle beds was available. Some Irish islands escaped conversion to intensive farming through isolation and small field size. Iris-swathed wet flushes and winter-grazed pasture allowed to burst into lush summer meadow provides refuge for skeleton bands. Corncrakes like cool, fairly thick stands of herbage not much taller than themselves. They feed in shady, moist conditions that yield a bounty of insects and other invertebrates; the bulk of the diet is animal matter.

Ungainliness in flight belies an ability to perform an annual round trip to sub-equatorial Africa. In the past, accepted wisdom blamed drought, overgrazing and fire in the Sahel region of Saharan Africa as major factors causing decline. Quite what migration routes are followed by Ireland's Corncrakes – and to where precisely – are unclear. However, radio-tracked Scottish birds wintered in the Congo and passed through Spain. Hazards include trapping along the entire North African coast and, in Ireland, domestic cats. Migrants also have an unfortunate preference to fly low down, frequently resulting in collisions with power lines.

The rasping craking of males is unmistakeable. Calling is little more than a clue to the approximate number of males and gives no inkling to the presence of females, which are silent. Nonetheless, it is possible to infer a good deal once the courtship ritual is understood. Because females migrate nocturnally, male voices crank longest at night. For some time after arrival, males call only in darkness. Daytime calling is erratic and, as the season progresses, is directed equally at potential rivals occupying adjoining cover. If paired, a territory is defended. When a mate fails to materialise, the suitor tries his luck elsewhere. In areas where several males compete for an unknown quantity of females, it is difficult to keep abreast of shenanigans. The situation is complicated by a tendency for both sexes to take more than one partner. A resumption of calling following a June lull is believed to portend a second brood. Other male sounds take two forms: a snoring rumble and a ghoulish gasp. Individuals viewed on Inishbofin, County Galway, made these sounds for no apparent reason. By late July all fall silent. Adults commence a root-and-branch moult of head and body, and regrow the wings and tail, thus becoming flightless. By late August most are attired with new robes and are ready to leave. Some choose to depart earlier in worn plumage. Adults found in Holland in late July had travelled there to moult. Logic suggests that juveniles raised in first broods could migrate any time after fledging. In other long-haul migrants, only adults were capable of achieving high deposition rates of fat that endowed them with sufficient fuel to fly continuously for up to 100 hours (Neto, Encarnacao, Fearon & Gosler, 2008). If juvenile Corncrakes cannot accumulate such a high fat loading, their smaller fuel store would commit them to several flights of shorter duration. Emigration from Ireland continues throughout September and

CORNCRAKE Six images depict males (blue-grey plumage on face and chest is less colourful on females). **PHEASANT** Bottom right, female.

presumably the last to leave are those from second broods. Early October turns up a few tail-end Charlies, probably migrants from elsewhere. In the nineteenth century, when Corncrakes were more or less ubiquitous, some were encountered during winter.

PHEASANT *Phasianus colchicus*

Although incontestably spectacular, Pheasants are no more Irish than Budgerigars. Cocks are more heavily decorated than communist generals whereas female plumage, when motionless among stalks and stems, becomes invisible ink. When introduced onto offshore islands their presence has a harmful effect on native grassland birds (see final paragraph, p. 120).

LAPWING *Vanellus vanellus*

Lapwing is a beginner birdwatcher's dream: it is unmistakeable. Adults, especially when they moult into breeding plumage, have head plumes that would bring tears to the eyes of any milliner. Males are blacker-faced than females and, when flight comparisons are possible, their wing tip is broader and even more like a table-tennis bat. Flocks feed on pasture or plough and scatter over fields and wetlands, taking a few brisk steps and periodically pausing. When quarry is located – worms, grubs or insect larvae – stalkers lunge forward with a stoop suggesting that a high heel must have snapped. Quite how they detect prey is a mystery. Big obsidian eyes confer wondrous vision but highly tuned listening may be an indispensable complementary means of guiding the hunter to targets. A habit of trembling one foot against the ground is an integral part of feeding behaviour, although its benefit is not understood. The tattoo might serve as a sensory means of pinpointing living organisms – or does such drumming trick invertebrates into making a fatal wriggle that registers on Lapwing's equivalent of sonar?

Small huddles of local breeders gather on traditional haunts in late January. The species is sociable and fine days – or calm, moonlit nights – trigger aerial displays. Males strut and peacock themselves at rest, then tumble in flight; frying-pan wings whump the air, powering biplane-style swoops and rolls. Landings are often languorous with wings raised to show off. The performance is accompanied by operatic hiccupping whose cadence matches jerks of the caller's head. The sound is as uplifting and unforgettable as the roar of the crowd at a Croke Park final. At other times a plaintive keening denotes wariness. Rivals join the pyrotechnics that are embellished by the twinkling of white underwings contrasting against bottle-green backs. Having wooed a mate, beaux fuss and squat on potential nest sites, elevating their hindquarters and wagging chestnut-orange undertail plumage to signal a suitable nest scrape. Females have the final say on location and four speckled eggs are laid at the end of March. If the first attempt fails, efforts to produce a family continue until June. Chicks feed instinctively on insects – vital protein to build muscle, tissue and feathers – and require the edges of ditches, sun-warmed marshland or insect-rich, tussocky sward.

In late summer, adults moult and dress down for autumn and winter. Juveniles and adults now look essentially similar. All ages have stumpy crests, buff-washed faces and back plumage scalloped with sandy-bronze, more extensive on first-winters. Post-breeding packs of Irish Lapwings move to winter quarters, probably nearby grassland, lakeshores or the coast. Serried ranks roosting on mudflats during short winter days give a clue to nocturnal feeding; darkness virtually eliminates predation risk. At dusk, gatherings rise and disappear inland. European Lapwings are migratory and trek west. Ireland hosts thousands each winter, numbers being highest when ice and snow entomb feeding grounds across the Continent and Britain.

Calamity has befallen our native population that once bred in every county. Overseas hordes still arrive, although their numbers have diminished too. Local pairs are beset by a litany of woes. Field drainage, spring-ripening crops and suffocating silage monocultures have changed the face of much of pastoral Ireland. Where suitable habitat still exists, a roster of predators beleaguers Lapwings and other ground-nesting birds. In a European study (Rickenbach *et al.* 2010) radio-tagged chicks suffered greatest mortality nocturnally at the jaws of foxes. In these changed times skeleton bands of breeding pairs find sanctuary on islands free from the red peril. Redoubts include the Aran Islands and the string of unploughed pearls that lie off the coasts of Galway, Mayo and Donegal. Western flower-filled commonages and turloughs still throb to the sound of displaying Lapwings, chiefly in the shadow of Croagh Patrick, Ireland's holy mountain. Elsewhere, pockets survive and may indeed prosper when given sanctuary, as at Lough Booragh, County Offaly – proof that the raffish jester of field and farm can yet be snatched from the jaws of agricultural Armageddon.

LAPWING Middle and top right: adult males in breeding plumage (also p. 2). Lower left: adult in winter plumage (buff fringes to back and 'chamois leather' face colour).

GULLS: A SWEEP OF IMAGERY

To many, gulls are as welcome as door-to-door salesmen. Unloved they may be but gulls are conspicuous, prevalent and fairly confiding; qualities that provide a head start in learning identification. Most confusion arises not when confronted by an adult (a simple check of back and leg colour will identify any adult of the common species) but when presented with a brown or partly pale immature. Although the offspring of other bulky species, such as Buzzard, resemble their parents, young gulls take up to four years to reach respectability through a series

HERRING GULL Top, swimming: adults in winter plumage (head streaked). Two brown-flecked immatures are far left and centre right. Upper middle, left: first-winter; centre: adult winter; right: adult breeding plumage. **LESSER BLACK-BACKED GULL** Lower middle, left: first-winter; right: adult breeding plumage. **GREAT BLACK-BACKED GULL** Bottom left: first-winter; middle: adult breeding; right: adult winter (streaked head). Dark bill smudge is variable.

of moults. Drab feathering is replaced in a regular sequence, not randomly. Interim stages are the equivalent of teenage acne and are at their worst during summer, when moult is protracted and universal. With large gulls it is important to remember that, except when a standard juvenile or adult, transitional garb is at the whim of the bird and is not the prerogative of field guide illustrations. The larger the species, the greater the number of costume changes. Hence Black-headed Gull, the smallest commoner, completes metamorphosis in just over one year. For all gulls, size is a convenient determinant that distinguishes two tribes, each comprising several species of comparable stature. Large gulls share broad wings less suited to the tight manoeuvres performed by smaller gulls, whose wings are more streamlined and pointed. Consequently, large gulls tend to scavenge rather than engage in dipping over water or hawking insects in warm weather. All adult large gulls are goat-eyed with stocky yellow bills that glint a scarlet spot during the breeding season. The spot is a target for hungry newborns that peck it to stimulate regurgitation. Smaller gulls have slim and lightweight bills that, along with dark Bambi eyes, foster a benign look.

HERRING GULL *Larus argentatus*

As the Latin name suggests, adults are silver-backed (and perpetually pink-legged). The species is so widespread that it is used as a yardstick against which others can be compared. Juveniles, even after they have moulted head and body plumage during autumn are mottled brown with, in flight, a broad blackish tail band and trailing wing edge. Importantly, the inner block of primary flight feathers stands out as a lighter unit. Although seemingly insignificant, this amounts to a sure-fire method of distinguishing the species. At around fifteen months, a root-and-branch moult unveils a new coat. Despite being far from adult-like, the emergence of pearly-grey plumage on some of the upperparts is a firm identification guide. Great Black-backed Gulls and Lesser Black-backed Gulls of equivalent age upgrade to dark back plumage, not clean pale grey.

LESSER BLACK-BACKED GULL *Larus fuscus*

For the most part only here during spring and summer, Lesser Black-backed Gull is a 'front-of-house' player in urban areas. Rooftop colonies exist in several cities and whinnying calls fill streets below. Adults with young nearby perceive humans as unwelcome and – understandably – sometimes attack. Slate-grey upperparts and legs as vivid as egg yolk render adults unmistakeable and undeniably elegant. At rest, youngsters are often identical to Herring Gull peers. However, the spread wing provides an infallible guide: juvenile and first-winter Lesser Black-backed Gulls have dark inner primaries.

GREAT BLACK-BACKED GULL *Larus marinus*

With a cosh for a bill and boxer shoulders, the big podge is not short of macho accoutrements and is capable of killing rabbits. The silhouette is distinctive: a bull in feathers. Ergo, immature Great Black-backed Gulls can be identified on profile alone. Pink-legged adults are, by a degree, darker-backed than Lesser Black-backed Gulls. Large white 'jabs of paint' at the tip of the wing clinch identification. Compared to brown-pigmented young Herring Gulls, juvenile and first-winter Great Black-backed Gulls are more monochrome and chequered, with a whiter head and, in flight, a snowy rear framed by a narrower inky tail band (or series of concentric bars). The full sweep of the outer wing is basically dark. Unlike a young Herring Gull, a well-demarcated pale 'window' is not appreciable on the inner primaries of a moving bird. Great Black-backed Gulls live along the coast. They patronise harbours and do not loiter around fast-food outlets. When settling on water among inferior hordes they plane to a halt on massive wings and put down like a heavily laden bomber among lightweight fighters.

BLACK-HEADED GULL *Chroicocephalus ridibundus*

'Seagull' is a term that is barely earned by this agile and cheerfully noisy occupant of coast, inland waterways and fields everywhere. They follow the plough and cackling, circling flocks are as commonplace as pigeons in urban areas. Year-round presence is complicated and masks a busy, well-travelled lifestyle. Adults attain courtship signage, a chocolate-brown hood, as early as January. During March they depart to breed. For many the destination is the Baltic States. Thanks to tameness, ringed birds whose number codes have been read in car parks, reveal a regular transit from the shores of Lough Neagh to Lithuania. Truthfully, Ireland is home because the birds return to moult during summer and spend almost two-thirds of the year here. Irish colonies exist on islands on lakes and sea loughs. A proportion of offspring emigrates and probably emulates British youngsters, some of which travel to Africa. At all times, red legs and bill distinguish Black-headed Gulls; wine red on adults during the breeding season and orange-tinted in young birds. As early as July the masked head begins to disappear through moult. During the rest of the year the head is white, save for blackish 'headphones'. Juveniles are ginger-brown above with beautifully patterned, tortoiseshell upperparts. They are strikingly different from their parents until, in late summer, they moult and become pearl-grey above; some brown coverts are retained through the following spring. Not until they are almost two years of age will final traces of parvenu plumage be replaced. Only then will they be accepted as breeding partners. All ages show a blinding white leading edge to both the upperwing and underwing. In flight, young birds during their first winter possess a black tail band and the clash of brown youthful plumage, leavened by the acquisition of some pristine adult-like upperparts, produces a piebald wing pattern.

COMMON GULL Top, left and centre: adult winter (head streaked); right: first-winter. Upper middle row, far left: adult breeding plumage; centre left: second-winter; centre right: first-winter; far right: juvenile. **BLACK-HEADED GULL** Lower middle row, left: first-winter; centre: adult winter; right: adult breeding plumage. Lower left (standing) and lower right (swimming): juvenile. Bottom row, from left: four first-winters (out of focus) and (bottom right) adult moulting into breeding plumage.

COMMON GULL *Larus canus*

In terms of plumage, adult Common Gull is similar to Herring Gull. At rest, each is white-bodied and grey-backed. In flight, a shared pattern consists of a black wing tip dabbed with white. Where, then, do distinctions between the two lie? Size is one. Common Gull is scarcely larger than a Black-headed Gull and is dwarfed by Herring Gull. Singletons – or even homogeneous flocks – are also recognisable by structure. Common Gull is a gentle version of Herring Gull. A dove-like head and dark eye are peacenik attributes reinforced by a slim bill, designed to tug earthworms out of pasture and sports fields. All ages appear streamlined, lightly built and 'well mannered'. The species is not demonstrative and, except on breeding territory, is generally quiet. Among a raucous melee of bread-snatching Black-headed Gulls, opportunist Common Gulls tend to keep shtum, although they do have a voice – a pleasant canine whinny, as commemorated in the Latin name. Adult bill colour brightens to lemon in spring then fades to lime during summer and develops an asymmetric dark band that persists during winter. Unlike Herring Gull, the leg colour is yellow or greenish in all but one-year-olds. With practice, the adult wing pattern becomes easy to recognise. Bordering a dark tip, two large white blobs fuse and form a roundel surrounded by a sea of black. On Herring Gull, the amount of white is insufficient to form a 'bulls-eye'. Young Common Gulls have a grey saddle that contrasts with brown, neatly edged wing coverts. Their white tail has a black terminal band and the (blackish-tipped) bill and legs are dull pink; on some, bill colour is as bright as nail polish. Common Gulls do not develop a hood but sport a variably streaked head during winter. Ireland's breeding population has declined over the past four decades and the vast majority now breed on lake islands in Connacht and Ulster. During late autumn, influxes arrive from Scandinavia.

ROCK DOVE *Columba livia*

All modern birds evolved around 2 million years ago, during the Pleistocene period, when our planet was restructured through natural processes. Fossils from ancient aeons establish the existence of roughly 900 species that are still with us today, pigeons included. Quite when *Columba livia* diverged from an older ancestor is unknown but, as a species, Rock Dove has been a citizen of earth for many millennia.

Feral Pigeons are derived from wild Rock Doves and have been domesticated longer than any other bird. Mesopotamian writings and Egyptian hieroglyphics show they had been tamed by 3,000 BC and domestication could date back to 10,000 BC (Blechman 2007). Breeders of birds, animals and plants produce strains sourced from the natural variety present within wild species. By ensuring that offspring survive, the artificially derived population is maintained. In the wild, variability forges small mutations that only endure if they are an improvement. In a nutshell, this is evolution. Even Darwin was amazed at the myriad types of Feral Pigeons spawned from one wild ancestor. Today, the world is populated with infinitely more feral 'Rock Doves' than unblemished forebears. Moreover, across the bird's native range – from Ireland through Europe to the Middle East and North Africa – feral individuals freely intermingle and breed with Rock Doves. Where populations are small and isolated (the species is sedentary and does not migrate) the gene pool can be swamped and any trace of the natural type is diluted through inbreeding. The result around Ireland's rocky coast has been a steady replacement of the pristine by the impure. Only in remote parts of the west have populations managed to avoid adulteration, although even there strays arrive and, naturally, attempt to join the breeding ranks of wild brethren.

Feeding birds ambulate at ground level by flexing the legs and shuffling quickly forwards. Food is mainly small seeds and, if available, grain. Rock Doves have the longest breeding season of all Irish birds because the sexual organs only regress in response to shortening daylight during the depths of winter. Distinctions between Rock Doves and Feral Pigeons are more than feather deep. Rock Doves are broader in the beam and slightly shorter-tailed; they look heart-shaped in outline when viewed from above. The bill is more slender and the cere (a twin-sided pad at the base of the bill) is consistently smaller. Adult females are slightly less colourful than males, although the difference is only appreciated when seen together. Juveniles have smoky eyes and dusty-pink feet. Seen well, real McCoy adults are a delight. Ladybird eyes and mother-of-pearl neck iridescence flash during social interactions. Feeding flocks are permanently poised on a hair trigger and flee noisily at high speed. Along cliff lines, escape flights hug contours, presenting grey topsides relieved by a sharp-sided white rump often invisible at rest but unmissable from above in flight.

Researchers in California (Palleroni 2005), over a seven-year period, compared the proportions of successful attacks by Peregrines on urban flocks of Feral Pigeons containing both white and plain-rumped varieties. Peregrines caught far more plain-rumped birds. The researchers concluded that, during high-speed swerves, the blink of the white dorsal patch momentarily wrong-footed the assailant. An inference from a wild Rock Dove population

ROCK DOVE
Six adults are shown. Although sexes are broadly similar, females (top, second from left; bottom row, centre) have a smaller cere – the bulbous bare skin surrounding the nostril at the base of bill. Flying bird, pursued by Peregrine, shows white rump plumage normally obscured at rest.

FERAL PIGEON By selective breeding from Rock Doves, many varieties of pigeon have arisen. Offspring are genetically viable and interbreed with each other and with populations of wild Rock Doves whose uniqueness, as a result, is being lost.

on the Faeroe Islands, where dark morphs were occasionally produced yet failed to persist (Salomonson 1935), appears to substantiate this contention. During 2006–2013, two interloping Feral Pigeons were the only witnessed fatalities to Peregrines among roughly thirty-five Rock Doves on Inishbofin, County Galway, both of which stood out due to plumage anomalies (A. McGeehan). Some authorities (Murton & Clarke 1968) have indeed argued that, were it not for Rock Dove's anti-predator colouring, the latent – genetically recessive – tendency to melanism would emerge as a dominant stereotype. One advantage of dark feathers is that they are stronger and abrade less easily than pale plumage. If urban Feral Pigeons represent an evolutionary test-bed then it would seem that darker, more uniform plumage is favoured. However, when survival-of-the-fittest rules are applied, the tables are turned and white-rumped fliers persist in any preyed-upon population.

WOODPIGEON *Columba palumbus*

Despite grande-dame proportions – big-boned and heavyweight – Woodpigeon is remarkably light-footed, as evidenced by delicate craning to pluck out-of-reach berries and scissoring tiny segments off cloverleaves before swallowing. Adults have yellow rheumy eyes and a bulbous 'Irish navvy' forehead. White neck furrowing suggests smears of toothpaste or a map cartouche.

WOODPIGEON Top row (three right-hand birds) and both middle rows. Juvenile – lacks white brooch on neck – at right in lower middle row. **STOCK DOVE** Bottom row and (flying) top left.

Youngsters are dark-eyed and grey-necked. Whatever age, airborne signage consists of a white half-moon on the wing's knuckle. When startled into flight, thrust is maximised by deep beats slapping the wings together on the upstroke. Displaying birds use the same ploy, this time using the sound to draw attention. An undulating Big Dipper, climbing high with clattering wingbeats and then descending like a swooping marionette, is a sight regularly seen alongside motorways. Perhaps Woodpigeons have an engineer's mind because they have a preference for flying in straight lines. Settled birds revert to producing in-house sound. The deep accent is foggy and cranked up by inflated air sacs located in the side of the neck. Perched Billy Bunters pulse to the rhythm and lean forwards. Cooing starts erratically in the first quarter of new year and continues until autumn. The verse seems to be a basic salutation rather than a territorial proclamation. Many published recordings miss the opening salvo, which is distinct from the subsequent two or three verses, each of which is identical. The first verse has four notes; all others have five notes. Put another way, the first verse is missing a note, the AWOL component being the second note, which is included in the following three or four verses. Confused? Part of the problem with the way field guides represent sound is the use of phonetics. Lines of vowels and consonants rarely convey the sense of what is heard. As a 'cheat', try the following. First four notes: *Who cooks for you?* Second and subsequent verses: *Who NOW cooks for you?* The new word, 'now' is emphasised. It may be slightly higher, louder or more slurred. The point is, it stands out. The opening verse is delivered more softly than those that follow, making it sometimes inaudible. Indoors listening shielded by double-glazing can filter out the sotto voce opening line. The ditty ends with an optional single note, which feels like a full stop. Woodpigeons habitually flock. Numbers are greatest in winter, all the more so because of communal roosting. Immigration is low-key. The species seldom flies out to sea and is a rare visitor to western islands, despite being common on adjacent mainland. An annual large-scale exodus from northern Europe does not result in significant arrivals in Britain where, as in Ireland, winter concentrations appear to consist of local birds en masse.

STOCK DOVE *Columba oenas*

An uncommon and timid species, Stock Dove is unlikely to be seen in gardens. Smaller than a Woodpigeon and superficially like a Rock Dove, a virtual lack of any prominent field marks conspire with a retiring nature to bolster anonymity. What is more, Stock Doves are not particularly social. Seeds, leaves, buds and flowers of cultivated ground are a mainstay. Or were. Agricultural land has become a mean street and Stock Doves a casualty. Distribution is patchy with most in eastern parts. Wintertime Woodpigeon flocks feeding on grain fields may harbour a few. In flight, Stock Dove is smaller, shorter-tailed and rounder-winged than Woodpigeon. The head is neat and held in a distinctive pose with the bill pointing downwards. The wing pattern – grey hemmed with dark – leaves the central wing looking curiously blank. The lack of a white rump and grey underwings exclude Rock Dove. At rest, plumage signage is low-key. Two half-hearted bars straddle the folded hind-wing. However, with a bluer colour cast than any of its cousins and an endearing dark eye, Stock Dove is really the fairest of the tribe. Pairs nest in holes. Trunk cavities created when large branches are shed, rabbit holes, and nooks among the masonry of abandoned wallsteads are used. The bird's name is derived from 'stoc', Old English for tree stump, reflecting choice of tree hollows as a breeding site. Calls are deep yet impetuous. A bassoon-like *oo-er-oo* is repeated several times and reaches a peak of orgasmic frisson before stopping abruptly.

COLLARED DOVE *Streptopelia decaocto*

Younger readers will not remember a time when this beige, spool-shaped dove was not part of Ireland's parks and gardens. In the wake of a spectacular march across Europe that began in the 1930s, colonists vaulted the Irish Sea in the 1960s. Even today, a pioneering spirit manifests itself. Youngsters launch themselves and arrive, usually in May, on islands off the west coast unsuited to breeding. Undaunted, they leave but nobody knows if they turn around and look for *Lebensraum* near their birthplace or if they disappear out to sea, questing for Utopia but likely to meet a watery grave. A few stragglers have reached Iceland.

COLLARED DOVE Top left: fresh juvenile (forehead and chin bare, no collar, pale feet). Middle and lower left: older youngsters with mixture across upperparts of pale-fringed juvenile feathers and browner, later-grown (adult-type) feathers. Bottom right, adult (neck ring deep, plain upperparts, red feet). Top right, probable adult.

Juveniles lack the Ash Wednesday half-collar on the side of neck and their plumage often combines two shades of fawn. Many of the first feathers were grown in the nest and are paler with delicate pale fringes. Once independent, 'latecomer', more adult-like plumage emerges from tracts that have not yet produced feathers. The population surge was achieved by an ability to wean squabs on crop milk, produced by both parents. On the one hand, this limits the number of young per brood to two; on the other hand, multiple generations can be reared in a breeding season spanning March to September. Calling accompanies courtship; the sound repertoire includes a distinctive wing whirr. Especially around dawn during late spring and summer, endless song repetitions can be as infuriating as a vuvuzela. Soloists like to perch on rooftops and aerials out of reach of disturbed slumberers. Unlike the deeper, mostly five-noted cooing of Woodpigeon, Collared Dove's phrase has only three notes: *who who, huh*. Series are long (exceptionally up to 25 verses) and the rhythm may change when *huh* is dropped: *who who, huh … who who … who who*. Hearing a couplet for the first time, some listeners understandably proudly announce that they have just heard 'the Cuckoo'.

CUCKOO *Cuculus canorus*

Male Cuckoos start calling upon their return from Africa in late April. Curiously, they appear to reach all parts of Ireland simultaneously, suggesting that some arrive by overseas routes that make landfall in Munster as well as along the Irish Sea coast. In contrast, July departures of adults, followed by juveniles in August and September, are thought to be largely via Britain towards the Mediterranean. Youngsters from Ireland have been recovered in Holland and Italy. Migration then carries them southwards to the Congo. Tracking of British-tagged males (www.bto.org/cuckoos) has been revelatory. Most spent no more than eight weeks on breeding territory. By mid-July several had crossed the Sahara; one made the 3,000km trip from Sicily to Lake Chad in just three days.

Although the same length as Collared Dove, Cuckoo is longer-tailed. In almost all other aspects, it resembles a small hawk. Unlike true birds of prey, however, it is thin-billed. Further distinguishing marks include a small head, a dark fan-shaped tail with a white tip and an eye-catching pale underwing tract. Without the trademark call, the species would slip unseen through bushy countryside and moorland, haunt of its chief victim, Meadow Pipit. Its cheating habits make the bird an outcast. Songbirds mob it, playing into the Cuckoo's hands in the process (see THERE IS ALWAYS ONE, p. 32). Females sport a fawn wash across the chest and broadcast a subtle bubbling trill, while both sexes utter a hard, gagging *gowk* when rivals are nearby. Stationary callers crane forwards and sway the tail. Caterpillars and beetles are captured from a perch. The bird drops to the ground and shuffles awkwardly like a pantomime dame before lunging at prey that seems incongruously small. Juveniles come in shades of brown or slate and are even more hawk-like than their parents, including a barred throat and underparts. A tuft of loose white nape feathering is probably an attempt to mimic

CUCKOO Adults have hawk-like silhouette, plumage and flight style. However, the small bill and light stripe across the underwing are reliable distinctions. Juvenile on p. 34.

a nestling Sparrowhawk. The artifice is reinforced by aggressive behaviour and a formidable red gape, opened wide like the bow of a receiving mother ship. Given the prolonged fledging period and sustained conspicuous begging, the hawk-like impersonation is designed to ward off crows and ground predators. Should all else fail, the feisty orphan produces foul-smelling faeces if handled.

LONG-EARED OWL *Asio otus*

The species name is unfortunate but we are stuck with it. Normally flat and invisible, the 'ears' are tufts, raised to startle when a roosting bird is rumbled during daytime. Small birds mob detected owls furiously. In reality, the sprig of plumage looks no more intimidating than an archbishop's leylandii eyebrows. Even to a human, the bird's glowering orange eyes are scarier. Long-eared Owls are secretive and elusive. Mature timber lies at the heart of most breeding territories. Innocuous disused crow nests are used for breeding and an incubating owl resembles a jumble of lichen-encrusted flattened sticks. Bats, frogs and roosting songbirds are all nabbed, although rodents form the mainstay. Often the first clue to presence is the sound of large young calling to be fed. The sound is remarkably like a squeaky gate swinging in the dark. One reason why adults escape detection is because, throughout most of the year, they are silent. Even the male's courtship flight, during which the wings are clapped together below the line of the body, can pass unnoticed. Famous for roosting communally during winter, several congregate year after year in the same location, such as thick corsets of ivy around wide trunks

LONG-EARED OWL Adults and (right inset) partly fledged juveniles. Although youngsters remain hidden, often perched among a tall conifer, their 'unoiled gate' begging call is a bead to presence.

or dense sprays of foliage in Scots Pine canopy. 'Whitewash' on branches and regurgitated pellets containing indigestible bones, mandibles and fur lying on the ground below are a clue. Immigrants from Scandinavia, mainly Norway, arrive in autumn. Airborne and caught in the glare of headlights, the paleness of the underwings is exaggerated and the apparition can look ghostly, erroneously suggesting a Barn Owl.

BARN OWL *Tyto alba*

Ireland's population of Barn Owls stands at a paltry 450 pairs. Most are in Munster and parts of Leinster. Hunting grounds consist of rough pasture, overgrown ditches and interfaces where tussocky and gappy vegetation adjoin tree cover: a commuting network for rodent traffic. Motorway verges, especially steep banks sown with saplings, amount to patches of pioneer woodland, beloved by furry prey. Unfortunately, given the speed of modern traffic, such habitats are death traps. Barn Owls float and weigh not much more than the herald angels that they resemble. Buffeted by air turbulence and suction, more than 1 per cent of the nation's population can be slain in a single year. Some measures have been taken to mitigate the carnage, although much more is spent to prettify roadsides with mediocre public art exhibits. Worse still, Barn Owls are resident and busy thoroughfares become permanent killing grounds that cull attempts at recolonisation.

In flight, Barn Owls are ghostly puppets-on-a-chain. The face is heart-shaped with dark, sleepy eyes. In Ireland, the species is strictly nocturnal, a lifestyle for which good night vision is a prerequisite. Although owl eyesight is more sensitive to low light levels than our own, moonless or cloudy nights curtail hunting. Hearing is more important. The face of a Barn Owl is a listening dish containing two forward-facing ears that are placed asymmetrically to pinpoint low-frequency sounds. Payne (1971) demonstrated Barn Owl's reliance on sound as its key hunting sense. Confined to flying around an enclosed space where mice were provided, light levels were steadily reduced to pitch darkness over several days. Thanks to the rustle of quarry among a floor of leaves, hunts were still successful. To eliminate sound, foam rubber was added as a substrate. Movements made by a mouse could no longer be discerned so a dry, swishing leaf was attached to the animal's tail. Swoops were made on the leaf, not the mouse. An acquired knowledge of the darkened hunting space also proved to be essential. If moved to another pitch-dark room, the owl was reluctant to fly even when the telltale patter of dinner was audible. Soft-toothed edges to the flight feathers ensure that owl wings are noiseless, enabling long legs and claws to skewer silently. Furthermore, one of the foot's outer toes is reversible, which makes the grip versatile. A ghoulish, hissing shriek is sometimes given in flight. Because breeding abodes include secluded nooks in abandoned mansions and tumbledown Blair Witch wallsteads, the sound has a banshee pedigree.

BARN OWL Although a Barn Owl's flight looks stiff – as though the wings are splints – the action is soundless. The disc-shaped face is a sound-capturing device and works in the same way as cupping your hands behind your ears to concentrate and pinpoint sound.

GREAT SPOTTED WOODPECKER *Dendrocopos major*

As an outpost of Europe, Ireland pays dearly by way of a dearth of wildlife either unable or unwilling to grace our shores. Woodpeckers have not inhabited Irish woodland for centuries. Timber clearance that accompanied settlement during the late sixteenth century and which continued until the twentieth century consigned any surviving Great Spotted Woodpeckers to extinction. Philip O'Sullivan Beare, exiled to Spain in 1602 after the Battle of Kinsale, linked the bird with the Ireland of his childhood. In 1625, he wrote: 'the woodpecker is very common in Ireland. A bird of several colours: white, black, red, beautiful bluish, with a longish tail, strong beak and hooked nails with which it can hollow out trees and build its nest …' (O'Sullivan 2009). The attribution of 'bluish' is consistent with the bluish gloss of Great Spotted Woodpecker's black crown, back and rump (Cramp 1977–94). Furthermore, femurs found amongst Bronze Age remains in County Clare consolidate the bird's Irish credentials.

Sporadically, winter visitors arrived from Scandinavia, precipitated by high population levels or food shortages in their homeland. When this happens a migratory urge develops and some disperse southwest before returning home in spring. Based on minor differences in plumage and structure, strays reaching Ireland were assigned as Viking nomads, not pioneering colonists. Very occasionally a British emigrant came west, deemed a considerable feat for a sedentary race believed to be virtually allergic to sea crossings.

During the last century, events in Britain led to a nationwide spread. Maturing conifer plantations were tapped for nest holes and food. By wedging cones in clefts, pine seeds could be extracted. In places, the food supply was almost inexhaustible. One bird worked over 3,000 cones in six weeks. An increasingly catholic choice of habitat, including hillside birch woods, well-timbered parks and gardens replete with peanuts and fat-balls, aided the boom. A less endearing habit is that of chiselling into occupied nest boxes: in Sussex, four pairs attacked over one-third of 190 nest boxes, devouring 113 young titmice (Mountfort 1962). The BTO's Common Bird Census and the Breeding Bird Survey are the strongest indicators of population trends of British birds. During 1970–2001, Great Spotted Woodpecker showed the fourth highest level of increase, 185 per cent (Tate & Tyler 2005). By 1994 Britain's population was estimated at 40,000 pairs and, by 2010, numbers were still rising. All the same, the propensity of a few recruits to cross the Irish Sea still came as a shock. Probably, the sight of distant land was sufficient to trigger exploratory flights. The main axes of expansion, from Galloway into County Down and from North Wales to Leinster – the Isle of Man was probably also a vital stepping stone – suggests that Ireland had merely to be seen to be explored, especially by youngsters yet to establish territory. By 2005, Irish reports started to amount to more than just flashes in the pan. The first breeding pair was discovered in County Down in 2006 but others soon followed, from County Antrim to County Wexford, with a concentration in County Wicklow. A steady blitzkrieg has continued. Just after the turn of the millennium, the Irish Wildlife Trust announced plans to reintroduce Great Spotted Woodpeckers. Fortunately such eugenic manipulation of the country's birdlife was rendered stillborn by the very creatures

GREAT SPOTTED WOODPECKER Top left: juvenile (probably male due to extensive red crown); bottom left, adult male; right, adult female. Right: groove used to wedge cones prior to hammering them open.

themselves: proof that the best policy is to let nature take its course, although by all means restore habitats or redress a balance that was once natural.

Great Spotted Woodpeckers are unmistakeable, as are their vocalisations. Drumming, whereby the bird strikes a dead branch with a series of rapid blows producing a machine-gun resonance, is heard during late winter and spring. It is initiated by the male and is the equivalent of song. A sharp *tchik!* is a clue to presence throughout the year. Nest holes are seldom used more than two years in succession although a new chamber may be excavated nearby. Young are fed a wide variety of invertebrates. Freshly fledged red-capped juveniles, clambering about in the vicinity of the nest, are rarely of similar size and come in 'steps and stairs' due to the habit of woodpeckers beginning incubation as soon as the first egg is laid, resulting in unsynchronised hatching.

MAGPIE *Pica pica*

By sight or sound Magpies are unmistakeable and are, like all birds, intrinsically beautiful. Moreover, being a member of the crow family means that the bird is avian Mensa material. Just as Cuckoos are genetically programmed to cheat by laying an egg in another bird's nest, thereby inflicting loss on the foster parent's brood, Magpies are born pirates that reconnoitre songbird homes within their breeding territory and then plunder them. The righteous suffer while the wicked prosper. Moral argument aside, the impact of such behaviour should not, long term, jeopardise the supply of stolen eggs and young. However, if sustained by other factors – availability of roadkill, animal feed and food waste – Magpies proliferate. Such basic birds-and-bees truths would, you might think, be common knowledge. In reality, the harm done by the villain has been glossed over. Magpie predation of songbirds and vulnerable others, notably Ireland's dwindling Lapwings, is presented as a process by which a scientific-sounding 'doomed surplus' (RSPB 2007) is tapped. This is fallacious – no species invests time in producing offspring prefigured to perish – but it reassures a concerned public that observe raids on broods of garden birds at first-hand. Are opinion leaders purblind or is callous indifference being shown? As it is an unsavoury topic, bird protection charity memberships might be lost if culling of Magpies was to be condoned, nay advocated. Establishing facts is difficult and are not helped by contradictory research. Despite publication in scientific journals, some data are dubiously interpreted yet cited as if holy writ, exonerating Magpies of suppressing songbird numbers. For Britain, Gooch *et al.* (1991) retrospectively compared a nationwide increase in Magpies during 1966–1986 and found that, during the same period, overall songbird nest success did not decline, nor was it linked to Magpie density on farmland or woodland. 'Density' is key and crunching global numbers is hardly a restless search for True Light. Groom (1993) conducted fieldwork on parkland sites within Manchester during three breeding seasons and reached opposite conclusions: 'Fewer than five per cent of Blackbird nests produced young. Predation caused most of the failures … of identified predation, the majority was attributable to Magpies. The results suggest that Blackbird populations in urban parkland would be unlikely

to maintain themselves [unless] sustained by immigration from other habitats.' In other words, exposed to high densities of Magpies, songbirds take a significant hit. However, three years of research in the suburbs of Paris (Chiron & Julliard 2006) found much less impact on songbird populations, although the authors urged caution in their conclusions: 'because the colonisation of Magpies is not finished in urban areas.' On Irish islands, Song Thrush often becomes the victim. On a bad day, listening to the chain of panic from distraught thrushes traces murderous actions.

MAGPIE Like all crows, Magpies (top row) mate for life and remain on home turf throughout the year. **JAY** The most colourful of crows, the fretwork of blue feathering on the outer wing is used as a fishing fly. Although shy, its raucous calls easily belie its presence.

JAY *Garrulus glandarius*

Jays are secretive and wary, a pity because they are sublime. Flight views reveal a conspicuous white rump, highlighted by a black tail and accompanied by the most raucous one-off squawk of the crow tribe. Short fat wings produce a peculiar stroke. The bird lurches through the air like a mother duck flailing the water when leading ducklings out of danger. Jays gambol rather than fly through tree canopy; the scampering silhouette can be mistaken for a squirrel. Once rare, the bird is increasing, making appearances in leafy suburban gardens and startling beginner birdwatchers into thinking that they have discovered an exotic rarity. Jays are almost exclusive to forest. They eat a variety of foods, including an unfortunate fondness for songbird eggs and chicks, but acorns are the most important. Each autumn, thousands are buried and then dug up and eaten during the rest of the year. Because some are missed, the bird is inadvertently responsible for sowing oak saplings that spring up above or beyond the timberline. Ireland's Jays are resident and may have been with us since the last Ice Age, around 10,000 years ago. Commencing in Tudor times, Irish woodland was decimated and several native birds became extinct. Jay might have been one of them. Migrants from Britain probably occasionally arrive and, as with recent recolonisation by Great Spotted Woodpecker, may have provided founders. However, Ireland's Jays are reputed to differ slightly from those across the water. Basically, the body plumage has an overall darker hue. Curiously, the middle pair of Jays in the plate is English and seems similar to the Irish Jay (below).

CHOUGH *Pyrrhocorax pyrrhocorax*

Ireland's Choughs live along the wild Atlantic coast and their twanging calls and eccentric mannerisms enhance the great outdoors. Airborne pairs and small groups rise and fall, as though bouncing off an invisible trampoline. Sharp nosedives are part of the performance. The broad blown-inside-out-umbrella wings are cupped against the body and their wrists are thrust forwards, morphing into a Stealth Bomber silhouette. Performers show gay abandon when riding updrafts along cliffs. At a distance, cavorting troupes resemble newspaper pages caught by the wind. In flight the red decurved bill looks straight. At rest its kinked shape becomes discernible, so too long red legs topped by black 'leg-warmer' thighs. Youngsters have a shorter, yellowish bill. A drunken sailor walk is interspersed with occasional pauses during which the bird strikes a rooster pose, flicks its wings and calls. The sound – an electric *chow* – begat the species name but the pronunciation has been lost in translation. Except for a black costume – leavened by a wondrous metallic purple and blue sheen – Choughs are scarcely crows at all. They are insectivorous and feed by probing, Curlew style, among short heather and grazed pasture adjoining headlands and low-lying coastal districts. Piles of decayed seaweed along storm beaches make a happy hunting ground. Likewise, shallow, friable earth is gold dust.

CHOUGH Like an artist's quirky signature in the margin of a frieze, Choughs embellish rock-hard coastal landscapes. Airborne antics are announced by namesake calls; the bird is a parrot dressed like a crow.

Free-draining and warmed by the sun, places such as exposed banks or the foundations of stonewall field boundaries are easily worked for ants and beetle larvae. Solitary pairs seek out a roomy rock cavity for nesting and are mostly silent in the breeding vicinity. Choughs disappeared from the coast of County Antrim when permanent pasture bounding cliff tops was converted into alternative use. For more detailed discussion, see McGeehan & Wyllie (2012).

JACKDAW *Corvus monedula*

Jackdaw may be Ireland's smallest member of the crow family but if a cocksure, pigeon-footed walk is anything to go by, it is the most confident and bullish. Frequent chuckling *Jack!* calls announce presence, and gangs or pairs are talkative. Other sounds include a snappy, querulous *kyow* and a double-note aptly used in Polish as the bird's name, *Kawka*. Intelligent yet mischievous, the bird delights in swooping over assembled flocks of other birds – roosting shorebirds or nesting terns – just for the hell of flushing them. If Jackdaws had matches they would be pyromaniacs. Unlike other crows, wing shape is neither rounded nor fingered, but tapered. Flight action is quick and often rapid enough to sow the seed of a cruising bird of prey rather than a lithe crow. A gregarious nature extends to uniquely coordinated wheeling flight manoeuvres, particularly in updrafts. Further hallmarks are a short, fairly stubby bill and whitish, goat-like eyes. Only the upperparts and fore-crown are truly black (juveniles are swarthier overall). A sooty face grades into slate-coloured underparts and the nape is ash-grey. Across the east European range there is a tendency for a whitish collar at the base of the nape. Some Irish winter visitors show this feature, thereby suggesting that they are far-travelled. An entirely different phenomenon that is occasionally noted in all bird plumages is the dilution of pigment or the appearance of pale, whitish patches. Such 'leucism' (from

JACKDAW Top left: adult emerging from nest cavity; bottom left: bill deformities occur in all birds – note the elongated bill tip; top right: East European Jackdaws show a frosty collar; some winter in Ireland; bottom right: piebald plumage is unusual, although not uncommon among crows.

Greek *leukos*, meaning white) is caused by a reduction in melanin, the pigment that darkens feathers to black or brown. For some reason, crows are prone to the condition. The Jackdaw (bottom right) and Hooded Crow (p. 167, top left) are examples. Jackdaws nest in holes and small colonies spring up in favoured nesting haunts such as quarry faces, abandoned mansions or aged Ash or Beech trees with heart rot. Their fascination with building nests in chimneys can result in a blocked flue and a fire hazard. In the depths of winter, males keep watch on the home place and some old hands roost there rather than join more populous gatherings with Rooks in tree plantations. Early in the new year, clacking hordes visit breeding sites. Established pairs maintain a lifelong bond and often feed together and snuggle against each other, for example, when sheltering under eaves during a downpour. They use the same nest site annually and domestic pride among neighbours leads to high jinx. A scene of harmonious living is deceptive. Hole-entering birds often emerge with pilfered nest material.

HOODED CROW *Corvus cornix* /
CARRION CROW *Corvus corone*

Ireland is the most far-flung outpost of the Hooded Crow. Across the Irish Sea, all-black Carrion Crows rule the roost, except in western Scotland where 'Hoodies' hold their own. Hooded Crows are generally encountered in pairs. Inland feeders eat earthworms and beetles – as well as carrion – whereas coastal inhabitants comb shorelines for shellfish and crabs, suggesting an aboriginal attachment to intertidal habitats. To extricate dinner, molluscs are dropped from on high. Man-made surfaces littered with shells testify to the ingenuity. Hooded and Carrion Crows share a stoic countenance. The bill's ridgeline (culmen) is noticeably decurved, unlike Rook's longer, more pointed and level-topped bill (see McGeehan & Wyllie 2012). Vocalists intone lazy 'Texas accent' caws. Calls are delivered in set pieces. Typical are two or three *kraah* notes repeated in a cycle of long gaps (anywhere between ten and thirty seconds). During calls, the body is elongated and the head is pumped. Broadcasts may elicit a response, most likely from the caller's mate. Compared directly, the two voices are not identical and differ slightly in pitch. Birds of prey are pinpointed with a grating, tar-voiced *grrikk* alarm.

Carrion Crows are regular along the east coast, chiefly in Ulster and Leinster, areas that face Carrion Crow populations in southwest Scotland and north Wales. In Scotland, Carrion Crows have pushed west and former Hooded Crow country has been subsumed. A dearth of Hooded Crow observations across the water suggests that movements are one way. To Thompson (1849–52) Carrion Crow was a rarity, occasionally encountered 'in the north, east and [curiously] west of the island'. A degree of scepticism attaches to west-coast claims; some museum specimens from eastern counties have been found to be young Rooks (Ussher & Warren 1900). As recently as the 1950s (Kennedy, Ruttledge & Scroope 1954) the bird was still classified as a 'rare vagrant … [that] has interbred with Hooded Crows in Dublin, Down and Antrim.' A fresh impetus in

HOODED CROW Top row, left: individual with abnormal pale patches on outer wing (not infrequent in Hooded Crow and Carrion Crow). Top row, centre: Hooded Crow. **CARRION CROW** Top row, right. Middle row: three birds. **HOODED x CARRION CROW** Lower row, paired with Hooded Crow (right). Bottom: Hooded Crow nest.

the new millennium has led to the establishment of an annually reinforced bridgehead; autumn influxes are followed by spring emigration. Around the County Down coast it is possible, during winter, to see equal numbers of both. In zones where the two meet, mixed pairings produce hybrids. Progeny, even from the same nest, are a hodgepodge. There appears to be no basis for believing that the sex of one parent exerts dominance on the genetic shadow cast over offspring. Variation generates dusky Carrion Crow-types that ghost the pattern of Hooded Crow, to piebald Hooded Crow-types with black scapulars and abdomen. As well as clear-cut hybrids, the plumage of others in the same general vicinity is undermined by minor inconsistencies, such as Hooded Crows that are slightly darker than normal and whose grey scapulars are, to a variable extent, dark-centred. At the other extreme, some 'Carrion Crows' show smoky grey whorls among black undertail plumage. On the other hand, brown wings and tail are a hallmark of normal fading. Young crows moult juvenile body plumage in autumn but not the wings and tail. A pose that seems peculiar to Carrion Crow arises when head plumage is raised, principally across the nape. This creates a bigheaded, lion's-mane appearance.

Hybrids may be fertile but research in an Italian contact zone suggests that they produce fewer chicks. If such lower fecundity were confirmed, then pure pairs would, in the long run, overhaul the reproductive contribution of hybrids. Not surprisingly, both species prefer to mate with purebred counterparts. Plumage character is not the only criterion that determines mate selection. Behaviour and choice of foraging habitat may drive mating preferences. In Sweden, a northward spread of grassland farming is believed to have aided Carrion Crow at the expense of Hooded Crow. Quite why Carrion Crows are reaching Ireland with increasing regularity is a mystery. Is the species enjoying a boom in Britain and sending recruits west in search of *terra nova*? While early pioneers had to make do with cousins as breeding partners, subsequent arrivals are swelling mate choice. Careful interpretation is needed. Rather than a breeding increase per se, the rise in sightings may, for now, reflect a change in the scale of numbers wintering in Ireland.

ROOK *Corvus frugilegus*

Rook has a more enunciated, plummy accent than the drawling caw of a Hooded Crow. Gabbling is part and parcel of a busybody lifestyle, although young Rooks are seen but not heard during their first winter. Adults are sometimes caught off guard, lost in a quiet reverie that sounds like the creaks of a galleon at anchor. From dawn, workers disperse from overnight roosts and scatter over fields and waysides – they are commonest in wooded, agricultural landscapes – picking and poking with a bill resembling a bony banana. Flocks, spread over grassland with Jackdaws or following the plough with gulls, make a familiar sight. They walk with swinging hips but occasionally hop, as though suddenly prodded by a hatpin. Time-outs for cawing are frequent. The bird pauses, points forwards and declaims a salvo of notes, pumping and ruffling its plumage. Foraging resumes and the caller 'falls in' like an infantryman taking up duty among a company. Diet includes unearthed grain and grubs: a combination that offsets bad with good in the mind of most farmers. Rook society is highly ordered and deferential bowing reaches Japanese proportions. Gossiping peaks just before bedtime, when groups from disparate districts assemble in favoured timber redoubts to pass the night. Stick nests dot tree canopies; large colonies straggle for hundreds of metres. Refurbishment starts as soon as daytime lengthens in the new year and unwanted nests are stripped down and recycled. Young Rooks are shorter-billed than adults. Black feathering sheaths the inner half of the upper mandible and surrounds the base of the bill. This pattern is dramatically different from an adult, which has a bare bill and pimply whitish skin on the throat. In autumn, young Rooks often consort in dark-billed peer groups and wander, strongly resembling Carrion Crows, from which distinctions are subtle. On a young Rook, the crown has a domed peak and the forehead meets the bill at a sharp angle. In addition, the bill profile is lumpy at the base but relatively flat towards the tip. Overall, the head and bill say 'Concorde'. On Carrion Crow, the crown is sleek and rounded and the bill's culmen is curved – resembling a butter knife. See McGeehan & Wyllie (2012) for further points of separation.

RAVEN *Corvus corax*

Ravens have presence. The biggest and blackest of crows, a meat-cleaver bill and tar-lined voice box cement the impression that Mr Big likes cigarettes and biker leathers. Deep and croaking calls are versatile and may amount to conversation pieces. Acquaintances holler to each other.

ROOK Top left: first-winter; top right and upper middle row: adults. **RAVEN** Lower middle row (left): juvenile harried by Hooded Crows; bottom left: perched juvenile. Lower middle row (right) and bottom right: adults.

A questioning '*Gruk, gruk, gruk?*' elicits a disgruntled '*Quok, quok*'. Nattering may continue for as long as a tennis set and exchanges are batted back and forth like a tiebreak. Perched on sentinel crags, the callers' silhouettes impart gusto. A talking head leans forwards and the throat distends. Akin to a pumping Adam's apple, a shaggy sable beard pulsates to the rhythm. The basso profundo has all the charm of an extra in a horror movie. Airborne, its Edward Scissorhands wing tip and whumping wingbeat engender a sinister 'flying undertaker' character. Menace is palpable. Sheep carrion has nearly doubled numbers across Ireland's uplands in recent decades but the vulnerable and weak – including baby birds and sickly gulls – also constitute fair game. Ravens have a hunting streak and the wherewithal to become angels of death. Starlings converging at roost have more to fear than dusk raids from Peregrines and Sparrowhawks; their attackers may include villainous Stuka-diving Ravens. But enough of the bad PR! Ravens are regal. Most times the wing shape is long and tapering. The deeply slotted primaries are raked back into a loose point and circling birds suggest a big-boned falcon rather than a crow. Flight profile is streamlined; the head and bill protrude, as does the spool-shaped tail (depending on flight attitude, more like a fan). Ravens fly high and soar. They are disliked by Hooded Crows. Gruff caws from a renegade band of lesser crows often draw attention to a passing caliph. The sovereign shakes off the rabble with a few deft half-rolls and continues, deriding the riff-raff with a sonorous honk.

BLUE TIT *Cyanistes caeruleus*

Blue Tit has become the poster child of the wild-bird food market. Males are more colourful, noticeable when members of a pair are compared. Like all celebrities whose mugshot is used in advertising, there is an element of retouching. In Blue Tit's case, colour saturation is overcooked, leading to complaints that a nesting pair is drab and second rate. Indeed, there is a belief that urban dwellers are grimy through exposure to pollution. Yet, with each moult for the first three or four years of life, plumage should become more vibrant. Research into variation in carotenoids in tit diet (chemicals with nutritive properties and that exist in the pigment of feathers, fruit and vegetables) focused on sexual, seasonal and environmental variation (Isaksson *et al.* 2007). Carotenoids have dual functions in establishing feather pigment and producing essential vitamins. Researchers found that urban titmice were in poorer condition

BLUE TIT Middle row, left: adult male. Bottom row (l–r): male and two females. Variation in yellow hue is linked to diet and also food variability between years. Blue Tits see the UV spectrum of light and females assess reflectance from male crown plumage to pick a mate. **GREAT TIT** Top left: adult male; top right and middle, right: female. Centre, upper: juvenile (atypical whitish plumage probably diet-related).

than rural birds, resulting in duller hues. Irrespective of age, by late summer the plumage of breeding birds is close to its expiry date. Only the tips of the feathers of the underparts are yellow, the bases are sooty. Hence, wear and tear exposes underlying darkness, which can despoil appearance and cause blotching or a 'thinning hair' appearance with dark tramlines peeping through yellow plumage. Like other family members, Blue Tits have stout, sharp bills. Hard food items are clasped, if necessary, below one foot and pummelled with pecks. The feeding action is anything but genteel yet the 'sweet and cute' esteem in which the bird is held has led to bird illustrators downsizing the bill. Juveniles have yellow cheeks and a greenish cap. Breeding strategy is high risk. Just a single brood is produced to coincide with the greatest abundance of small, nutritious caterpillars. Up to a dozen eggs are laid in woodland that, if the season is kind, will be replete with caterpillars. In gardens, clutches tend to be only half this size (Hume & Cady 1979). Unlike Great Tit and Coal Tit, much of Blue Tit's vocabulary contains trills and pure notes 'trembled' in a high key. In other respects the bird is, like its peers, a polyglot (see p. 102).

GREAT TIT *Parus major*

The largest of the tribe, Great Tits can be told from other black-capped species not only by size but also by yellow underparts bisected by a black bandolier. In males, the black band widens behind the legs and extends over the ventral region. Youngsters have washed-out, duller colours and pale yellow (not white) cheeks. In flight, white outer tail feathers catch the eye. Because both Blue Tit and Coal Tit are plain-tailed, the flash of white immediately identifies Great Tit. A hefty bill bolsters a reputation for toughness, and occasionally Great Tits kill small songbirds and roosting bats. Rapid tapping sounds pinpoint a hazel nut or oak gall being hammered apart. Unlike other tits, Great Tits often forage at ground level where they toss leaves aside and tear up moss and fungi to check for fallen or buried plunder. Although widely distributed among all sorts of tree cover, the bird is less at home in cities than Blue Tit. Ireland's population is sedentary and even short sea crossings are shunned, making it a rare visitor to inhabited islands not far offshore. Nonetheless, some migrants cross the Irish Sea. These are drawn from Continental populations that periodically irrupt. One ringed bird reached Belgium from northeast Europe and travelled 1,200km in twenty-one days; an average of 57km per day. During the autumn of 2012, a spectacular movement with origins in western Russia dispersed individuals across Western Europe. Some crossed the North Sea and reached Ireland. Invaders were distinguished on the basis of an idiosyncratic call (first distinguished by German listeners) and led to the remarkable discovery that the first Great Tits ever recorded on Inishbofin, County Galway, were not Irish but Russian! Hole-nesting habits endear the species to us when a pair occupies a nest box. Plumage distinctions attest to separate roles for each sex. Males, with their wide black abdominal stripe and glossy black cap, play little part in nest building, a female prerogative. Great Tits have a bewildering vocabulary and are accomplished mimics (see p. 104).

COAL TIT *Parus ater*

A black-and-white head pattern does not, of itself, distinguish Coal Tit. Great Tit is superficially similar but lacks its smaller relative's badger-striped nape. Coal Tit is marginally smaller than Blue Tit but shape-wise is a lot less butch and would not look out of place as a Christmas tree decoration. In fact, the bird is the only Irish titmouse that is totally at home in coniferous plantations, although all types of woodland are occupied. While certainly not as tweezer-billed as commonly portrayed, the bill tip is longer and finer than other members of the family and well suited to gleaning tiny insects among pine needles. Perrins (1989) indicates that, within the bird's range, the bill shape varies quite markedly, being relatively thinner where conifers are frequented, stouter where broadleaved woods are occupied. High in the canopy of dark plantations, Goldcrests are frequent companions. In severe weather both species feed from the undersides of branches not covered in snow. They also roost 'above the shop' in dense foliage. Two short wing-bars, the upper consisting of a row of Tippex-like dots, is diagnostic. The sexes are similar and youngsters have a sooty cap. Furthermore, plumage areas that on adults are white during the breeding season are creamy-buff on juveniles. By autumn, adults and young have moulted into fresh body plumage. Variation in the shade of light-coloured plumage on the face and nape spans white through magnolia to pale primrose. A yellowish pallor is most intense on the rear cheeks and nape and a few individuals look almost waspish. However, as plumage is progressively blanched by sunlight and also becomes worn, any buttery glow fades. By late winter, except for cream-coloured rear cheeks, buff flanks and an olive cast to grey upperparts, all Coal Tits in Ireland possess an essentially monochrome, black-and-white head pattern. At feeders, visits are frequent and action is fast. In reality, the diminutive dynamo is carrying away items and hiding them for later use by burying them in soft ground, under leaves or in mouldy wood. By rolling seed and coating it with saliva, it also manages to glue seed among evergreen hedges and conifer foliage. In summer, quantities of insects are balled up and stashed. A high, driven voice chimes with small size and hyperactivity (see p. 103). One frequent *tit wee* couplet serves as a useful handle that combines sound and size as an identifier: Coal Tit really is 'Tit Wee'!

LONG-TAILED TIT *Aegithalos caudatus*

Long-tailed Tit is unique in spades. The long appendage apart, stature and weight only slightly exceed that of a Goldcrest. Close cooperation in food searching and roosting increase survival; breeding pairs may be assisted in nest building and chick rearing by helpers (see TERRITORY & NESTS, p. 17). Encountering a troupe is like being caressed by a moving, calling wave. A baby bill and diet of teeny insects requires constant foraging. Acrobatics are the norm and flock members appear to tumble and fall through the latticework of twigs at the ends of branches. Short whirring wings propel a ball-and-stick shape. Parties seem leaderless but when

LONG-TAILED TIT
Top row: three adults. The stubby bill is designed to gather insects rather than peck seeds. The nest is built from interwoven moss and spiders' webs. **COAL TIT** Apart from a juvenile (right of centre), all are adults. To a limited degree, geographic location and time of year affect appearance. In northeast Ireland many are monotone (bottom left); elsewhere, olive upperparts combine with buff underparts (centre); yellow-tinted cheeks are commonplace (also see p. 43).

it comes to crossing a boreen to reach inviting tree canopy across open space, they proceed in an orderly fashion – like parachutists jumping over a target zone. Sound accompanies every action. Bursts of stutters evoke *syrup, syrup, syrup* and suggest a coughing Tom Thumb outboard engine being tugged into life. Of other vocalisations, one is a pulse of high-pitched and bouncy *zee-zee-zee* notes; the other is disorganised tapping akin to hailstones hitting windows and rattling pavement. General racket envelops excitement and alarm. Each vocal element probably has a tailored function. The chorus mixes and alternates because, acting on whim, individuals utter any of the components. At times all can be heard simultaneously. Candyfloss-pink 'shoulder-pads' and fluffy underparts complete the avant-garde trim. Flocks often transit through gardens that form part of a line of trees or bushes. Occasionally, despite a puny bill, fat-balls and peanuts will lure a mob that hang and dangle like badly thrown darts.

KINGFISHER *Alcedo atthis*

Small is, indeed, beautiful. Kingfishers are barely larger than a Robin. Descriptions are superfluous but it is worth remarking that, depending on the incidence of light, the upperparts can vary from cobalt blue to emerald green. Adult males are ebony-billed; females have a variable amount of red at the base of the lower mandible. Adults have vermilion feet with blackish toenails. Youngsters have dull-coloured feet, although mature tones soon develop along the back of the tarsus and their orange underparts are dappled with brown. Patient fishermen sit motionless on perches overhanging clear water, then plunge suddenly after finny prey, occasionally hovering before striking. Successful high dives from overhead cables have been measured at 11m.

Successful pairs, if they survive the winter, reunite for the breeding season and occupy an excavated nest site defended year round by the male. Broods contain up to five nestlings that queue in line for food before retreating to the back of the tunnel. Parents beat small fish into submission and then drop them in the water, enticing fledglings to quit the nest. Novices also hone skills by diving to retrieve small twigs. Adults are fastidious and bathe after tending young. Uniquely, they groom crown plumage by sleeking it down using the underside of the wing. Hard weather can decimate the population by denying access to food, although one intrepid individual dived under ice to catch fish. However, especially in Ireland, coastal areas always remain open so cold weather is unlikely to have a major impact. Across Europe it is a different story and many migrate to Mediterranean shores to escape winter's icy grip. In extreme weather, some cross the North Sea: one Polish-ringed individual was discovered in Kent. In Ireland, pollution, the removal of bank-side vegetation and the re-profiling of slopes that offer a secure overhang for nest burrows are the chief problems facing the bejewelled dart with a voice like a dog whistle.

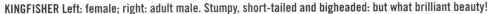

KINGFISHER Left: female; right: adult male. Stumpy, short-tailed and bigheaded: but what brilliant beauty!

DIPPER Top left: juvenile. Adults are white-breasted with chocolate-coloured upperparts. Wren-like proportions are not accidental: the two species are related and share nest type (domed) and distinctive musty smell.

DIPPER *Cinclus cinclus*

Dippers seem umbilically connected to their habitat. Unless your home borders theirs, you are unlikely to see one. They skim low, tracing each bend of serpentine streams. When not submerged, foraging for aquatic insect prey among pebbly beds, they perch stoically on exposed rocks. Movements consist of bows and curtsies, wing flicks and regular winking of a white eye-protecting membrane. Riverside acoustics demand metallic and piercing calls. Wintertime courtship song is fast and scratchy, loud enough to transcend the din of tumbling, frothy water.

Irish Dippers are darker-backed with narrower legs than their British counterparts. Grandiose nests tucked behind waterfalls and under bridges are used by successive generations. Once reared, youngsters leave home and take their chances on unoccupied stretches, biding their time until prime real estate becomes available, complete with breeding partner and heirloom home. Dippers are well adapted to chilly water and have dense plumage that extends down to the nostril. The long, strong tarsus has stout claws and sharp toenails designed to grip slippery rock. Adults feeding young among wet recesses can climb perpendicular gradients.

Much has been written about Dipper's underwater locomotion and was convincingly settled in contributions to journals (Madon 1934, Dewar 1938). Long-standing myths were exposed, such as an ability to fly underwater. Submerged Dippers occasionally spread their wings but the action is incidental and used to maintain balance when buffeted by strong currents. The main confusion rested on how Dippers could walk on the bottom with closed wings and not grasp rocks for stability. They bob quickly to the surface, suggesting that staying under requires considerable muscular effort. In 1938 Dr J.M. Dewar simulated Dipper behaviour by using a piece of wood manoeuvred by string. If gently tugged and maintained at a slant, wood can be steered against flowing water. Once the slant is released, it regains buoyancy. Ergo, when a Dipper walks on the bottom of a stream, it generates a slight current containing two components, one resisting forward progression, the other holding the bird down, creating a state of equilibrium. The glory, however, lies with a forgotten French ornithologist, Comte G. de Vogue, who reached the same conclusion in 1934 (Ingram, Salmon & Tucker 1938).

SKYLARK *Alauda arvensis*

Pinpointing a black speck filling the sky with sound is one way to see a Skylark. Once tabbed, the dot's progress can be tracked. Its oratorio is rich, febrile and continuous. Then, like a breaking wave, it dies. The singer stops treading air and sails earthwards like a parachutist. A follow-up search is unlikely to reveal the maestro – songsters scarper when they hit the deck. They sneak away, so low to the ground that belly and terra firma seem magnetically connected. A surge of powerful, broad-winged flaps carry it away in shallow bounds, accompanied by rippling chirrups. In autumn and winter, the same call locates overhead flocks. Aloft, hordes are loose; playful dogfights are a hallmark of travelling troupes. Other field marks are a narrow white trailing wing edge and bold white outer tail feathers. Seen well at rest, on a wall or shuffling on bare ground, its feathered fretwork can be admired. By spring, plumage has already taken two seasons of wear and has the texture of tawny, weathered rope. The effect boosts the camouflage of an already cryptic costume.

At ease, a Skylark is a joy. Gone is the frightened-rabbit squat. A relaxed lark is long-legged and upright and walks with a Norman Wisdom roll. The comet-shaped beady black eye is set in an orbit of pale plumage suggesting goggles. Depending on mood, the crown may be raised to form a crest. There is no true tuft so when the bird sprouts a headdress – usually when threatening a rival or courting a female – a gap appears at the rear crown, giving a scalped appearance. Meadow Pipits have plumage affinities to Skylarks and share the same universe of tussocky pasture, short heather and dune grassland. Although Skylarks are a trifle larger, gauging the size of lone individuals of either species is virtually impossible. Points of separation include Skylark's chunkier bill, designed to handle seeds (swallowed whole rather than dehusked) and seize beetles, grubs and grasshoppers in the breeding season. Meadow Pipit is tweezer-billed and employs a sprightly, mincing gait as it shoulders through vegetation snatching insects. Skylarks are ground nesters and incubation time is the shortest of all Irish birds, as little as twelve days. Flightless, partly grown youngsters decamp when just over a week old (see p. 40). Quite where our indigenous population spends the winter is unclear, although many are probably sedentary. In some areas arable stubbles hold sizeable flocks. Breeding haunts are evacuated during late summer and territorial singing resumes in February. Immigrants arrive in autumn and, depending on the severity of winter overseas, droves of British and European refugees head west.

In the past, the bird was everywhere. Inexorably, as agriculture intensified during the last millennium and into this, Skylarks have been blighted by a litany of bad news. Declines in Ireland, while difficult to quantify, have been immense. A similar situation has slashed UK populations where numbers plummeted by an estimated 1.5 million pairs during the last quarter of the twentieth century (Donald 2004). They are decreasing as habitats are modified or lost and more nests fail, more chicks starve and adults make fewer nesting attempts. In Britain, the 'factory production' scale of arable fields, exacerbated by a switch from Skylark-friendly spring-sown crops to autumn-sown varieties that are tall and impenetrable during

SKYLARK Sexes are similar. At the end of the breeding season adults and fledged juveniles undergo a root-and-branch moult of all plumage. By autumn, all are identical. To increase chances of survival, speckled youngsters (bottom right and p. 40) quit ground nests and hide as soon as they can walk. Skylarks are famous for filling the sky with song.

the breeding season, broke the relationship that once existed between larks and farmers. The introduction of silage systems has turned much pasture into a green death mask where spring is silent. 'Weed'-killing herbicides that in turn decimate insects have further degraded the spectrum of life nurtured among soil and vegetation. Agricultural intensification is the sum of a multitude of different and complex policies, many influenced directly by that handmaiden of the EU's Common Agricultural Policy, national government. Luckily for Ireland, Skylark reservoirs remain across moorland, on islands and in low-intensity farm systems in the west. Given a chance, the fields of Athenry – to name but a few lifeless acres – could resound once again.

SWIFT *Apus apus*

Screaming overhead with a souped-up engine and sleek Darth Vader bodywork, Swifts live in paradise. The heavens are their home; they sleep there, cruising on autopilot with one eye half open and their brain on 'snooze'. Alas, they need to make contact with earth to breed. Once an emblem of warm sunny evenings and found over every town, populations have crashed. Little did the species realise that, by choosing to nest unobtrusively in inglenooks below roof tiles and among the recesses of masonry, it was signing a death warrant. Building regulations have become malefactors that take no account of the other life that shares our homes, offices and places of worship. Cavities are outlawed and legislated out of existence. Even church walls, that resound to biblical lines such as 'And God said, "Let the waters bring forth swarms of living creatures, and let birds fly above the earth across the dome of the sky",' have been plugged and transformed into an Iron Curtain. Dwindling numbers of Swifts wing all the way back from their winter quarters over the Congo only to find that the myopic march of Health & Safety has rendered even more of their tribe homeless. A few people care and nest boxes are a simple solution. In Ireland, there is little enough to draw our gaze upwards and regale our ears. The loss of Swifts is avoidable, which makes the disaster indefensible. So-called green tiers of government and bird conservation charities north of the border largely ignored the bird's plight until the indignation and efforts of a few (www.saveourswifts.co.uk) stirred some last-ditch action. The contrast with other EU countries could hardly be greater. Municipal authorities, including a growing number in Britain, offer succour not sabotage. Replacement homes are a legal requirement in several Dutch and German boroughs. Identifying a Swift is a no-brainer. Unlike a Swallow or House Martin, the top-flight aeronaut appears all black with sickle-shaped wings and a short, notched tail. Insect prey is snatched rather than trawled. Despite zooming at high speed, the bird discriminates between female worker bees armed with a sting and stingless male drones. How does it tell them apart? Perhaps it recognises the tubbier abdomen of a drone or avoids worker bees that, apparently, emit a different buzz. Nobody knows for sure but it is not surprising that, after 50 million years of trials, practice makes perfect. Chicks are fed balled-up collections of bugs. Cold, wet summer weather interrupts deliveries. Undeterred, young become torpid, analogous to entering a persistent vegetative state, until the clouds roll away.

SWALLOW *Hirundo rustica*

We see Swallows at their best. Ultramarine upperparts shine like armour and attenuated tail feathers scribble the air like a conductor's baton. Such swank is missing during winter. Swallows moult before they leave Africa and head north. Only then do they acquire a fresh coat of blue coverts and a full-length tail whose needle length serves as a badge of machismo and, in the estimation of females, elevates lanky-tailed males to the status of matinee idols.

SWIFT Top left and centre: adult. Far left and top right: juvenile. SWALLOW Left of centre and bottom left: juvenile (also p. 80). Two perched on long rope: adult males. Bottom right and centre: adult female (shorter tail and some chestnut plumage in breast band).

By late summer, adult plumage has taken a pounding but the new kids on the block more than compensate. Juveniles have cinnamon faces and a shorter tail with blunt-tipped outer feathers. Unlike adults, the upper-wing coverts are dark matt brown, not shiny blue-black. Readying themselves like D-Day troops, all ages sit like rows of fattening dots on wires. Several broods are reared to offset expected heavy losses on a migration that entails a small 20g bird completing an annual round trip of at least 30,000km (see MIGRATION, p. 79). Airborne Swallows are more dashing and erratic than Swifts and martins. One regular habit involves a fast upswing immediately followed by a sharp backwards tack, as though colliding with the inside of an invisible sphere. A lot of information is encrypted in a fast twittering song. Among the discourse a rubbery rattle signifies the male songster's status. As if to emphasise the proclamation the gob is opened wide, evoking a patient in a dentist's chair waiting for cotton wool to be removed after treatment. Aerial views mean that Swallows are quick to spot birds of prey. Panicky *veet! veet!* calls raise the alarm. Suspicious husbands looking for spouses use the same sound. By deliberately false alarming he summons all hands, thereby revealing where – and with whom – his partner and peers have been.

HOUSE MARTIN *Delichon urbica*

Along with rabbits, deer and shy birds such as Bullfinches and Jays, House Martins make a meal of flashing a warning and use the signage of a white bum to do so. For us, the feature is an instant field mark. To make matters easier, the eye-catching blaze is not shown by Swallow, Sand Martin and Swift. White-feathered legs, glossy cobalt upperparts and a white throat complete a fetching outfit. On the wing in late summer, youngsters have monotone upperparts, an off-white rump and a dusky wash on the side of the chest which, depending on

HOUSE MARTIN Top left: juvenile (fresh wings are unworn with white tips; blue plumage emerging among first-generation brown upperparts). Adults: top right and three in upper middle row collecting mud. In flight: left-hand two (note white rump). SAND MARTIN In flight: right-hand three birds. Bottom row: at nest holes in sandbank. Fledged juvenile on far left.

angle of view, hints at a breast band. Sparrow-like chirps accompany most activities. House Martins often fly high to catch insects; familiarity with the gritty chirrup earmarks a speck in the sky. Flight style is somewhat different and distinguishable from that of a Swallow. House Martins fly in straight, level lines and usually 'indicate before turning'. The manner of feeding may explain what they do in Africa during winter. Strange as it may seem, the whereabouts of Europe's estimated population of 20 million is largely unknown. Most likely, they feed over the Congo and stay aloft, napping like Swifts on the wing. Termite hatches, whipped high during daily thunderstorms and stretching over many kilometres, are probably tapped. Before people constructed dwelling places, House Martins nested on cliffs and in caves. Some still do along parts of the coast. Most, however, opt to build under eaves. An adobe home is fashioned with mud pellets rolled like dough inside the bird's mouth. Each gobbet is neatly plastered into place and attached using trembling movements of the chin, acting as vibrating plate. Drought delays operations. Once the edifice is secure, a smooth internal cup is lined with grass and feathers and a clutch of four or five tiny pointed eggs is laid. At this point disaster often strikes. Householders, rather than allow the birds a chance to raise a family, power-hose the lot for the sake of keeping whitewash off a gable wall or driveway. With a look of satisfaction syruped across chops, 21st-century Neanderthals snuff out unborn life programmed to live within the means of this planet and adorn skies from Ireland to the heart of Africa.

SAND MARTIN *Riparia riparia*

Riparian. The word means 'of, or inhabiting a riverbank'. So Sand Martin's Latin name is an apt descriptor of the bird's nesting requirements. By burrowing with tiny feet, they can excavate a tunnel up to 6m long and dislodge intervening stones four times their own body weight. The titch of the Swallow tribe feeds over water and lives in colonies in a matriarchal society. Motherhood is not deeply ingrained and some females copulate with more than one male, relegating the first to a Mrs Doubtfire role. Group sync is a constant theme and feeding flocks fly about in a cloud, like an insect swarm. The air at a breeding citadel suggests a cicada chorus. A dry, buzzing *vrrt, vrrt* double note can be matched to *rabbit, rabbit*. The first to spot danger utters an incongruous-sounding *keeer*; this serves as a panic button. Tail length is slightly shorter than House Martin and noticeably shorter than Swallow. Sand Martins fly using fast flicks rather than slalom glides. Typically, the wings are crooked at half-mast, creating a dart shape. In this aerial pose the raked tips exceed the length of the tail: a silhouette foreign to both Swallow and House Martin. Uniquely, Sand Martins are brown-backed and have a brown breast band. However, among fast-moving spirals of Swallows and House Martins – all species feed collectively over lakes – colour distinctions are lost. At all times, the best identification steer to Sand Martin is dusky, dark brown wing-pits (linked to the breast band). On Swallow and House Martin, the equivalent area of the wing's underside is whitish and offers no contrast against white chest plumage.

WILLOW WARBLER *Phylloscopus trochilus*

The month of April produces an out-of-Africa flood of Willow Warblers that, as the name suggests, descend on pussy willows. The tree's male catkins, before they come into flower, are covered in fine soft down (the fancied likeness is to cat fur). As they turn yellow with pollen, insects either fresh from hibernation or newly emerged are attracted. For a nimble, slim and hungry warbler, the awakening life is a magnet. The sylph is brownish-olive above with a watery yellow bib and has perfect 'bare willow tree' camouflage. However, many come close to looking brown above and white below with a buttery waistcoat sandwiched between a fluffy white throat and belly. Chiffchaff is a lookalike that reappears during late March from winter quarters around the Mediterranean but prefers to snatch minute prey from among bursting buds and unfurling treetop foliage. Nonetheless, freshly returned migrants of either species sometimes occur in the same habitat. Luckily, song is an instant distinction. Willow Warbler is a minstrel; Chiffchaff's monotonous ditty is about as adventurous as an I-speak-your-weight machine: a one-trick pony that can say its name. Willow Warbler's madrigal is delightful; if a fairy could sing this would be its tune. The melody is a continuous soft ripple that tinkles downscale, gathering momentum and volume before ending with sweet notes that are clearest of all: *seep-seep, tie-tie, tay-tay, wirri-wirri-wee*. As countless leaves unwrap, they provide hiding places that mask views, although song always serves as a beacon. A single brood is produced from a secret bower in grassy basement. Quickly the parents moult and prepare to depart. By late summer the population is at peak. As spotty juvenile Robins upgrade fledgling feathers and replace them with an adult-like red tuxedo, so juvenile Willow Warblers emerge with canary-yellow underparts. Their parents, following moult, are also yellow-chested although whiter-bellied. During August, bushy wild corridors are a-flicker with troops feeding up for migration. Call notes, rather than song, fill the air, although apprentice broadcasts given by young males are recognisable, despite being a poor copy. Most call notes are angelic and soft, a soothing *who-eet* that rises slightly in pitch. But not from the youngest juveniles, whose voice has not yet broken. Their salutation is rougher, a husky and scraping monosyllable. However, as the parvenu moults out of loose and somewhat dishevelled plumage grown in the nest, its voice 'matures' and becomes sublime. During summer and early autumn, nationwide migrants flit through greenery. Gardens everywhere become part of their universe. By late September they are gone, a useful watershed in the calendar because migrant Chiffchaffs, closely similar in appearance, travelling in small numbers into Ireland from northeast Europe, are encountered in coastal gardens during October and November, some even staying for winter.

CHIFFCHAFF *Phylloscopus collybita*

Discussion of Chiffchaff inevitably invites comparisons with Willow Warbler (see above). Splitting hairs, Chiffchaff is smaller and dumpier yet, especially in autumn, prettier. In spring

WILLOW WARBLER Top row: autumn migrants (moulting juvenile in August, far left). Bottom row: spring adults (also pp. 8 and 133). **CHIFFCHAFF** Upper middle row: autumn migrants. Lower middle row: spring adults (also p. 86).

and summer, chalk and cheese songs immediately differentiate the two. Indeed, *collybita* means 'moneychanger', a nod to the simple coin-counting rhythm of its binary verse. Ireland's breeding Chiffchaffs and Willow Warblers spend the winter in sunny climes, whose rays progressively bleach plumage. This explains why, before adults renew plumage in summer, the olive and yellow signage commonly depicted in field guides is, in reality, drab and faded. No wonder the twosome is troublesome to tell apart. Autumn unveils more faithful looks. By then all ages of Willow Warblers are fresh plumaged and yellow-breasted. Looking as though they are lit from within by a saffron glow, they are quite distinct from Chiffchaffs. Although Chiffchaff lacks didactic colours, its face is more demure. Separation by means of expression is feasible but usually impractical because the models never sit still. Identification is, therefore, best achieved by assessing leg and foot-sole colour. Chiffchaff is blacklegged with 'sickly' yellow soles. Leg colour in Willow Warbler is variable but even the darkest are no darker than nut brown and all have 'juicy' yellow soles. Chiffchaff actions are almost always accompanied by robotic tail dipping; Willow Warbler, although similarly active and sprightly, is a far less predictable tail-pumper.

BLACKCAP *Sylvia atricapilla*

By nature, Blackcaps are restless sleuths. Although dapper, plumage is fairly nondescript and the bird's knack of not staying still whilst slinking through undergrowth restricts views to glimpses. Because the species has undergone a spectacular change in status, it is more easily observed during winter in gardens, when diet comprises berries, fruit, scraps and some feeder seed, notably sunflower hearts. The warbler-for-all-seasons is a bossy customer and drives away all comers (including other Blackcaps) from food items over which proprietorial rights are enforced. Males are grey-faced with a black beret. Ashen plumage rides up in front of the eye, reducing the cap to a sliver. Body plumage is smooth, like a grey velvet sky, and contrasts with 'gloomy' olive-grey upperparts. Partially obscured and proceeding by jerky movements among bushes and brambles, the dove-grey nape, sandwiched between the black cap and smoky back, often catches the eye. Female upperparts are more olive-brown, less tinged with grey than the male; similarly, the underparts are pale brown, rather than grey. Female beret colour is reddish-brown; bright ginger in adults but more sombre chestnut-brown in youngsters, a distinction that holds good until first-winter females moult at around one year of age. During autumn, some first-winter males show a mixture of brown juvenile feathers among the emerging black crown. Narky, scolding call notes are an important guide to a presence that would otherwise be invisible. The sound is a randomly repeated *tac … tac*, a tooth-sucking, petulant rebuke that can also be imitated by knocking two stones together, which sometimes prompts the caller to risk a peep. Song bursts are fast and dense; Blackcaps do not sing in short sentences. Like a pan of milk rushing to boiling point, the outpouring is a conflagration. The opening notes stutter slightly and suggest a sprinter rising hesitantly. Once up and running, acceleration is palpable. Then, like phone credit dying, the notes suddenly cease in mid-climax. Carollers are fickle and surreptitiously shift position without warning. As ever, irascibility is de rigueur when it comes to Blackcap behaviour.

WHITETHROAT *Sylvia communis*

Unlike other warblers, the sound of a singing Whitethroat is usually a bead to a visible songster. There he is, rattling off jabbering bursts of a song of such high energy that no mnemonic fits the metre. Lines evoke a terse question asked heatedly in a foreign language. The singer is animated and his trademark white throat puffs like cotton wool during broadcasts, leaning forward like a rutting stag and bellowing. Prominent perches are used as a stage and sometimes the bird yo-yos into the air, combining sound and semaphore. Scolding, hoarse *charr* contact calls are reminiscent of the raucous simpering of juvenile Starlings. In late summer and early autumn Whitethroats are much more secretive but can still be tracked by voice. All ages and sexes have rusty edges to the wing feathers and their coverts, creating a colourful appearance to the closed wing and contrasting with a dun-brown back and buff-coloured underparts. Females and young have a subdued face but are still white-throated. Leg colour is pale, almost sandy or flesh-coloured. Adult males are the most debonair. Their underparts are flushed with pink and a morning suit grey cap descends below the eye, illuminating a snowy cravat. Males arrive in late April and take up station in wide battlement hedges and sunlit scrub. Embankments run wild with briars and nettles, especially when intermixed with sapling trees or tall gorse, are especially beloved. Whitethroats are sprightly and slip with ease into cover. Although home turf may be shared with Willow Warblers and Blackcaps – co-stars in a rousing springtime eisteddfod – a disappearing Whitethroat flashes white outer tail feathers; both other warblers are plain-tailed. Whitethroats are a worry. In common with all Irish summer insectivores that winter in Africa, disaster can strike along migration routes prone to multiple jeopardies. In the spring of 1969 most of Ireland's breeding population never made it back. Thankfully, the survivors fostered a recovery, although it took a decade to repopulate many areas.

BLACKCAP Of upper four, lower right is a brown-capped female (males are black-capped, including first-winter males). **WHITETHROAT** Lower four: spring adults. In males (such as bottom left) brown head abrades to reveal grey; ashy chest acquires pink bloom. Middle right is probably female due to brown head and greyish-buff chest.

GRASSHOPPER WARBLER *Locustella naevia*

As the Latin name suggests, this small warbler's voice sounds as if it has been piped in from an insect. Grasshopper Warblers live among the filigree of long-stemmed vegetation and twisting briars that wreath ditches, young plantations and ground that has escaped cultivation and become bushy. Much habitat is transient and so too its complement of Grasshopper Warblers. Perhaps year-on-year variation is linked to feeding conditions among savannah grassland along the southern margins of the Sahara, an important springtime staging area. In years when rains fall, vegetation blooms, nectar and insects abound and migrants are good to go. To boot, when southerly tail winds bless onward passage, many arrive nocturnally. Were it not for the thin

GRASSHOPPER WARBLER Bottom four. Note variability in 'glow' of plumage from yellowish-olive to smoky-brown. Singing birds remain motionless but can be located by puffed-out pale throat. SEDGE WARBLER Upper two, adults; middle left, juvenile (gorget of speckles on chest).

whirring trill, rising and falling as the bird turns its head from side to side, little would be seen of the wraith. Bursts of song can last for minutes on end and the greatest output occurs during the still of the night. The secret songster is mouse-like and drops out of sight when disturbed. Among its underworld of stalks and rank grass it prefers to run and hide rather than emerge and fly. Patience reaps a rich reward. Territorial males like to sing from a low, exposed perch. A stealthy approach is often tolerated; sometimes the need to broadcast trumps the instinct to hide. Streaked on a palate of sombre olive and brown, the colour scheme harmonises with the surroundings. Porker-pink gangly toes clasp vegetation with the gentle touch of newborn fingers and the face is innocent, more pipit-like than any other warbler. A frail build is no bar to energetic outpourings, however. Body and soul pulsate in time to the shrill soliloquy that, in calm air, carries up to 0.5km or more.

SEDGE WARBLER *Acrocephalus schoenobaenus*

If ever a bird could be accused of burning the candle at both ends that species would be Sedge Warbler. Migrants return from mid-April on the first warm zephyrs of spring, hightailing it from south of the Sahara and taking up station in tangled bushy habitats, usually near water. Males sing virtually around the clock and do not pipe down until offspring leave the nest. When that happens, parents moult body plumage and retire to the sanctuary of reed beds where they pig out on aphids like a pre-race marathon runner guzzling pasta. Corners are cut to get back to Africa and migrants depart with the same set of increasingly worn wing feathers that carried them north. The troops are evolution's infantry. Mortality stands at 90 per cent for fledged juveniles and between 50 and 87 per cent for adults (Hockey, Dean & Ryan 2005). Not wonder they look as edgy as kamikaze pilots. Songsters are flat-crowned, hunchbacked loudmouths, but plumage details more than compensate. The crown is dark but wet-combed with tawny striations and the supercilium is bold enough to stand out on Google Earth – even on a flying bird, when a ginger rump is also distinctive. Patterned upperparts are a faint echo of Meadow Pipit but smooth underparts glow cream or tan, depending on angle of view. Songsters sound grumpy and look narky. A troubadour will often sidle up a stem to sneak a peep if a passing human has breached a territorial boundary. Belting males also perform aerial sweeps over breeding demesne. The song is a jazzy jumble, intermixed with incongruous random notes. The overlay of extramural sounds often suggests that a second species is singing close by but is being drowned out by the front-of-house chattering. In fact, Sedge Warbler lives in an eavesdropping universe and has a predilection for copying alarm notes and flight calls of other species. It seems addicted to simulating stress. The repertoire is freighted with mimicry. Frequent impersonations include Swallow's *veet veet* alarm, squeaky *seep seep* flight notes of Meadow Pipit and the dry, rapid-fire click-stops of passing Linnets. Sedge Warbler's personal alarm calls are, not surprisingly, angst-ridden. Monosyllabic muttering sounds like the word '*thick*', which may be further embellished into a drawling '*jerk*'. Does it understand English? It is hard not to become anthropomorphic and ascribe Victor Meldrew tendencies!

GOLDCREST *Regulus regulus*

Weighing slightly less than a 20-cent coin, it is no surprise that Goldcrest is Europe's smallest bird. What is surprising is that migrants from as far away as Russia reach Ireland every autumn. For visitors and those that breed here, winter is a challenging time. The titch is insectivorous and burns considerable energy as it flits among greenery and twigs looking for prey barely visible to the human eye. Year-round foliage on conifers is a lifesaver. Many Goldcrests nest in plantations. Catching sight of the mite reveals a quizzical peppercorn eye and a furrowed gape evoking Fu Man Chu. Prominent black stripes border a golden crown. On males, flame-orange lies at the heart of gold. During courtship display or tussles between rivals, the crown plumage is flattened to expose maximum colour. Juveniles, until they moult during summer, lack head stripes. Aft of a whitish wing-bar on the greater coverts, sooty bases to the secondaries stand out as an eye-catching 'black box'. Earwax-orange feet connected to dark shanks complete the outfit. Goldcrest is the only small bird that has perfected moth-like hovering as a feeding technique. A hunchbacked silhouette employing tit-like locomotion as it edges through greenery or along twigs can be identified as a Goldcrest once it breaks into a hover. Blurred wings look opaque and pale. High-speed wing and tail flicking accompany twitchy movements and changes of position. Calls are often the first clue to presence. During winter, mixed troupes of tits often contain Goldcrests, verified by high-pitched 'needling', repeated like a simpering mouse. Song, if anything, is even thinner. The discourse has a rolling, squeaky-bicycle rhythm. After three or four 'revolutions' the verse dies, almost spluttering to a halt. A useful analogy is a car ignition turning over but failing to start.

WREN *Troglodytes troglodytes*

Wrens possess an iconic shape. Peeping out from foliage like a nosy curtain-twitching neighbour, the impression is not of a titch but of a mystery warbler with a substantial schnozzle and bold supercilium. However, unlike a slinking warbler, Wrens are noisy lookouts. A tetchy 'tapping ball-bearings' burst alerts the district and the half-bird pops into view, or buzzes off on whirring bumblebee wings. Most are resident and adult males are sedentary. Year-round territory is important; song proclaims occupancy of a patch of ground. Diminutive size is no impediment to loud singing and songsters let rip with operatic aplomb. In open-mouthed, tail-cocked full voice the body pulsates and orange flashes from the gape. Complete recitals last around five seconds and consist of separate components that are stitched together without a break. A whirring trill is frequently included. 'R' sounds roll and the Edith Piaf of the undergrowth uses the fricative effect in much the same way as the famous French 'Little Sparrow' did in 'Non, Je ne Regrette Rien'. Local inhabitants know each other and often abbreviate songs rather than repeat full compositions. Sexes are virtually identical. In spring, the male constructs several domed nests but does not line them. The female, who picks one, then adds a lining of

GOLDCREST Top row, male; second row, female or male. On males, orange feathers among the yellow crown plumage become visible when the bird is agitated. **WREN** Although sexes are similar, plumage condition related to wear is apparent. Photographed in March, the singing bird shows the effect of six months' wear. The three others, photographed in October, are freshly moulted.

feathers. During summer, fledged juveniles glow ginger and contrast markedly with threadbare, fawn-chested adults. Following moult in autumn, all ages look the same. The brightest russet plumage is found on the rump and upper-tail coverts. Wrens need sheltering undergrowth to survive. Woodland understorey, hedge bottoms, dry reed beds and boulder slopes in uplands and at the foot of sea cliffs are all suitable. Insects and their larvae is the mainstay. Live food becomes difficult to find in hard weather and losses are often severe. Communal roosting combats cold. Ten were recorded roosting regularly inside a coconut shell (Witherby 1940) and over 60 have been watched entering a standard-size nest box. Some migrate across the Irish Sea and several have struck Irish lighthouses. Three foreign-ringed birds have been found in Britain, one from Russia (Toms *et al.* 1999). Bearing in mind that the ancestral home of the world's wrens is the New World, from whence 'our' Wren colonised the Old World, the poppet's pioneering spirit should not be underestimated.

STARLING *Sturnus vulgaris*

Starlings sound as though they have kissed the Blarney Stone. That Bjorn Borg face and restless swagger with the air of a strutting Human Resources ogre, suggests irascibility. The bill is bayonet-shaped and used to stab ground, whereupon both mandibles are prised slightly open, creating a looking space to check for prey. Mobs are intimidating – like a rugby team sprinting onto a pitch before a big game – and other birds yield. Hordes multitask and pluck blackberries and elderberries, then cruise on flat wings for insects. Swooping for flies, they are as graceful as Swallows with shark-fin wings and a short tail, the latter a good distinction from Blackbird. During winter, all are pebble-dashed with stardust plumage evoking a planetarium. Come the new year, pale tips wear off and males are transformed into sheen-rich courtiers with an azure-based yellow bill (see p. 30). Male body feathers, especially on the breast, are long and pointed. Vocalising males, with silky spiky throats, look Brylcreemed. Minstrels in full flow ruffle plumage, raise the rump and pump wings as though they were bellows. The head is periodically turned to achieve maximum broadcast radius and, in an effort to dominate the airwaves, soloists often lay down a burbling backing track to which they add autobiographical notes. Some are old favourites, such as the screams of Swift, which persist in areas from which breeding Swifts have been lost. Plagiarisms include a whine resembling a falling bomb, a pitch oscillation uncannily like tuning a radio and a whistled *pur-dee* couplet that, with minor improvisations, is used by residents throughout the year, often from the same song post.

Female body feathers are shorter and broader; the bill has a watery yellow or pale grey base and their nut-brown iris has a pale rim. Males are dark-eyed. Adults moult during late summer and new plumage is copiously sprinkled with spots. Before that, unspotted and mousy juveniles fledge and quickly band into homogenous flocks. From July onwards they start to moult, acquiring a Frankenstein look as plain feathering is progressively replaced with the polka dots of adult winter plumage. The transition proceeds headwards, generating the stark contrast of a plain front attached to a patterned body. By late September the bonce will also have changed, although some youngsters still retain a sandy-brown bonnet or cheeks at Halloween. In many coastal districts, notably in the windy west, salt-tolerant New Zealand Flax *Phormium tenax* is planted for shelter. Starlings suck nectar by reaching deep inside the flower-stalk and their head becomes coated with yellow-orange pollen, often culminating in reports of a *rara avis* (see p. 115).

Ireland's breeding population has crashed. Gazing at pastures that were once dotted with Starlings, Skylarks and Lapwings, the contemporary scene is not permanent pasture complete with a hidden larder of invertebrates but silage fields inaccessible to ground-feeding birds. Reseeding with grass monocultures, involving ploughing that progressively diminishes insects and plant associations sustaining a web of life, as well as regular applications of fertiliser, herbicide and insecticide, have been as destructive as Agent Orange, except that the rural death mask is green and looks deceptively benign. How does this square with the incontestably vast numbers of Starlings that congregate at winter roosts? These are overseas visitors, largely from Scandinavia, the Baltic States and Russia. Arrivals throng Ireland from October onwards and as many as 1,000 have been seen arriving and passing Copeland Bird Observatory, County Down, in a few hours. Departures are in March. Before then, pilgrims host epic trysts in gathering gloom, coalescing along ley lines that stretch up to 50km from daytime feeding haunts and surging to bed like black bees returning to a hive.

STARLING At top: roost swarm. All ages grow a full set of new feathers during late summer. Plain-plumaged juveniles (in flight at left, spring) develop large polka-dot flanks (inset, late summer) that progress headwards (bottom right, autumn). During winter, flank markings on males (bottom left) are V-shaped but more circular on adult females (top pair).

BLACKBIRD Top: adult female and nestlings. Centre, left: juvenile male moulting into first-winter. Centre, middle and right: first-winter males (also first-winter male, p. 51). Bottom right: adult male. Bottom centre and left: juveniles (female to left of male).

BLACKBIRD *Turdus merula*

Originally shy inhabitants of woodland, Blackbirds utilise rural and urban habitats nationwide. In the past, gardens were patronised once nesting was completed and not until the twentieth century did stakeholders settle close to people. In Britain, city dwelling began during the 1920s. Across large parts of Eastern Europe they are still unwilling to trust humans and remain a phantom of the forest. Earthworms are a staple throughout the year. Caterpillars that drop from leafing trees are eagerly snapped up and fruit and berries provide winter fare. Unlike Song Thrushes, they lack the knack of cracking open snails. Instead, if tapping is overheard, a Blackbird saboteur lies in wait and attempts to steal a thrush's dinner.

The breeding season runs from March to July and three broods can be reared, each from a new nest built by the female. Some parents show favouritism. Fathers may provide for one sibling and leave others in the care of mother. Short-tailed and blunt-winged, juveniles appear loose and fluffy, spotted below and streaked above. Males have slightly darker wings and a 'cold' brown body lacking the ginger glow that typifies young females. For lone individuals, cheek colour often proves decisive: sooty on males, tan and more patterned on females. From July, offspring begin moulting into adult-like plumage. Commencing with the body and smaller wing coverts, moult proceeds headwards where progress slows, creating a bizarre vulturine appearance. By early autumn, young males have replaced a speckled body costume with matt black against which the retained kelp-coloured juvenile wings contrast. At first, a dusky bill and faint yellow eye-ring distinguish the yearling. As winter advances, signs of immaturity disappear. Ageing females is harder; their body and wing colour is similar. Young females are dark-billed until at least Christmas. Adult females show variable amounts of yellow on the bill. Older females are peat-coloured while adult males are satin black. On some males the underparts are subtly scaled, due to the edges of breast feathers being less glossy than their centres, resulting in a 'knitted' texture, most marked on young males in spring.

Blackbirds segue together beautifully modulated phrases, rounding off the discourse with a hoarse chuckle emphasised by a rise in pitch. Erratic, tentative song regales the airwaves during February. March outpourings are prompted by mild weather and lengthening daylight. Competition is rife and young pretenders begin auditions before dawn. Older males listen and watch, preferring to sing later in the day. Every voice is slightly different and individuals vary song rate and style of delivery, ranging from repetitive, almost staccato, to laid-back and ethereal with long gaps. June brings languid last hoorahs, usually at vespers. Courtship battles are over and songsters seem to embrace 'Auld Lang Syne' sentiments. During the breeding season, males often fly in a hesitant manner, cupping the air and simultaneously uttering a few garbled phrases. Flight prompts a high-pitched rippling *tseeerrrp*. At dawn and dusk, noisy 'chinking' is commonplace in the vicinity of roost sites. The ratcheted notes are also used during mobbing and often morph into a deeper-voiced *chuck, chuck, chuck*, the closing syllables stalling and portending unease. Outright panic is conveyed in a caterwauling fusillade. Unease and social interactions utilise a piercing, almost ultrasonic *zeee*. A parping *pook…pook*, used during communal feeding in winter, seems to function as pacifying mood music. Fledglings keep a low profile but maintain parental contact via a loud skirl. Summer dispersal of Irish juveniles probably takes them no further afield than a few kilometres. During winter, they wander widely, although they lack a strong migratory urge. All the same, young generations are imbued with a sense of exploration and some probably emigrate before returning to seek out their roots. In Britain, 93 per cent of juveniles ringed as fledglings and subsequently retrapped were nesting within 10km of their birthplace. Populations breeding across cold countries from Scotland to Russia migrate west. Sometimes Ireland is awash with hard-weather refugees. Ringing data showed that 25 per cent of nestlings from northern England and 33 per cent from Scotland were later recovered in Ireland.

FIELDFARE *Turdus pilaris*

Like Redwing, its smaller cousin and frequent companion in mixed flocks, Fieldfare is a winter visitor from central and northern Europe. Scaly chevrons, reminiscent of the fretwork of a metal grille or curly black copperplate, girdle its underparts on a 'golden toast' breastplate. For a thrush, Fieldfare signage breaks all the rules. Colourful plumage abounds. A leather-brown saddle sits between a blue-grey head and rump. The tail is blackish, as is facial mascara that sets off a black-tipped yellow bill. In flight, the underwing and belly glisten white but are separated by a slipstream of the chest markings that pepper the flanks. Aerial squadrons fly with a powerful, measured pace and the longer tail creates a more cruciform silhouette than other thrushes. Calls assist identification. A scissoring salvo, forceful and reminiscent of garden shears, is hard to miss. Flocks often keep up a constant clamour. Less striking is a keening *kleep* or tremulous *quee*, given in flight and recalling the anxiety of some Lapwing calls. Fieldfares are cocky and swanky. Hard-weather immigrants enter gardens and set about monopolising food supplies. A lawn strewn with apples that accommodated many diners will be commandeered by one zealous green-keeper. Trespassers are dealt with severely. During mild weather roaming flocks feed together in fields or rough pasture, landing first in a tall hedgerow before swooping to the ground like trainee hawks. On the deck, troops fan outwards, running a few steps and then halting to look for food and scan for danger. Posture is upright, alert and militaristic. If one becomes nervous, all shift in unison (chuckling calls and grey rumps to the fore) and take to the nearest vantage point to review the threat. Unlike Blackbirds and Song Thrushes, fleeing Fieldfares do not dive into cover but perch up and, as a general rule, face the same way.

REDWING *Turdus iliacus*

Flanks and a wing-pit the colour of dried blood may be diagnostic, yet Redwing's long creamy supercilium is more easily seen, especially when troupes 'hop and halt' among grass as they forage for worms. Although Song Thrush size, Redwings can look smaller and darker-backed; a moving carpet of half-hidden ground feeders can suggest Skylarks or even Starlings. The species is a winter visitor from Scandinavia and Iceland. If weather is mild, parties stick to fields and hedgerows where they strip haws. Skittish and well fed, they explode if approached and deliver supersonic *seeeep* calls as they scatter. The same note, when heard from night skies in late autumn, signifies passage. If bitter weather strikes, everything changes. Ground becomes inaccessible either through frost or snow. And, because cold snaps tend to occur in the new year, most hedgerows fruits have already been devoured. Freeze-ups drive Redwings into gardens in search of berry-laden ornamental shrubs, chiefly Cotoneaster and Pyracantha. Refugees that have headed west from Britain and Europe swell numbers. Some must continue to a watery oblivion with the lucky ones making it to the New World and even a research

FIELDFARE Bottom three. Left-hand bird female due to brownish wash to head and nape, less rich chestnut-brown back and duller flank markings. **REDWING** Top three. The bird at top right is a first-winter. Moult details enable ageing. Many young birds retain old juvenile greater coverts alongside new adult-type feathers. On this Redwing, five juvenile feathers are discernible — smaller and more pale-fringed than the three adjoining adult feathers to their right.

vessel off Brazil. Among the hungry hordes are Fieldfares, Song Thrushes and Blackbirds. Threatened by starvation and guzzling any available fruit, the birds suspend natural wariness. For us, close-up views of the will-o'-the-wisp are mouth-watering. Sharp *Jack!* calls intersperse feeding activities. The sound is more upbeat than an equivalent note made by Blackbird; Redwings sound like they have sat on a hatpin. As soon as a thaw arrives, the lodgers up sticks and revert to worms. Airborne, Redwings are sharp-fronted and flick-knife the wings to full stretch, then half-close them. However, when top speed is needed, such as when zooming into roosting cover, cruise control is overwritten and the whole wing is flexed.

SONG THRUSH *Turdus philomelos*

All thrushes sing but Song Thrush earns full entitlement to its eponymous epithet. The bird does not so much sing as holler. Stanzas emerge at a volume resembling a backseat passenger in a Tiger Moth shouting to the pilot. Cranked-up decibels and repetition of phrases make identification a no-brainer. MC announcements begin on calm days in the dead of winter and sometimes start or end in the dark. When not performing, the diva is shy and stays close to cover. Calls chime with a retiring persona. A Blackbird-style alarm fusillade is tinny and downbeat and a perfunctory *tix* flight note hits a choirboy register. In flight, a yellow-orange

SONG THRUSH Bottom four. Juvenile at far right, worn adult at bottom left. Along Atlantic coasts, increased exposure to UV light causes plumage in resident breeding birds to fade and wear more rapidly and to a greater degree than elsewhere in Ireland, hence the grey back and whitish ground colour of this bird (resembling Mistle Thrush) photographed in June on Inishbofin, County Galway. MISTLE THRUSH Top three.

wing-pit is diagnostic. Unlike Blackbird and Mistle Thrush, Song Thrush shuns open feeding spaces and seldom parks up and guzzles hedgerow fruits. Worms are its preferred staple; snails only become popular when dry soil makes worming difficult. A knack of cracking open snail shells on a makeshift anvil is demonstrated in front of fledglings that are then fed bits of mollusc. Song Thrush has a sad, kindly face. Blotched cheeks resemble tracks of tears. The chest and flanks are butter-coloured – warming to buff on the flanks – and bleed to white on the belly. Much of the breast spotting is arranged in zip-fastener rows; the spots are comet-shaped, not circular (except in juveniles). Compared to other brown-backed thrushes, its upperparts are relatively plain. Telling sexes apart is impossible and even differentiating first-winters from adults is challenging. Although ostensibly resident, local breeders disperse and a proportion of youngsters and adult females emigrate. Individuals ringed in Ireland have reached Spain. North European winter visitors melt away among woodland and mature gardens. Song Thrushes are not gregarious and do not flock. Only in the west of Ireland is the true scale of numbers revealed. Forced to pass the winter in more open habitat, particularly islands with permanent pasture bounded by thickets of fuchsia, Song Thrush outnumbers all its relatives.

MISTLE THRUSH *Turdus viscivorus*

Most gardens are not big enough for a ground-feeding Mistle Thrush, although a berried tree or bush in any neighbourhood will attract a watchman that vigorously enforces proprietorial rights over the food supply (see BERRIES AND BIRDS, p. 49). Mistle Thrush is larger than a Blackbird. Unlike a coy Song Thrush, it has a fondness for open grassland and green spaces in town parks. Its confident deportment has the uprightness of a girl riding a dressage pony. A relatively puny bill and small head is compensated for by a muscular neck and a bulging 'just swallowed a tennis ball' belly. The underparts are extensively spotted and the markings are more spherical than the arrowheads of Song Thrush. Spot density is greatest at the side of the chest where a cluster-cloud forms. Mistle Thrush upperparts exude a gravestone look and the underparts have a dead-skin cast. Feather tracts on the folded wing are well differentiated and stand out like pleats of a skirt. Large, ponderous and often stationary, there is no better bird upon which to locate and memorise wing parts. Flight is bounding – except when driving away others – and the tail corners and tip are off-white. White underwings are distinctive, although shared with Fieldfare. Intimidating rattling calls have a pneumatic-drill feel. Rather than given purely in alarm, the sound also accompanies offensive sorties. Song is delivered from a high perch and commences early in the new year. The singer always sounds distant, partly due to the somewhat melancholy nature of the phrases. Clear articulation is the bird's strong suit. Words rather than a tune are delivered in a monotone that would be the envy of a NASA anchorman at Mission Control. After a few verses the limited repertoire comes across as monotonous. Unlike the richness and melody of Blackbird, with which the song is confusable, Mistle Thrush is austere – a Scottish Presbyterian minister carefully choosing his words.

SPOTTED FLYCATCHER *Muscicapa striata*

Reliance on bite-sized flying insects means that Spotted Flycatcher is the tail-end Charlie of summer visitors. Southerly winds in May carry them home to glades and woodland edges where they take up station among fresh greenery. A stock-still, guard-duty stance is a giveaway. Scrutiny reveals a combed crown and 'dusty-edged' wing feathers. Where are the eponymous spots? The underparts are, it is true, diffusely striated across the chest. It appears that the moniker owes its origin to the teardrop-shaped markings shown by juveniles across the shoulders and some coverts. These spotted feathers are short-lived and replaced by plain grey-brown plumage. Elsewhere in Europe the bird is more appropriately known as 'Grey Flycatcher'. Despite drab colours, it is a spectacular acrobat. Perched lookouts explode into action and combine swoops and hovers with tight 'turn on a sixpence' manoeuvres. Snapping sounds are a clue to presence. Elasticised skin along the corner of the mouth allows the mandibles to seize prey with the rapidity of a mousetrap clanging shut. Call notes are heard more often than song. A thin pressurised wheeze is often linked to an emphatic *tup!* The combination almost matches the sound of a tin-can ring pull. Timbered gardens are favoured by breeding pairs. These days, with expanding populations of Grey Squirrels and Magpies swamping woodland and raiding songbird eggs and young, Spotted Flycatcher's open-nesting habits cost it dear. Pairs in western districts fare best thanks to isolated breeding habitats that escape predation. Females commence a second brood if fine summer weather and later-emerging insects bless the rapid development and survival of chicks. Time is tight, however. Assisted by her partner, she feeds the fledged young of the first brood while incubating a second clutch. Although not yet supported by any meaningful data, wholesale declines in large flying insects are likely to depress the breeding population.

TREECREEPER *Certhia familiaris*

At first flush this feathered fridge magnet suggests a mouse jerkily climbing a trunk. Treecreepers are slightly built, dinkier than a Robin, with upperparts resembling a dappled brown carapace. Except when viewed in profile, silvery underparts remain mostly hidden. Born to shuffle, they have feet like an arachnid. The arched hind-claw is longer than the toe to which it is attached; claws rather than toes grip bark. The arrangement is a trestle, supported by a 'knuckle joint' on the underside of the hind toe. The tail is all-important and used as a brace. Two large central feathers curve below the line of the body and have a rigid point, strong enough to serve as a prop. Even during moult, the uniquely important central feathers are not dropped until all the other feathers have grown to full length and can act as a substitute until the core regrows. Forward-facing eyes peer from below the bill and curved mandibles, as fine as a dentist's descaling spike, probe and snatch insect prey among pitted bark and decaying wood. The base of the bill is broad and topped with two nostrils. Is a sense of smell important during foraging? Other

SPOTTED FLYCATCHER At bottom. Sober colouring and – except when fly-catching – a stationary pose, make the species easy to overlook. Ivy-covered trunks provide popular nest sites. **TREECREEPER** At top. Anorexic toes grip bark while a splint-like tail jacks up the body. The only way is up. When they run out of trunk, Treecreepers swoop low and recommence foraging on the next tree in line.

peculiarities include a regular habit of folding one wing over the other and sometimes freezing if startled. Its progress, as it spirals upwards around a trunk or along a bough, is usually easily followed until the target peels off and swings, with a deep undulation, onto the lower girth of an adjoining tree. Intermittent and shrill 'hearing-test hiss' calls may be so high-pitched as to be inaudible. The sound is anonymous and even when loud and close, it can be hard to pin down. Treecreepers are resident and have a short song period, chiefly during fine weather in late winter or early spring. The tune is lively yet high-pitched; its opening recalls Willow Warbler but the ending has a Chaffinch flourish. Sometime in the past the bird made the ingenious discovery that the cardboard bark texture of introduced Wellingtonias can be scraped to create a shallow cup for roosting (see p. 58). Most mature specimens in Ireland have become pockmarked as a result. Despite being an inveterate tree-hugger, Treecreepers sometimes visit scrubby woodland and gardens by joining forces alongside insect-hunting Long-tailed Tits; they do the acrobatics whereas Treecreepers stick to the beams.

STONECHAT *Saxicola torquatus*

Endearing and almost as trusting as a Robin, Stonechats are half-pints that perch on briars, bracken and fences. Insectivorous, they drop for food into tangled vegetation – overgrown ditches, field boundaries festooned with brambles and coastal scrub of gorse and thorn. Where land is wild and settlement sparse – as in parts of Connacht and Munster – nature and Stonechats begin at the bottom of the garden. Affairs are conducted in the open and the watchman likes to see the sky at all times; some hunting forays are airborne. Dumpy and peculiarly big-headed with an afterthought of a tail and a big beguiling eye, pairs keep company and draw attention by flicking the tail and calling. The sound has two components. A fast, short whistle is attached to signature stony tapping (hence the bird's name). The two sounds combine and are interchangeable: *wheest, trek-trek* is typical. Juveniles, fledged but still hanging around parental apron strings, emit a buzzing note that sounds remarkably like one half of Lesser Redpoll's trademark *jut-jut* flight call. Males commence singing during calm days in February. Because many are already partnered, song is erratic. Hence, the wheezy warble is not uttered with much regularity. Males in breeding plumage are black-headed with a white half-collar and a terracotta 'bleeding heart' breast. Females ghost the same pattern. Following moult in late summer, all ages don a chequered russet coat. In winter, head markings are muted and the white collar of males is duller. Fresh juveniles are not unlike scaly baby Robins but have bright copper wing panels. Because up to three broods are produced, youngsters can be encountered any time between May and September.

WHEATEAR *Oenanthe oenanthe*

Except for a gap in northern Canada, Wheatears occur across the Northern Hemisphere and migrate back to their ancestral home in Africa for the winter. Irish breeders frequent bare hillsides, short pasture along Atlantic coasts and barren rocky places. Offshore islands are especially popular; drystone walls are used as perches and grazed commonages rich in invertebrates represent nirvana. Wheatears are active and restless. They charge over the ground in high-speed hops that resemble running. Brief pauses on small prominences – dry cowpats are a favourite – entice an observer to approach the Dapper Dan. But the blighter is having none of it and flits maddeningly ahead. Flight views are dominated by a white rump, made more conspicuous by white bases to the outer tail feathers. 'White-rear' is a handy mnemonic. The first males arrive around St Patrick's Day and, in March, are the prettiest spring migrant. China-blue upperparts combine with blackish wings and a masked face. In sublime counterpoint, the chest is honey-coloured, bleeding to white across the abdomen. The decadent colours are effective camouflage. By remaining still, a sentinel blends in with rocky terrain and the bumpy contours of walls. Brown-backed, plainer-faced females arrive in April. Towards the end of the month a second larger tribe passes through. Populations breeding in Iceland, Greenland and northeast Canada must

STONECHAT Top left: adult male, breeding. Top middle and top centre, juvenile. Top right and centre right, female. Also see pp. 3 (breeding pair) and 121 (adult male). WHEATEAR Middle row: left, female; centre, juvenile; right, adult male. Bottom row: left, male in flight; centre, female; right male. Also see pp. 3 (male), 28 (juvenile) and 84 (autumn migrant).

time migration to coincide with the later arrival of summer in the subarctic. Especially in May, they decamp to Ireland and fatten up for the last leg of their journey. Disputes with ensconced Irish inhabitants are commonplace. 'Greenland' Wheatears (the term is used as a catch-all for tundra nesters) are bigger, heavier and longer-winged (averaging 10.8cm, compared to 9.5cm) but defence of hearth and home favours local Ghurkhas. Irish-born youngsters fledge just as the last migrants pass through, an incredible example of one breeding cadre leapfrogging another. August signals departure. Rather than return via Ireland, northern groups prefer to reach the European coast further south and make use of brisk tailwinds that slingshot 25g aeronauts across a vast sweep of the North Atlantic (see MIGRATION, p. 84). Depending on the vicissitudes of weather, migrants pepper Ireland's coastline and islands, although benighted travellers are not gregarious. Irrespective of age or where they bred, autumn migrants look similar. A pervasive 'false tan' replaces courtship tuxedos. However, adult males, which acquire a rudimentary mask, are still subtly distinct. Migrants are silent but breeding birds frequently utter a hard double tap, prefaced by a high, scraping note. In combination: *weet … chack, chack.* Songsters are among the fastest wordsmiths. A fizzy discourse contains hints of Skylark mingled with rasping, creaky notes. Mimicry of other species is often interwoven but executed with such rapidity that the impersonations are lost on untrained ears.

ROBIN *Erithacus rubecula*

Approachability and doe eyes foster an impression of shivery vulnerability. Song, a sweet lyre whose notes are never the same twice, is delivered day and night throughout the year. It betokens ownership of a territory, whether for breeding turf, a winter home or a rest stop on migration. Most Robins are migrants and large numbers arrive from Scotland and northern England. The verse appears to get no further than a few pleasing opening bars, as though the singer has run out of ideas. Attentive listening reveals a spiralling, ethereal beauty. Stalling, metallic click-stop ticks serve as a call sign. If agitated, an ultrasonic gasping *seeeeh* may not register with human ears. More easily audible versions of the same note are given randomly and function as a kind of Robin intranet because the caller's position is hard to pin down but not its presence per se.

Juveniles, until they moult during summer, lack red and are scaly-breasted; their upperparts are sparsely streaked in a 'falling raindrops' pattern. The virginal plumage in which they fledge is lacy and lightweight. The body feathers, although complete, contain a bare minimum of filaments and have to be upgraded. As the makeover progresses, a Bambi look is superseded by the emergence of a foxy-orange bib and then face. The trademark colour earned the bird its original name: Redbreast. Sexes are similar. On account of trusting habits and the possibility of a close encounter, it is sometimes feasible to determine a bird's age – whether youngster or adult – during autumn and early winter, although the distinctions are forensically detailed. The key is to scrutinise the small band of greater coverts that cloak the flight feathers along the folded wing. Here, some individuals possess a row of pale tips, which form a thin bar. On adults that possess the feature (many do not and are plain-winged), the tips are rusty, somewhat wedge-shaped and decrease gradually in size over the full feather tract. On first-years, they are broader, buff coloured and more uniformly sized. In addition, young birds have fewer pale tips (as little as three) that are restricted to just the outermost feathers.

DUNNOCK *Prunella modularis*

If function follows form, then creeping hops with flexed legs are the optimum way to scrutinise the ground in front of your face. This seems to be a Dunnock's station in life. The bill is slightly decurved and slim, ideal for apprehending small fry, mainly creepy-crawlies augmented by tiny seeds in winter. Sobriety pervades appearance. All ages and sexes are similar, although juveniles

ROBIN Top left, moulting juvenile; top right, juvenile; inset right, adult. See also adults in worn and fresh plumage, p. 67. DUNNOCK Middle left, inset: adult. Bottom left, juvenile; bottom right, adult. Juveniles are brownish with streaking on crown and chest. The foreparts of some adults, presumably older males, are blueish-slate. See also p. 25.

are more heavily streaked. Closer inspection reveals sublime upperparts etched in pine-cone brown with a wood-smoke head and chest. Recognition of a shuffling silhouette among bushy undergrowth is made easy thanks to frequent calls and a peculiar wing-flicking habit, involving raising and quivering just one wing, which seems to function as an appeasement gesture by supplicants in the presence of higher-ranking individuals. Formerly inappropriately known as Hedge Sparrow, Dunnocks are sylphs compared to true sparrows. Often polygamous, threesomes may amount to a breeding unit that stays together until young fledge (see p. 25).

Outpourings of song cheer up late winter and persist until the final broods become independent in July. A complete sequence of male song is around four seconds long. The discourse is fast and cyclical. Phrases are stitched together like sharp shards. Many deliveries are short snatches exchanged by male neighbours. Although pleasant on the ear, the sound lacks gravitas – a text message not a letter. Rather than broadcast full versions repeatedly, they dash off brief salutations as if issuing a trailer. Furthermore, to denote prior acquaintance akin to 'mateyness', they splice excerpts of each other's songs into the compilation. Calls come in single or multiple syllables. In each, the core note – *seeep* – is a thin plaintive pipe with a forlorn undertone recalling a lost chick. Call rate ranges from three *seeep* notes per second to just one in three seconds. If anxious, there is a slight rise in pitch that, even to our ears, conveys trepidation. By compressing several syllables into a homogenous shuttling burst – *zee/zee/zee/zee* – the sound morphs into a sibilant trill. This is used in flight and occasionally at rest. Migrant Dunnocks from Scotland and Scandinavia arrive across Ireland in autumn. Trill notes often belie their location, especially when freshly arrived and announcing presence.

HOUSE SPARROW *Passer domesticus*

House Sparrows occur wherever English settlers set up home. Within a century, pilgrims had become established across the entire American continent and evolved cold-hardiness capable of withstanding temperatures of minus 30 °C and have also widely penetrated Amazonia. They adapt quickly to local conditions and have largely abandoned migratory instincts. A cheeky stance, characteristic hop and fearless persona have become trademarks. The chirruping of sparrows is reassuring to hear when we awake in a foreign city. Among concrete canyons dividing high buildings the sound has a sharp-edged clarity. Most nests are stuffed out of sight but are sometimes given away by an untidy train of dead vegetation protruding from an eave or gutter. House Sparrows are omnivorous. Adult diet is nearly 97 per cent vegetarian, while bare-skinned infants are fed roughly 70 per cent animal matter, mainly aphids. Declines have been attributed to a low survival rate for chicks and may be as a result of a dearth of nestling food in an increasingly sanitised environment. However, one study showed that cats accounted for 30 per cent of all deaths in one English village (cited in O'Sullivan & Wilson 2008). Disease is a fact of life in bird populations and outbreaks have the capacity to cause local extinctions (McGeehan & Wyllie 2012).

Black-bibbed males are distinctive at all seasons. In winter, feathering is unworn and pale-flecked 'stubble' peppers areas of plain plumage, such as the nape and sides of the head. During spring this gradually disappears and, in particular, the bib becomes more extensively black. Bill colour also undergoes a change when hormones instigate a switch from horn-coloured to slate black in males and a less noticeable, partly graphite-grey bill in females. Cock sparrows have a grumpy countenance. The leaden crown bears down like a tight-fitting cap and impinges on the upper face, just forward of the eye. A pale squiggle contributes to a furrowed brow. Close behind the eye, a whitish fleck emphasises the piqued look. Females are regarded as dowdy. Such a blinkered assessment overlooks a broad supercilium and upperparts that sport a desert-fatigues palette. Juveniles resemble females, but as young males moult during summer they acquire a sooty chin. Flight style is level and barrelling: a clockwork blur of wingbeats interspersed with a 'fast float'.

TREE SPARROW *Passer montanus*

Forget the underwhelming inept title, Tree Sparrow is dinky and swanky, true sparrow aristocracy. Just as Coal Tit is more petite and dumpier than Blue Tit, Tree Sparrow is fatter-headed but shorter-tailed than House Sparrow. On the ground, feeding actions are fast and finch-like and the tail is constantly cocked. Foragers are animated and constantly ready to explode into flight. Sexes are similar and juveniles closely resemble adults. Appearance is standard throughout the year, apart from an indistinctly pale bill base during autumn and early winter. The cheeks are snow-white, not sea-fog grey, and are anointed with a diagnostic black

HOUSE SPARROW Top row: left and middle, black-billed males in relatively unworn plumage at start of breeding season, March; right, worn male, July. Upper middle row: left and middle, females in unworn plumage, October; right, female in breeding condition (bill changes to olive-grey), April. Lower middle row: males in new plumage, October (bill yellowish; right bird showing some leucistic plumage – not uncommon among House Sparrows). TREE SPARROW Bottom four. Left-hand pair in fresh autumn plumage with pale bill base (black-billed by late winter, right-hand pair).

thumbprint. Extending from the forehead to the nape, a chocolate-brown bearskin dispels any lingering thought of House Sparrow. Chiming with a svelte costume, vocalisations have the air of a Dublin 4 accent. Although paralleling House Sparrow's vocabulary in most utterances, Tree Sparrow enunciations sound 'neater'; more cut glass. Distinctive in flight is a muttered tapping *chet … chet*, as if delivered through clenched teeth.

In the past, Ireland's population periodically dwindled but is currently enjoying a boom. Formerly exclusive to arable farmland in coastal districts, inland populations occur and small companies wander widely and are capable of establishing breeding nuclei. In the last century, most human-inhabited but sparrow-free Irish islands were colonised. Curiously, to fill the vacant niche, Tree Sparrows often adopted a House Sparrow lifestyle (a habit that makes it the default urban sparrow across China). Ordinarily, the species takes grain and seeds and shuns human proximity. They breed in holes and readily accept nest boxes. Young are fed insects gathered by adults in damp habitats such as wet ditches and marshland. Wild bird cover has sustained sizeable winter flocks and the birds typically associate with Yellowhammers and Chaffinches. Except in rural areas within the breeding range, the species is an unlikely garden visitor.

GREY WAGTAIL *Motacilla cinerea*

Yellow plumage on Grey Wagtail's underparts, especially noticeable in flight beneath the tail, causes confusion and pops 'Yellow Wagtail' into the mind of many. In truth, Yellow Wagtail *Motacilla flava* is a rare migrant to damp coastal meadows, whereas Grey Wagtail is widespread year round along fast-flowing upland streams, ponds and localities where sluggish tributaries meet the coast (also frequented by Pied Wagtails). More elegant and nimble than Pied Wagtail, the tail is longer, which exaggerates its pivot. Flight manner is deep and bounding – like a skipping kangaroo. The call is sharp-edged and disyllabic: *jeet-jeet*. A Grey Wagtail is routinely encountered standing on a stone in the middle of a frothing current, bobbing its long tail vigorously before launching into a near-vertical slam-dunk after a passing insect. Territory holders sing sporadically. Occasionally a full twitter develops but the commonest discourse is a repetitive lisping *zee-zee-zee-zip* that has undertones of Long-tailed Tit but is louder with an emphatic, abrupt conclusion. Males develop a black throat in the breeding season, bounded by a wiggly white whisker. Unlike Pied Wagtail, the head is marked with a thin pale supercilium and the legs and feet are pink. Immigration enlivens coastal areas in winter. Across northern parts of the European range, Grey Wagtail is highly migratory. Indeed, many winter in Africa, including South Africa.

PIED WAGTAIL *Motacilla alba*

The eponymous name is Route One to identification. Except in late summer or autumn, when facial feathering is fresh and a few show a primrose glow to white cheeks, Pied Wagtail is monochrome. Some plumage is moulted in early spring and 'booted and suited' males are black on the back, crown, throat and chest. Irrespective of age, they have two white wing-bars. On males, the bars are broad and almost meet. Hard-to-miss white edges also pick out the three large tertial feathers that cloak and conceal the folded wing at rest, providing good practice in locating this feather group that may be tricky to pin down on other species whose upperparts are plain. Female Pied Wagtails are grey-backed and the nape is blotched with black. Juveniles lack snow-white underparts and are ashen-faced with a dark-bordered crown and a double-banded upper chest (dark throat sides braid into a breast bib). Following moult, first-winters resemble adults, although some 'stubble' often remains on the ear-coverts as a badge of youth. Pied Wagtails are chatterboxes and specific calls are used to forge feeding partnerships (see TERRITORY AND NESTS, p. 17). During daytime foraging and at pre-roost gatherings, an assortment of two-parted syllables maintains vocal presence, even when alone. A burst of polysyllables sounds like song but is reserved for 'giving out' to any bird or beast (including us) that piques curiosity. Once airborne, polyglot utterances are replaced by a standardised flight call – an emphatic *chissick*, *chiddick* or *fizzup* – that often keeps pace with dipping undulations. Pied Wagtails are insectivorous and frequent open spaces everywhere. Habitat

GREY WAGTAIL Top row, adult breeding plumage. Left: female; centre and right, male. Second row: left, female; centre and right, winter plumage. **PIED WAGTAIL** Monochrome at all seasons. Centre right: male high-stepping and (below) wing-stretching. Bottom right: juvenile. Centre lower and bottom left: female. **WHITE WAGTAIL** (migrant to Ireland, analogous to Pied Wagtail in Iceland and Europe): two left of centre, against pink background. Male at top.

preference is hard to define and although frequently near water, garage forecourts, tarmac playgrounds and freshly mown lawns appear to lack a unifying thread. However, winged prey, when drifted across open space lacking protective vegetation, is exposed and quickly snapped. Pied Wagtail roosts are almost as famous as those of Starlings. The relatively safe, 'splendid isolation' of avenues of mature ornamental trees in town centres can draw hundreds. In the 1950s, over 3,000 once roosted in three Plane trees in Dublin's O'Connell Street.

White Wagtail is Pied Wagtail's more migratory counterpart across Europe and Iceland. In a similar vein to Iceland's Wheatear population, which transits through Ireland en route to Africa, White Wagtails do likewise. The title is unfortunate. In reality, back colour defines the stranger. All ages are pale grey above. Spring adults are particularly fine and show maximum contrast between pearly upperparts and a black nape. Revved up and bound for Iceland, they are skittish and behave quite unlike their common-or-garden cousins. Passage peaks in late April and migrants occur on coasts and the shorelines of large lakes. In August, southbound migrants travel west of Ireland and are scarce. Identification at this season is problematic and few genuine White Wagtails occur. Most claims are explained by variation in the appearance of first-winter Pied Wagtails.

MEADOW PIPIT *Anthus pratensis*

Meadow Pipit is one of several 'little brown jobs' whose natural constituency is grassy wild places, moorland and rushy fields. Because dung attracts insects, the vicinity of livestock is favoured. Although a common breeder, year-round presence is due to waves of migrants heading, in April, for Iceland and Scotland, then filtering south in autumn, en route to southwest Europe. Probably, Ireland's wintering birds are a late-arriving contingent from overseas. A brown livery with streaked underparts suggests a diminutive thrush. Unlike true thrushes, the back is patterned, not plain, and the bill is fine. Meadow Pipits have a closer affinity to wagtails, with which they share a jaunty high-stepping gait and occasional tail bobbing. The tail is shorter and the flight action lacks a wagtail's sense of purpose and surging dips. They are frail fliers and seem to be treading water due to an excess of flutter and a

MEADOW PIPIT Top three: left, spring (plumage at least six months old and most have lost olive-bronze glow); centre and right, fresh plumage, autumn and early winter. Note pale legs at all seasons. **ROCK PIPIT Lower four:** upper left, fresh plumage, November (also p. 70, lower); centre, worn, July (also pp. 68 and 70, upper); right and bottom left, slight wear, late winter.

somewhat erratic flight path. Timorous, squeaky *jeet* calls accompany take-off; travelling birds are vocal and seek company. Courtship flight is spectacular. Rising from the ground, a shrill *sip-sip-sip* tattoo reaches a crescendo in line with the songster gently parachuting to earth. During autumn, plumage is fresh and exquisite and permeated by a honey-pine glow. Some are almost olive-backed. Below, the undercoat colour ranges from cream to cinnamon. Head markings mainly consist of a striated, wet-combed crown and a creamy-buff supercilium. A white, monocle-like hoop encircles a sequin eye and a dark jawline delineates a light throat, hemmed in by blackish tramlines. These extend across the chest like widening meridians of longitude: thick, short and crowded below the throat, longer and more widely spaced along the flanks. The legs and feet are pale pinkish or horn-coloured and the claw on the hind toe is extraordinarily long and easily visible on a bird perched on wires, reminiscent of crampons. Upon take-off, snowy outer tail feathers contrast with a black inner tail.

ROCK PIPIT *Anthus petrosus*

Exclusively coastal, Rock Pipits forage above and below storm beaches, consistent with a life dictated by a clockwork tidal rhythm. The bird is mobile and ranges widely, seeking out a range of prey: sandhoppers flushed by the incoming tide, tiny molluscs ferreted from exposed seaweed, basking insects snatched off boulders or plucked over piles of rotting seaweed. Meadow Pipits frequently occur alongside Rock Pipits among any interface of seashore and rough grassland, creating identification problems. Compared to Meadow Pipit, Rock Pipit is larger and less svelte with a longer bayonet of a bill. On account of drab plumage tones, messy underparts and a huskier voice (a strident *feece*, usually uttered singly) the bird suffers indentured inferiority to Meadow Pipit. Although fascinatingly variable, it is often cast as an ugly sister, afforded soul-crushing stasis through being not pretty enough to impress but not sufficiently bland to be boring. The salty sift of spray, exposure to plumage-bleaching sunlight and shouldering feathers against rocky substrate produce a weathered appearance, like garden furniture left out for a year. During summer many adults are tatty but following moult completed in August all ages sport a sombre-but-sultry outfit for winter. Depending on light, the colour scheme takes on the pallor of a wax jacket, although a mousy soupçon is omnipresent. Plumage located between eye and bill is dusky. The result is a sooty face of overdone mascara, among which white-rimmed spectacles, split at the eye's corners, gleam like a *fáinne* ring. Adjoining a light bib, extensive chest markings are murky: grey, diffuse and disorganised, rather than crisp radiating lines. Some individuals are heavily blotched. Except for the snow-white bangles surrounding the eye, no part of the plumage is bright, even the outer tail feathers are ashy. Leg colour is variable, although most are fairly dark: kelp-coloured through mulled wine to unpolished amber (potentially resembling Meadow Pipit). Cat's-paw striations on the back of both species are similar. Courtship display and song is shared with Meadow Pipit, although Rock Pipit sounds more butch. Ireland's Rock Pipit population is comprised of residents and a proportion of winter immigrants from western Scandinavia.

CHAFFINCH *Fringilla coelebs*

Present year round and widespread in gardens, Chaffinches cannot fail to be identified by sight and sound. At rest, irrespective of sex or age, no other small songbird has so much white in the wing. On a flying bird, white is located on two discrete sets of coverts, producing dual bands of white. Unlike some other finches, there is no white rump but the outer tail feathers are white. Males are brightly plumaged with more vivid contrasts than females, whose underlying colour scheme is drawn from a palette of olive-brown. During autumn and winter, male colours dumb-down. To become tickety-boo for spring courtship, drab feather margins wear off to reveal full tints of a blue-grey crown, salmon-pink chest and cherry-brown back. Glimpses of an astro-turf rump add a tropical touch and are also shown by females. Dandy males develop a black forehead and the bill turns steel blue. Chaffinch has a rich vocabulary. A key call given at rest is a sunny, cocktail-clinking *pink!* Often the note is repeated: either quickly – *pink! pink!* – or randomly and, depending on mood, with more vim. The call covers contact, threat, alarm

BRAMBLING Top row: male (left) alongside female. CHAFFINCH Second row: female between two males (right-hand male in breeding plumage). Three lower rows: Chaffinches on left, Bramblings (winter males) on right. In bottom row, female Chaffinch is first-winter (narrow tertials) as is female Brambling (greater covert bar has two feather generations of different colour).

and distress. It is also a precursor to taking flight. When that happens an entirely different handle is broadcast. The flight note is softer and longer: *choop*. Although delivered singly and not part of a trill or a twitter, calls from members of a passing flock or a disturbed feeding party overlap; the resulting cacophony of muttered expletives erroneously suggests runs of notes. Because Greenfinch, a frequent companion, usually broadcasts a baritone *jup* in a short series, scope exists for confusion. Song is lively; males in full voice pulsate and occupy sentinel song-posts, thereby drawing attention. Hallmarks of a ratcheted trill are a 'gear-changing' momentum and a terminal flourish. Sometimes the final note attenuates and resembles *queer* or *beer*. Territory-holding males substitute shorthand *de-feat* rather than sing, especially during inclement, rainy weather. Ireland's breeding population is resident. Once youngsters acquire a territory they become attached to it for life. Familiarity with local surroundings appears to confer high survival rates and, for a small bird, a long life expectancy. Ringing recoveries show that some reach the age of twelve; a Swiss Chaffinch reached fifteen years. Where cause of death is known, cats are mostly to blame. Given that a recent study that attached cameras to domestic cats found that only around one-quarter of kills are brought home, the scale of death is hugely under-recorded. Each autumn a spectacular exodus from Scandinavia brings many immigrants here for the winter. These swell local populations and large flocks comb farm fields, running and hopping through stubble for unharvested grain and intermingling with buntings, Skylarks and Tree Sparrows. The majority are youngsters and females; older males attempt to tough it out closer to home. During summer, diet switches to insects. Chaffinches may not be as agile as warblers but they are artful flycatchers and, most un-finch like, they frequently hover among autumn leaves to snatch prey.

BRAMBLING *Fringilla montifringilla*

Bramblings are handsome winter visitors, small numbers of which arrive in association with immigrant flocks of Scandinavian Chaffinches. A summer inhabitant of northern taiga and Birch forest, millions head south each winter and scour Europe for nuts of Beech (mast) and Hornbeam. Beech in Ireland seldom produces mast and travellers settle for stubble grain or wild-bird seed proffered in gardens. Attracting one often produces others and a chance to admire a denizen of northern wilderness. Although similar in overall size to Chaffinch, Bramblings are slightly larger-billed and thickset. Hunkered on the ground and busily de-husking seed, they look nervous and raise the rear crown, making the head look pointed. Winter plumage is fresh and unworn; pale tips to black and tan create a mealy, almost tartan look. Depending on the bird's sex, the chest is orange (male) or apricot (female) and the belly is white. Orange-washed wing-bars and shoulder patches are further distinctions. In flight, the tail is plain and dark-sided, but the rump is white. A peculiar tooth-sucking flight note is characteristic but underwhelming. A better giveaway to buried treasure among a horde of Chaffinches is a whining, nasal *nyeeep*. The note has a braying, nose-wrinkling feel. A useful analogy is a tight-fitting wine cork being extracted.

GREENFINCH *Chloris chloris*

Despite being built like a bouncer, Greenfinch is graceful with soulful ball-bearing eyes and dainty porker-pink legs and feet. In flight, broad shoulders continue the weightlifter impression, reinforced by a stocky tail with a distinct cleft. The Latin name is derived from Khloros, a Greek god of leafy vegetation. Greener than a shamrock, males are a chlorophyll dream. The back is brassy, paling to grape-green on the rump and blushing grey on the cheeks. The folded wing has a yellow hi-viz strip along the base of the primaries, also evident at the wing's wrist. In flight, yellow explodes from the base of the tail. On more bland females, hints of streaking adorn a browner back and the face has an uncomplimentary jaw-line due to a 'five o'clock shadow' whisker radiating from the gape. Youngsters are stony white below with widespread fine, pencil-line streaking. Based on wing pattern, determining the sex of an individual is relatively straightforward, even in juvenile plumage. Females have narrow, herringbone yellow edges to just the outer primaries; on males, yellow covers most of the outer vane, forming a solid block. The macho bill extends the range of seeds that can be split and eaten, although Greenfinches are equally content to eat blackberries and buds. Rose hips are, however, a speciality. In gardens, flock members are aggressive and tend to commandeer feeders and park at seed ports. Recaptures of ringed birds indicate that home-bred birds are sedentary. In autumn small parties wander to offshore islands and will remain if a plentiful supply of *Rosa rugosa* hips is discovered. In early spring males perform a Swallow-like 'floating butterfly' display and glide by, slowly flapping their wings. The production is accompanied by twittering that gathers momentum, then climaxes into a long wheeze whose crescendo suggests that a point of tension has been reached. During summer, juveniles pestering parents keep up a barrage of reverberating metallic monosyllables, varying in pace but reminiscent of hammer taps. The petulant utterance is a forerunner of the adult flight call, a burry trill consisting of three to eight tightly spaced *chup* notes that, to our ears, may come across as a 'fast bouncing *djururrup*' (Jonsson 1992).

GOLDFINCH *Carduelis carduelis*

Goldfinch is an eyeful of bullet points. As if colourful 'get seen' signage at rest and on the wing is not enough, the dancing flight is a further advertisement. As close-knit as a shoal of fish, the birds probably adhere to the same philosophy of safety in numbers. They are not exactly peaceniks, however. At feeders, bee-pollen wingbars in jostling flurries resemble yellow sparklers but the argy-bargy is for real. Open-mouthed hissing and fluttery kickboxing are less than angelic. Hence 'charm' is an absurd collective term for a flock; coven is more apt. Even so, group harmony is important and pre-roost evensong has a unifying feel. Over two months juveniles acquire an adult 'bloodstained bandage' red-white-and-black head pattern and fawn-headed young are a common sight into late autumn. Tinkling flight calls – sharp-

GREENFINCH Lower middle row: left, juvenile; right, first-winter male. Bottom row: left, adult male (broad tertials and blue-grey greater coverts); centre, first-winter female; right, adult female. GOLDFINCH Top: autumn flock containing many juveniles. Goldfinches rear two or more broods, explaining the presence of fawn-headed youngsters as late as November. Upper middle row: left, adult; right, juvenile.

edged and popping – are difficult to convey phonetically. The momentum never falters and the unintelligible jumble has a fax-machine feel. Goldfinches have increased dramatically over the last fifty years, partly because they are no longer trapped as cage-birds. Ironically, garden feeders have fuelled newfound abundance. Elsewhere, flocks swirl around thistles. From the time the seeds are formed in midsummer, and throughout autumn and winter, birds search the dead tops. Strong jaw muscles prise open dried-up plant heads, having first pierced them with the bill's dagger tip. Male bills are longer than those of females. Although the difference is small – 1mm – it allows mainly males to access the seeds of teasel *Dipsacus*, which lie at the base of long spiked tubes. Darwin (1871) was made aware: 'I am assured that the bird-catchers can distinguish the males by their slightly longer beaks … [they alone] are often found feeding on the seeds of the teasel, which they can reach with the elongated beak.'

LINNET *Carduelis cannabina*

Linnets rise as a twittering cloud when disturbed from low vegetation. The bill is insubstantial and best suited to munching green seed and minuscule grains. Favourite plunder is the base of Dandelions that are slit open and disembowelled for feathery filaments each containing a tiny capsule. Hotspots include gorse commons, heather hillsides and 'wasteland' replete with low-growing seeding wildflowers. Among agricultural landscapes, stubble, rough pasture and field margins along hedgerows may offer food and sanctuary if management practices are not severe. Wild bird cover has become salvation in many areas. Except during spring when feather tips abrade to turn male chests and foreheads lipstick red – the same process yields a smooth grey head and clay-coloured back – the standard dress is brown and streaky. At rest, white fishbone edges to the primaries and tail may be obvious, although their visibility is tempered by overlapping plumage. Across the outer wing in flight, a 'Venetian blind' effect is more noticeable, thanks to the juxtaposition of a contrasting dark knuckle composed of blackish primary coverts. The best field marks are found on the head. A beady eye is clamped between pale upper and lower haloes

TWITE Top two rows. Twites are, compared to Linnet, more stereotyped in appearance. All share a buff-yellow face that suggests a custard-pie attack (N.D. McKee). **LINNET** Top centre, red-fronted adult male; far right, female; bottom right, juvenile; bottom left, first-winter female; lower centre, winter male; far left, breeding male (see also p. ii).

and creased by a dark furrow. The cheeks are pale-centred, as if an underlying shade was erased, leaving a hollow. Fledged juveniles are fawn-chested and lightly streaked below; they look cuter than adults. Because up to three broods are produced, youngsters associating with parents are a familiar sight through spring and summer. At rest and in flight a hubbub of cheeps is maintained. Furthermore, because incubating females are indisposed, gangs of noisy offspring are often in tow with carmine-chested adult males and clamour to be fed right up until they moult body plumage in early autumn. Close views show their red gapes, derived from blood vessels in the throat lining. When sated, blood supply diverts to aid digestion and gape colour dims. The ingenious colour change determines which mouth gets the next food delivery. Year round, sociality and song go hand in hand. At vespers or during 'downtime' between feeding excursions, flocks settle in hidden conclaves and twitter. The nattering is an amalgam of song excerpts and calls. Full song is rich, fast and varied. In the past Linnets were trapped as cage-birds and deemed a poor man's canary. Talkative trills are de rigueur at rest and 'recycled' in shortened form as flight calls. Ascribing words to fit is difficult. A typical sequence commences with a few repetitions of around four identical notes (reminiscent of Greenfinch) and truncates into shorter fragments, some of whose notes are out of key. The 'broken biscuits' unconformity is characteristic. It is as though, once airborne, at-rest rehearsals of a smooth homogeneous trill fall apart. A similar pattern of good intentions gone pear-shaped can often be observed on television weather forecasts when prepared scripts run into trouble.

TWITE *Carduelis flavirostris*

So far as looks go, Twite and Linnet appear to be Tweedledum and Tweedledee. On the rare occasions when they share a flock, sharp wits are needed to tell the two apart. The Latin name is a cryptic clue: *Flavirostris* means yellow-billed. Compared to Linnet, other distinctions include a bland, curry-powder 'Mongolian' face and a pink-tinted rump. Watched squirrelling over the ground on a chilly day among vegetation scarcely tall enough to hide in, they appear round-shouldered, neckless and swaddled. Unlike Linnet, the base of the bill is feathered, which makes it seem puny. At times a troupe rises in unison, as though pulled by an invisible puppeteer. Conversational chatter attends feeding activities but volume increases when the flock is airborne. Downscale slurred *swee swee* notes stand out from a canvas of twitters. In recent decades Ireland's resident Twite population has gone down the pan. Some Scottish birds cross to northeast Ulster for winter but elsewhere the sight of breeding pairs high among heather or roly-poly parties at sea level, combing field and shore for the tiny seeds of Sea Aster and Thrift, is increasingly hard to find. West is, just about, still best. Because they live in such wild and beautiful places, Twites are not gifted to gardens.

LESSER REDPOLL *Carduelis flammea*

'I have Redpolls!' is not an admission of contracting a contagious disease. Rather, in the same way that diminutive stars of stage and screen captivate audiences – Charlie Chaplin and Judy Garland spring to mind – the feisty bundle that is Lesser Redpoll has a similar effect when recognised at a feeder. Most of its tribe live in the vast wreath of birch and taiga that girdles the planet from Scandinavia across Asia to America. Where proper forest ends and low-growing willows cling to tundra, thumbnail size is a liability, unsuited to withstanding bitter cold. A larger body loses less heat. Hence Arctic Redpolls are Chaffinch-sized with feathered legs and whiteout plumage that matches troops in an undercover ski patrol. We, in Ireland, on the other hand, reside in the same latitude as the smallest and swarthiest member of the crew. As the name suggests, adults are recognised by a crimson forehead. Equally distinctive is a sooty, chimney-sweep face. Although brown and streaky elsewhere, plumage is as neat as a bellboy. Crisp wing-bars pass for epaulets; furrowed tramlines comb the flanks and belly whiteness permeates the underparts. As feather tips abrade in January, the chests of some individuals beam pink. These are males, aged two and older. The oldest are radiant; even their rump is rose-coloured. Juveniles are a different matter. Lacking a red beret and all bar a hint of a smoggy face, they can be perplexing. A gingery wing-bar and petite size are useful steers. All ages show a whitish weave within the rump, peppered by dark streaking. In winter, feeding birds jostle among birch and alder cones to extract seed. Acrobatic, tit-like and often with Siskins, flocks associate with groves of deciduous trees along riverbanks and around lakeshores. Ground feeders hop. Meadowsweet and other tall plants are visited; swaying movements made by silent nibblers often denote presence. A jangling *chu chu chu*, interspersed with a pulsating wheeze during the breeding season, seems perfectly choreographed to fit a bouncy, undulating flight. The species has benefited from the expansion of forestry plantations across uplands and lowland bogs. Traditional habitats include hillside birch woods and the scrubby wet woodland of callow land across the midlands. They seem to be attracted to willow thickets in July and August, probably to feed on aphids that would boost protein intake during moult (Neville McKee pers. comm.). Depending upon the availability of food, numbers fluctuate. Moreover, unpredictable waves of migrants travel both within Ireland and to and from breeding haunts in Scotland and winter quarters in the Low Countries. Surging through gardens, they seek small seed. Tiny black nyger seed can exert an almost magnetic draw.

SISKIN *Carduelis spinus*

Siskins have scored a double whammy. Because they mainly breed in coniferous forest and, in spring, eat the seeds of pine and commercially grown Sitka Spruce, their population has soared. With breeding over, they switch to alder and birch. Crucially, they are confiding and have learned to visit gardens. During the 1970s, red-coloured net bags filled with peanuts were

LESSER REDPOLL Upper four; juvenile at top left. Males become pink-chested in spring when plumage tips abrade to emphasise reddish hues that are intensified further by UV sunlight. SISKIN Centre and left: first-winter males. Bottom left: adult male (broad pale-edged tertials). Centre right and bottom right: females.

in vogue. Siskins latched onto them. Feeding fashions change – nut bags are becoming old hat – but the garden-visiting habit has become enshrined. The upshot is that a once rare Irish breeding bird has skyrocketed. If food is scarce abroad, large numbers stream west from Britain and Europe. This has led to several spectacular overseas ringing recoveries of birds trapped in Irish gardens in winter: from Count Dracula Transylvanian Mountains in Eastern Europe to Dr Zhivago forests in Russia. Green, black and yellow colours, small-fry size and an agile and twisting modus operandi suggest a Blue Tit or Great Tit. Redpolls, a regular consort, are fundamentally brown. Males are particularly showy and adults of both sexes are longer-billed than youngsters, even during winter. The curved upper mandible is long and designed to prise seed from opening scales of cones. For this reason, shorter-billed youngsters may opt to feed on the ground on leftovers dislodged from above. Chatty most of the time, a shrill flight call is an instant bead. The sound is a zinging, descending *tzzzeeuu* with the 'Did you see that?' suddenness of glimpsing a shooting star.

BULLFINCH *Pyrrhula pyrrhula*

Like an unobtrusive devoted couple, pairs of Bullfinches keep quiet company and seldom sally forth from the innards of thickets, hedgerows or tall shrubbery where they feed on a wide range of seeds and fruits. Feeding action is clambering and adroit in the manner of a heavyweight boxer. A longish tail counterbalances pivoting actions and the unlikely acrobat rarely drops to the ground. Bullfinches have a penchant for ripening buds and a fastidious pair can snip a sizeable tree of blossom. The stubby bill is disc-shaped but as sharp as secateurs. Males are smartly dressed. An eyeless black cowl confers the anonymity of a hoodie yet a pouting sergeant-major chest is rosy-pink, set off by blue-grey upperparts. Females are drab and have a twin set and pearls consisting of a brown breast and grey shawl. Young birds are uncapped and plain-faced; the eye looks beady and gormless. The base of the black tail flashes a square-shaped white rump, often the first clue to an eloping pair. Low-key piping maintains contact and is used as a personalised intranet, rather than broadcast to a wider audience. A soft, rather forlorn whistle – *pew* or an intoned pronunciation of the name *Hugh* – is sometimes doubled. Youngsters seeking company call more loudly. Adult privacy settings apply to creaky warbling that is delivered sotto voce: pillow talk between couples rather than YouTube attention-seeking chatter.

WAXWING *Bombycilla garrulus*

Dark winter days are sometimes enlivened by the appearance of a small company of this exotic Starling-sized visitor from northern taiga. Waxwings disperse westwards in autumn and switch from swooping for mosquitoes to guzzling berries. A combination of good breeding success, easterly tailwinds and below-par food supplies across Europe propel sizeable flocks to Ireland. They scour hedgerows and gardens replete with berries. Haws are a favourite. Because they usually arrive after Christmas – having eaten their way west across northern Britain – the menu may be restricted to berries on ornamental shrubs such as Cotoneaster and Pyracantha, a predilection that brings them into parks and gardens. Berry after berry is swallowed whole and securely held fruit is yanked free with a hover. Sittings are punctuated with frequent time-outs for digestion, the purple results of which pebbledash pavements. Waxwing is the embodiment of a bird swaddled against the cold. The Cossack is remarkably round (a short tail and stubby bill truncate shape) and fawny feathering resembles fur that envelops most of the feet. Non-feeding birds ball up, fluffing up grey rump plumage. The costume is dense and remarkably waterproof. Nonchalantly, they stay in the open during downpours. One shake and they are dry. Silhouetted and arranged among bare twigs, flock members sit like lanterns. Starlings lean forward and are more slouched. Waxwings are crested, although the headgear may be sleeked flat and can be raised at will. The eye and foreface are masked and cue a resemblance to a Fedora hat: creased and pinched at the front and along the sides of the crown. A black cravat rounds off dapper looks. Technicolor is found across the wings and tail. Adult males are the most ornate; daffodil-yellow edges hook around the feather circumference. On youngsters, only one side of each feather is pale. Red waxy blobs adorn the bunched ends of several folded secondaries (formed by the fusion of the feather shaft with the tip of the inner vane). Adult males have several resinous red dabs; young birds may have none. The undertail is fox red and a yellow-banded black tail is a useful field mark in flight. Waxwings drink a lot and have a habit of flying perilously close to ground level when swooping down to puddles. Singles and troupes are vocal. Soft purring trills reminiscent of the peals of tiny silver bells appear to attract passing strays because flocks feeding in the same location often increase in number as days go by.

BULLFINCH Bottom row: left, male; right, female. WAXWING Five birds. Centre, far left: adult (herringbone pattern around all primary feathers forming wing tip). Far right and lower centre: first-winters (unilateral pale edge along primaries, fewer red waxy tips to folded secondaries).

YELLOWHAMMER *Emberiza citrinella*

On the world stage, a male Yellowhammer will always make heads turn. The bird is neon but never gauche. Day-Glo plumage may be for show but it also forms a canvas for a tweedy chestnut back and an unstreaked ginger rump, obvious in flight when a sleek willowy form delights the eye. Females undertake incubation duties and their plumage is, of necessity, more cryptic. A fan of streaks encircles the chest and yellow tints elsewhere are smothered beneath a wealth of detail. Yellowhammers feed on the ground. When disturbed they fly up into bushes, flashing white outer tail feathers and intoning a pebbly metallic click. Repetitions of the note and overlapping calls from flock members create a sense of insect calls, rather than birds. Across country districts, the 'A *little bit of bread and no – cheese*' mnemonic for the sleepy broadcast of males has become part of folklore. Nowadays silence reigns because the most

YELLOWHAMMER Bottom row: left, female; centre, male breeding; right, male (first-winter). REED BUNTING Top row: female flashing white outer tail feathers. Middle row: left, adult male; centre, female (first-winter based on sharply tapered tips to splayed tail feathers); right, female (probably adult due to impression of broader and more smoothly rounded shape of two outer feathers).

statuesque of buntings has been brought to its knees. Ireland's Yellowhammers are sedentary. Ringing reveals that 70 per cent of adults spend the winter within 5km of the nest site, which means that when they are gone, they are really gone. Breeding nuclei have become smaller and more beleaguered. The bird needs grains to get through winter and uncultivated field margins (adjoined by battlement hedgerows) that sustain seeding wildflowers and the bounty of insects needed by Yellowhammer broods. Will farming hearts bleed for a feathered fellow citizen?

REED BUNTING *Emberiza schoeniclus*

Human feet do not easily tread where breeding Reed Buntings go. Bushes bordering lakeshores or along the margins of reed beds are des res but wet thickets laced with bramble and rushes are equally acceptable. Insects and their larvae are the most important elements in the summer diet, replaced by small seeds of marsh plants and rushes for the rest of the year. By autumn, parties rove widely and occupy dry habitats such as unharvested crops – weedy runnels among rows of root crops are frequent feeding places – cultivated ground or grassy edges of young tree plantations. Gardens, except those surrounded by untamed countryside, are seldom visited. When disturbed, small clusters fly up and perch in nearby hedges, trees or overhead wires. The silhouette is blob-headed with a spool-shaped body and an ample tail that tapers from a narrow waist to a swollen tip. Identification is helped by a unique habit of opening the tail sideways. The flick-knife twitch unveils a flash of white, delivered intermittently in an undulating flight but seemingly 'compulsory' upon landing. Gingerly, one or more call softly to each other. The sound is a sliding coquettish *tzoooo* that has the elegance of a waltzing skater. In flight, a short grating note is given. By late February, flocks become weighted in favour of one sex or the other. Parties of males include winter visitors destined to depart overseas, probably Scotland but feasibly Scandinavia. Their plumage is in a state of flux, particularly the head. Controlled abrasion burnishes brown tips into black. In the throes of transition, males appear to don shades and resemble pall-bearers at a Cosa Nostra funeral. Overall stripy plumage in females and young recalls that of a small brown finch, such as a Linnet or Lesser Redpoll, although Reed Bunting is larger and House Sparrow size. Furthermore, no other contender marshals as much chestnut and russet in the weave and female and young Reed Buntings have a moustachioed appearance, absent in all common confusion species. By late spring, bachelors ensconced on breeding haunts sit high and courtship chases commence. Females lead suitors in a twisting pursuit that often concludes with several participants diving into the bottoms of bushes. Singing black-shrouded males, their white neck collars puffed up in bas-relief, bring to mind the formal dress of a magistrate. The notes are tapped out rather than sung. Reed Buntings are not divas; the delivery is pedestrian and the verbiage jerky. Two or three monosyllables drip by, followed by an underwhelming final jingle. The riff approximates to *Tim, Pat … Coogan.*

REFERENCES

Arendt, W.J. 1985. *Philornis* ectoparasitization of Pearly-eyed Thrashers. I. Impact on growth and development of nestlings. *Auk* 102:270-280.

Ash, J.S. 1965. The 'raptor flight' of the Cuckoo. *British Birds* 58:1-5.

Attenborough, D. 1998. *The Life of Birds*. BBC.

Aviles, J.M. & Garamszegi, L.Z. 2007. Egg rejection and brain size among potential hosts of the Common Cuckoo. *Ethology* 113: 562-572.

Bairlein, F., Norris, D.R., Nagel, R., Bulte, M., Voight, C.C., Fox. J.W., Hussell, D.J.T. & Schmaljohann, H. 2012. 'Cross-hemisphere Migration of a small 25g Songbird'. Biology Letters online, 15 February www.royalsocietypublishing.org, , DOI:10.1098/rsbl.2011.1223.

Bartholomew, G.A. & Cade, T.J. 1956. Water consumption of House Finches. *The Condor* 58: 406-412.

Bartholomew, G.A. & Cade, T.J. 1963. The water economy of land birds. *Auk* 80: 504-539 (October 1963).

Baynes, G.K. 1913. Blackcap and Swallow in England in winter. *British Birds* 6:279.

Benner, J.H.B., Berkhuizen, R.J., de Graaff, R.J. & Postma, A.D. *Impact of wind turbines on birdlife. Final Report, no 9247*. Consultants on energy and the environment, Rotterdam, Netherlands.

Bewick, T. 1804. *History of British Birds*. Newcastle.

Biebach, H. 1991. Is water or energy crucial for trans-Saharan migrants? *Proc. Int. Orn. Congr.* 20:773-779.

Birkhead, T. 2008. *The Wisdom of Birds*. Bloomsbury.

Birkhead, T. 2012. *Bird Sense*. Bloomsbury.

Blechman, A. 2007. *Pigeons – The fascinating saga of the world's most revered and reviled bird*. [http://andrewblechman.com/pigeons/learn_more.html]. St Lucia, Queensland: University of Queensland Press. ISBN 978-0-7022-3641-9.

Bonser, R.H.C. & Witter, R.S. 1993. Indentation hardness of the bill keratin of the European Starling. *The Condor* 95:736-738.

British Birds (notes from editors). 1912. Introduction of Nuthatches and Marsh Tits into Ireland. 5:229.

British Birds (notes from editors). 1913. A Swallow ringed in Staffordshire and recovered in Natal. 6:277.

Broome, D.M., Dick, W.J.A., Johnson, C.E., Sales, D.I. & Zahavi, A. 1976. Pied Wagtail roosting and feeding behaviour. *Bird Study* 23 (4): 267-279.

Browne, P.W.P. 1953. Nocturnal migration of thrushes in Ireland. *British Birds* (1953) 46:370-374.

Buchanan, K.L. & Catchpole, C.K. 2000. Song as indicator of male parental effort in the Sedge Warbler. *Proceedings of the Royal Society of London*. Bulletin 267: 321-326.

Campbell, B. & Watson, D. 1974. *The Oxford Book of Birds*. Book Club Associates. London.

Chiron, F. & Julliard, R. 2006. Responses of songbirds to Magpie reduction in an urban habitat. *The Journal of Wildlife Management*. 71 (no. 8): 2624-2631. DOI: 10.2193/2006-105

Clark, R.B. 1948. A display flight of the Skylark. *British Birds* (1948) 41:244-246.

Cramp, S., Simmons, K.E.L. and Perrins, C.M. (eds.) 1977–94. *The Birds of the Western Palearctic* (nine volumes). Oxford University Press.

D'Arcy, G. 1999. *Ireland's Lost Birds*. Four Courts Press. Dublin.

Darolova, A., Hoi, H. & Sleicher, B. 1996. The effect of ectoparasite nest load on the breeding biology of the Penduline Tit. *The Ibis* 139:115-120.

Darwin, C. 1871. *The Descent of Man*. Murray. London.

Davies, N.B. 1982. Territorial behaviour of Pied Wagtails in winter. *British Birds* 75: (1982) 261-267.

Davies, N.B. 1983. Polyandry, cloaca-pecking and sperm competition in Dunnocks. *Nature* 302: 334-336.

Davies, N.B. 1992. Dunnock Behaviour and Social Evolution. Oxford University Press.

Davies, N.B. 2000. *Cuckoos, Cowbirds and Other Cheats*. T&AD Poyser.

Dee, T. 2010. *The Running Sky*. Vintage. London.

Dewar, J.M. 1938. The Dipper walking under water. *British Birds* 32:103-106.

Dhondt, A.A. 1966. Bijdrage tot de oecologie van de koolmeus *Parus major* – verplaat-singen, mortaliteit. Lieenciaatsthesis, Rijksuniversiteit, Gent.

Donald, P. 2004. *The Skylark*. T&AD Poyser.

Gartner, K. 1981. PhD thesis. Hamburg University, Germany.

Gehringer, F. 1979. *Nos Oiseaux* 35:1-16.

Gibb, J. & Gibb, C. 1951. Waxwings in the winter of 1949–50. *British Birds* 44:158-163.

Glue, D.E. 1982. *The Garden Bird Book*. Macmillan. London.

Gooch, S., Baillie, S.R. & Birkhead, T.R. 1991. Magpie *Pica pica* and songbird populations. Retrospective investigation of trends in population density and breeding success. *Journal of Applied Ecology* 28 (no 3):1068-1086.

Groom, D.W. 1993. Magpie *Pica pica* predation on Blackbird *Turdus merula* nests in urban areas. *Bird Study* 40:55-62.

Hambler, C. & Canney, S.M. 2013. *Conservation* (second edition). Cambridge University Press.

Hanson, T. 2011. *Feathers*. Basic Books. New York.

Hockey, P.A.R., Dean, W.R.I. & Ryan, P.G. 2005. *Roberts Birds of Southern* Africa. John Voelcker Bird Book Club.

Hume, R.A.H. & Cady, M (eds.). 1988. *The Complete Book of British Birds*. AA & RSPB.

Ingram, G.C.S., Salmon, H.M. & Tucker, B.W. 1938. The movements of the Dipper underwater. *British Birds* (1939) 32: 58-63.

Irwin, M.P.S. 1956. Notes on the drinking habits of birds in semidesertic Bechuanaland. *Bull. British Orn.* Club 76:99-101.

Isaksson, C., Von post, M. & Andersson, S. 2007. Sexual, seasonal and environmental variation is plasma carotenoids in Great Tits. *Biological Journal of the Linnean Society.* 2007: (92) 521-527.

Jenner, E. 1788. Observations on the natural history of the Cuckoo. *Philosophical Transactions of the Royal Society, London* 78:219-237.

Jenni, L. & Winkler, R. 1994. *Moult and Ageing of European Passerines.* Christopher Helm. London.

Jonsson, L. 1992. *Birds of Europe.* Christopher Helm. London.

Kelso, L. & Nice, M.M. 1963. A Russian contribution to anting and feather mites. *Wilson Bulletin.* 75:23-26.

Kelty, M.P. & Lustick, S.I. 1977. Energetics of the Starling in pine woods. *Ecology* 58:1181-1185.

Kempenaers, B., Borgstrom, P., Loes, P., Schlicht, E. & Mihai, V. 2010. Artificial night light affects dawn song, extra-pair siring success and lay-date in songbirds. *Current Biology* 20: 1735-1739.

Kennedy, P.J., Ruttledge, R.F. & Scroope, C.F. *The Birds of Ireland.* 1954. Oliver & Boyd. Edinburgh, London.

Klump, G.M., Kretzschmar, E. & Curio, E. 1986. The hearing of an avian predator and its avian prey. *Behavioural Ecology and Sociobiology* 18:317-323.

Lohrl, H. 1973. Einfluss der Brutraumflache auf die Gelegegrosse der Kohlmeise Parus major. *Journal für Ornithologie* 121: 403-405.

Madon, P. *Alauda* 1934. Pp. 47–65.

Martin, G.R. 2014. The subtlety of simple eyes: the tuning of visual fields to perceptual challenges in birds. *Phil. Trans. R. Soc.* B 2014 369, 20130040, published 6 January 2014.

Marzluff, J.M., Walls, J., Cornell, H.N., Withy, J.C. & Craig, D.P. 2010. Lasting recognition of threatening people by wild American Crows. *Animal Behaviour* 79: 699-707.

Mason, E.A. 1944. Parasitism by Protocalliphora and management of cavity-nesting birds. *Journal of Wildlife Management.* 8:232-247.

McGeehan, A. & Wyllie, J. 2012 *Birds Through Irish Eyes.* The Collins Press. Cork.

Moffat, C.B. 1916. Richard Manliffe Barrington. *British Birds* (1916) 9:130-137.

Moss, S. 2003. *The Garden Bird Handbook.* New Holland. London.

Morris, F.O. 1856. *A History of British Birds.* Groombridge. London.

Mountfort, G. 1962. *British Birds* (1962) 55:42.

Mouritsen, H. & Hore, P.J. 2012. The magnetic retina: light-dependent and trigeminal magnetoreception in migratory birds. *Current Opinion in Neurobiology* 22:343-352.

Muheim, R. Behavioural and physiological mechanisms of polarised light sensitivity in birds. 2011. *Phil. Trans. R. Soc. B* (2011) 366, 763-771 doi:10.1098/rstb.2010.0196

Muheim, R., Phillips, J.B. & Akesson, S. 2006. Polarised light cues underlie compass calibration in migratory songbirds. *Science* Vol 313, August 2006.

Muller, W., Heylen, D., Eens, M., Rivera-Gutierrez, H.F. & Groothuis, T.G.G. 2013. An experimental study on the causal relationships between (ecto-) parasites, testosterone and sexual signalling. *Behav. Ecol. Sociobiol.* 67: 1791-1798.

Murton, R.K. & Clarke, S.P. 1968. Breeding biology of Rock Doves. *British Birds* (1968) 61:429-448.

Neto, J.M., Encarnacao, V., Fearon, P. & Gosler, A.G. 2008. Autumn migration of Savi's Warblers in Portugal: differences in timing, fuel deposition rate and non-stop flight range between the age classes. *Bird Study* 55:78-86.

Newton, I. 2001. *The Sparrowhawk*. Shire Publications Ltd. Buckinghamshire.

Newton, I. 2010. *Bird Migration*. Collins New Naturalist Library. London.

O'Sullivan Beare, P. 2009. The Natural History of Ireland. Book One, *Zoilomastix* (1625). Translated by Denis O'Sullivan. Cork University Press.

O'Sullivan, O. & Wilson, J. 2008. *Ireland's Garden Birds*. The Collins Press. Cork.

Palleroni, A., Miller, C.T., Hauser, M. & Marler, P. 2005. Prey plumage adaptation against falcon attack. *Nature* 343/21 April 2005/ www.nature.com/nature

Payne, R.S. 1971. Acoustic location of prey by Barn Owls. *Journal of Experimental Biology* 54: 535-73.

Perdeck, A.C. 1958. Two types of orientation in migrating Starlings and Chaffinches, as revealed by displacement activities. *Ardea* 46:1-37.

Perrins, C. *British Tits*. 1979. Collins New Naturalist Library. London.

Phillips, J.B., Muheim, R. & Jorge, P.E. 2010. A behavioural perspective on the biophysics of the light-dependent magnetic compass; a link between directional and spatial perception? *J. Exp. Biol.* 213:3247-3255. (doi:10.1242/jeb.020772)

Phillips, J.B. & Waldvogel, J.A. Pp.190-202 in *Avian Navigation*. Editors: Papi, F., & Wallraff, E. Springer-Verlag, Berlin. 1982.

Rickenbach, O., Gruebler, M.U., Schaub, M., Koller, A., Naef-Daenzer, B. & Schifferli, L. 2011. Exclusion of ground predators improves Northern Lapwing chick survival. *Ibis* (2011) 153: 531-542.

RSPB (Royal Society for the Protection of Birds) 2007. *The Predation of Wild Birds in the United Kingdom: A review of its Conservation Impact and Management*. RSPB Research Report 23, p. 12. Sandy, Bedfordshire.

Salomonson, F. 1935. 'Aves.' *Zoology Faeroes*, part 64.

Selous, E. 1933. *Evolution of Habit in Birds*. Constable. London.

Snow, D. 1958. *A Study of Blackbirds*. George Allen and Unwin Ltd. London.

Snow, D. & Snow, B.K. Territorial song of the Dunnock *Prunella modularis*. *Bird Study* 30: 51-57 (March 1983).

Soler, M. & Soler, J.J. 1999. Innate versus learned recognition of conspecifics in Great Spotted Cuckoo. *Anim. Cogn.* 2:97-102

Stoddard, M.C. & Stevens, M. 2010. Pattern mimicry of host eggs by the Common Cuckoo, as seen through a bird's eye. *Proceedings of the Royal Society B: Biological Sciences* Vol. 277 no 1686: 1387-1393.

Tate, M. & Tyler, O. 2005. *The Birdwatcher's Companion*. Robson Books. London.

Ticehurst, C.B. 1911. The British Great Spotted Woodpecker. *British Birds* (1911) 4: number 11, 335-343.

Tinbergen, N. 1948. Social releasers and the experimental method required for their study. *Wilson Bulletin* 60:6-51.

Tieleman, B.I., Williams, J.B. & Buschur, M.E. 2002. Physiological adjustments to arid and mesic environments in larks (Alaudidae). *Physiological and Biochemical Zoology* 75: 305-313.

Thompson, W. 1849–52. *The Natural History of Ireland*. Reeve, Benham & Reeve. London.

Toms, M.P., Clark, J.A. & Balmer, D.E. 1999. Bird Ringing in Britain & Ireland in 1997. *Ringing & Migration* 19:215-255.

Ussher, R. & Warren, R. 1900. *The Birds of Ireland*. Dublin and London.

Walls, G.L. 1942. The vertebrate eye and its adaptive radiation. Cranbrook Institute of Science, Bloomfield Hills, Michigan.

Welty, J.C. & Baptista, L. 1988. *The Life of Birds*. Thomson.

Whitworth, T.L. & Bennett, G.F. 1992. Pathogenicity of larval Protocalliphora (Diptera: Calliphoridae) parasitizing nestling birds. *Canadian Journal of Zoology* 70:2184-2191.

Witherby, H.F., Jourdain, F.C.R., Ticehurst, N.F. & Tucker, B.W. 1940. *The Handbook of British Birds* 2:214. H.F. & G. Witherby, London.

Yalden, D.W. 2002. Place-name and archaeological evidence on the recent history of birds in Britain. *Acta zoological cracoviensia* 45 (special issue): 415-429. Krakow.

INDEX

Note: pages in bold refer to photographs and captions